T0200875

UNSUPERVISED LEARNING

UNSUPERVISED LEARNING

A DYNAMIC APPROACH

Matthew Kyan
Paisarn Muneesawang
Kambiz Jarrah
Ling Guan

IEEE Press Series on Computational Intelligence
David B. Fogel, Series Editor

IEEE PRESS

WILEY

For general information on our other products and services or for technical support, please contact our
Customer Care Department within the United States at (800) 762-2974, outside the United States at
(317) 572-3993 or fax (317) 572-4002.

Wiley also publishes its books in a variety of electronic formats. Some content that appears in print may
not be available in electronic formats. For more information about Wiley products, visit our web site at
www.wiley.com.

Library of Congress Cataloging-in-Publication Data:

Kyan, Matthew.
 Unsupervised learning : a dynamic approach / Matthew Kyan, Paisarn Muneesawang,
Kambiz Jarrah, Ling Guan.
   pages cm
   ISBN 978-0-470-27833-8 (cloth)
   1. Database management.   2. Self-organizing systems.   3. Machine learning.   4. Big data.
I. Muneesawang, Paisarn.   II. Jarrah, Kambiz.   III. Guan, Ling.   IV. Title.
   QA76.9.D3K 93 2014
   005.74–dc23   2013046024

Printed in the United States of America

10 9 8 7 6 5 4 3 2 1

CONTENTS

ACKNOWLEDGMENTS

This book is dedicated to all the members of the former Sydney Multimedia Processing (SMP) Lab, University of Sydney; and to the members, past and present, of Ryerson Multimedia Processing Lab (RML), Ryerson University, Toronto.

In addition, the authors would like to thank Professor Sujin Jinahyon, President of Naresuan University; The Department of Physical Optics, University of Sydney; Sydney Vislab.

In addition, special thanks goes to Dr. Steven Liss and Dr. Ivan Zhou, of the Environmental Biotechnology Lab, Ryerson University, for their contributions for biofilm data and expertise.

CHAPTER 1

Introduction

With the explosion of information brought about by this Multimedia Age, the question of how such information might be effectively harvested, archived, and analysed, remains a monumental challenge facing today's research community. The processing of such information, however, is often fraught with the need for conceptual interpretation—a relatively simple task for humans, yet arduous for computers. In order to handle the oppressive volumes of information that are becoming readily accessible in consumer and industrial sectors, some level of automation is desirable.

Automation requires computational systems that exhibit some degree of intelligence, in terms of the ability of a system to formulate its own models of the data in question with little or no user intervention. Such systems must be able to make basic decisions about what information is actually important and what is not. In effect, like a human user, the system must be able to discover characteristic properties of the data in some appropriate manner, without a teacher. This process is known as *unsupervised learning* (sometimes referred to as *clustering* or *unsupervised pattern classification*; an essentially pure form of data mining).

This book primarily introduces a new approach to the general problem of unsupervised learning, based on the principles of *dynamic self-organization*. Inspired by the relative success of other popular research on self-organizing neural networks for data clustering and feature extraction, this book presents new members within the family of generative, Self-Organizing Maps, namely: the self-organizing tree map (SOTM) and its advanced form, the *self-organizing hierarchical variance map* (SOHVM). While the devised approach is essentially generic, the core application considered in this book is the automatic, unsupervised data clustering for multimedia applications and unsupervised segmentation of microbiological image data.

1.1 PART I: THE SELF-ORGANIZING METHOD

Computational technologies based on Artificial Neural Networks (ANN) have been the focus of much research into the problem of unsupervised learning, in particular,

Unsupervised Learning: A Dynamic Approach, First Edition.
Matthew Kyan, Paisarn Muneesawang, Kambiz Jarrah, and Ling Guan.
© 2014 by The Institute of Electrical and Electronics Engineers, Inc. Published by John Wiley & Sons, Inc.

for network architectures that are based on principles of Self-Organization. Such principles are in many ways centered on Turing's initial observation in 1952 [1], namely, that Global order can arise from Local interactions. With much support from neurobiological research, such mechanisms are believed to be analogous to the organization that takes place in the human brain.

Clustering algorithms use unsupervised learning rules to group unlabeled training data into similar or dense clusters. Unsupervised training algorithms depend upon internally generated error measures, which are derived solely from training data. The network has no knowledge of the correct answer during training and, consequently, must derive the errors and the necessary weight modifications directly from the statistics of the training data. As a result, input patterns are stored as a set of cluster prototypes or exemplars—representations or natural groupings of similar data. In forming a description of an unknown set of data, such network architectures are characterized by their adherence to four key properties [2]: synaptic self-amplification for mining correlated stimuli, competition over limited resources, cooperative encoding of information, and the implicit ability to encode pattern redundancy as knowledge. Such principles are, in many ways, a reflection of Turing's observations previously discussed.

Part I of this book consists of Chapters 2 and 3. It gives an extensive review of the general problems of unsupervised clustering, with emphasis placed on the inherent relationship that exists between unsupervised learning and Self-Organization. The unsupervised learning problem is first defined with respect to the concepts of similarity and distance. A survey of unsupervised techniques from the broader field is then conducted to establish the context for more focused surveys on self-organization-based principles and architectures. The issue of validating unsupervised clustering solutions in the absence of a ground truth is also addressed.

1.2 PART II: DYNAMIC SELF-ORGANIZATION FOR IMAGE FILTERING AND MULTIMEDIA RETRIEVAL

Multimedia processing has seen impressive growth in the past decade in terms of both theoretical development and applications. It represents a leading technology in a number of important areas that warrant significant need for data mining, namely, digital telecommunications, multimedia systems, high dimensional image analysis and visualization, information retrieval, biology, robotics and manufacturing, and intelligent sensing systems. Inherently unsupervised in nature, neural network architectures based on principles of Self-Organization appear to be a natural fit.

In Part II of this book, the SOTM and its recently successful application in multimedia processing is presented. This neural network architecture incorporates hierarchical properties by virtue of its growth, in a manner that is flexible in terms of revealing the underlying data space without being constrained by an imposed topological framework. As such, the SOTM exhibits many desirable properties over traditional self-organizing feature map (SOFM) based strategies. Chapter 4 of the book will provide an in-depth coverage of this architecture. Chapters 5 and 6 will then cover a series of pertinent real-world applications with regard to the processing of multimedia data. This includes problems in image-processing techniques, such as the automated modeling and removal of impulse noise in digital images, and problems in image classification in multimedia indexing and retrieval.

In Chapter 4, the SOTM algorithm is explored and developed, wherein a number of enhancements and modifications are proposed, justified, and tested, with the goal of rendering the SOTM more robust under application to different datasets. Specifically, alternative modalities for hierarchical control and learning are considered, in addition to more appropriate stopping criteria linked to aspects of the input data. The SOTM is then explored as a means of segmenting biofilm images, where its strengths and flexibility as a dynamic clustering model for segmentation are explored. Limitations and deficiencies of the SOTM are also identified.

In Chapter 5, the SOTM is applied to the automated modeling and removal of impulse noise in digital images. Improving the quality of images degraded by noise is a classic problem in image processing [3]. In the early stages of signal and image processing, linear filters were the primary tools for noise cleaning. Later, the development of nonlinear filtering techniques for signal and image processing was spurred by some drawbacks of linear filters [4]. However, one problem with nonlinear filers such as the median filter is that they remove the fine details in the image and change the signal structure. In addition, improved nonlinear filters, such as the weighted median filter, multistage median filter, and nonlinear mean filters, have better detail-preserving characteristics at the expense of poorer noise suppression. Here, a novel approach for suppressing impulse noise in digital images is proposed for effectively preserving more image detail than previously proposed methods. The noise removal system, shown in Figure 1.1a, consists of two steps: the detection of the noise and the reconstruction of the image. As the SOTM network has the capability to classify pixels in an image, it is employed to detect the impulses. A noise-exclusive median (NEM) filtering algorithm and a noise-exclusive arithmetic mean (NEAM) filtering algorithm are proposed to restore the image. This system is able to detect noise locations accurately, and thus, achieves the best possible restoration of images corrupted by impulse noise.

In Chapter 6, the SOTM is applied to problems in image classification in multimedia indexing and retrieval. The system architecture is shown in Figure 1.1b. In multimedia database retrieval, relevance feedback (RF) is a popular and effective way to improve the performance of image re-ranking and retrieval. However, RF needs a high level of human participation, which often leads to excessive subjective errors. Here, an automatic RF is present, using the SOTM, which minimizes user participation, providing a more user-friendly environment and avoiding errors caused by excessive human involvement. Unlike the conventional retrieval system, where the user's direct input is required in the execution of the RF algorithm, SOTM estimation is now adopted to guide the adaptation of the RF parameters. As shown in Figure 1.1b, the initially retrieved samples are labeled with the unsupervised module, and image re-ranking is performed by the pseudo-labeled samples. As a result, instead of

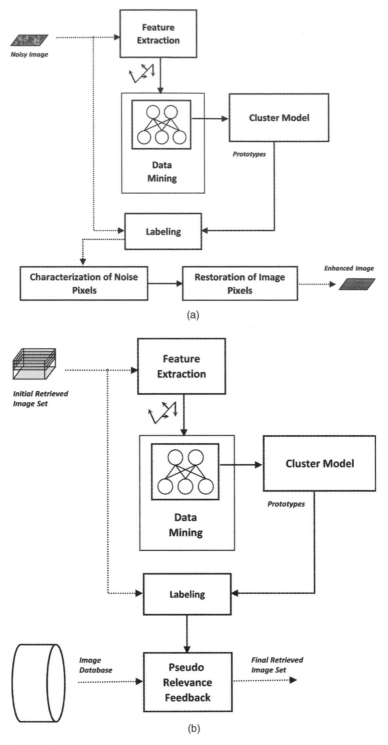

FIGURE 1.1 Unsupervised Learning–based framework for (a) automated modeling and removal of impulse noise in digital images and (b) image classification in multimedia indexing and retrieval.

imposing a greater responsibility on the user, independent learning can be integrated to improve retrieval accuracy. This makes it possible to obtain either a fully automatic or a semiautomatic RF system suitable for practical applications.

1.3   PART III: DYNAMIC SELF-ORGANIZATION FOR IMAGE SEGMENTATION AND VISUALIZATION

Much emphasis of this book is placed on Part III, on the developments of the SOHVM and its application in the unsupervised segmentation and visualization of microbiological image data. With recent advances in imaging, computer, and optical modalities for microscopy, a paradigm shift away from the purely observational toward the extraction of more quantitative information seems to be taking place. As such, data mining techniques are thought to serve as a useful basis for further processing stages. To this end this book demonstrates the capability of the newly proposed SOHVM over its predecessors and other popular self-organizing and partition-based clustering algorithms, for formulating a relatively stable clustering solution. Furthermore, avenues are explored for how the model can extract and use data associations discovered between clusters.

In the interests of assisting biologists in exploring previously unseen, unlabeled image data, unsupervised methods for attaining useful data-driven segmentations are explored, serving as a useful basis for further processing stages such as visualization or quantitative analysis.

In general, the approach taken is to identify characteristic biological materials present in the data, by identifying natural groupings (clusters) of similar voxel patterns—where an individual voxel pattern may be thought of as a vector of one or more different attributes, to which we refer as features. The framework for the approach taken is summarized in Figure 1.2.

In the most basic example, a voxel pattern from a single channel image might comprise a single feature only, namely, its intensity value. Alternatively, over a three-channel image, a voxel pattern may be a three-tuple vector, with one dimension for each channel. Under this framework, higher level, n-dimensional pattern vectors also become possible, allowing for the possibility of fusing local regional or other information extracted from the image into the description of each voxel. For instance, at a later stage in this study, the use of a classic texture feature (from the signal/image processing community) is incorporated into the description of a voxel for a single channel dataset, effectively transforming it into an 18+ tuple pattern vector.

Armed with an n-dimensional input data/feature space of actual pattern vectors, unsupervised learning or data clustering algorithms are aimed at parsing the space of possible patterns so as to locate regions of density that characterize the underlying data distribution. In this way, specific data samples may be associated and conglomerated into such characteristic groups. Each grouping is such that the data within demonstrates a certain level of *homogeneity*, with respect to some predefined similarity metric. Such metrics are typically implemented in the form of a *distance* mechanism, where the distance between two sample patterns gives a quantitative

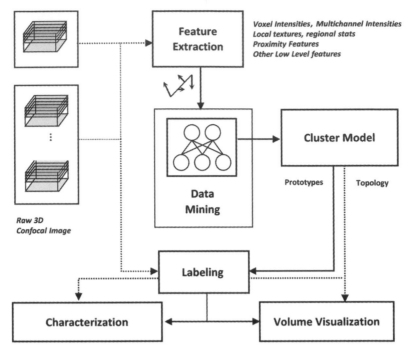

FIGURE 1.2   Unsupervised Learning–based framework for mining segmentations for visualization and characterization of microbiological image data.

measure of their relative dissimilarity (i.e., the smaller the distance, the more similar the patterns).

While there exist many classes of unsupervised learning algorithms in the literature (reviewed in Chapter 2), relatively few offer solutions to the problem of finding an appropriate number of pattern groups in which to break up the data at runtime. In fact, relatively few algorithms exist that are able to dynamically construct an appropriate number of groups as the data is parsed. The majority of unsupervised techniques available today are fixed, in that the number of groups (K) in which to partition the data is an argument to the algorithm, and it is more or less enforced. The current state of the art then, is to run a fixed algorithm multiple times, each with a different value for K, and then to evaluate the most suitable solution in an a posteriori manner, based on cluster validity analysis [5].

If an algorithm is able to dynamically construct a description of the input space throughout the course of parsing the data, then it seems natural that such a mechanism may be better suited to estimating an appropriate number of groups *on the fly*. ANN modeled on principles of dynamic (or generative) Self-Organization seem a natural fit toward this goal, as they possess the unique ability to grow and adapt over the course of time, while demonstrating heightened ability to generalize across a wide range of linear and nonlinear input pattern stimuli, by virtue of their inherently associative and parallel nature. Exhibiting properties found to have neurobiological support [6], self-organizing-based networked systems reflect a realization of what we know to be at work in the cerebral cortex in the processing of information, namely, the existence of topologically ordered mappings of sensory inputs such as tactile, visual, and acoustic stimuli [2]. Inspired by this notion, the proposal of a new algorithm for unsupervised learning, based on dynamic Self-Organization, forms the core of this book.

In Chapter 7, a new model for unsupervised learning based on dynamic Self-Organization is proposed, namely, the SOHVM. The impetus and motivation for the new model arise out of the desire to overcome limitations identified with the SOTM. In addition, the new model embeds a mechanism to adaptively extract higher level associations from the data (interclass or topological relationships), as well as a mechanism for estimating an appropriate number of optimal classes at runtime. The performance and characteristics of the new model are then demonstrated with both the SOTM and other algorithms through a series of visual simulations.

In Chapter 8, the first half of the chapter presents a more concrete validation of both the modified SOTM and newly proposed SOHVM model. Specifically, an extensive cluster validity analysis is performed, drawing comparisons across a range of popular unsupervised clustering models. Issues of regularity, quality, and optimality are addressed with respect to synthetic and real-world data. The second half of the chapter then returns to the problem of segmenting microbiological image data, and in this regard, the performance of both the SOHVM and modified SOTM are demonstrated against other techniques. The discussion of the experiments on microbiological data then concludes with an example for how topological information mined by the SOHVM can be used to simplify the three-dimensional (3D) visualization of a large stack of chromosome data.

1.4   FUTURE DIRECTIONS

The focal points of the book lay in the design and development of two models for unsupervised leaning or data clustering, based on dynamic self-organization— namely, the self-organizing tree map (SOTM) and the self-organizing hierarchical variance map (SOHVM). Specific applications presented outline the utility of these models in applications including the automated modeling and removal of impulse noise in digital images; image classification in multimedia indexing and retrieval; and segmentation and visualization of biomedical image data.

The real advantage of creating a self-organizing clustering lies in the functionality of the resulting topological map. Mining the topology can be leveraged for very specific tasks. The major categories of tasks are

- Dynamic navigation through information repositories, applied for image re-ranking and visualization, video browsing, summarization, and retrieval.

- Interactive knowledge-assisted visualization, applied for volume exploration of volumetric multimedia datasets through direct volume rendering techniques to actively re-render the scene based on the user's current cluster of interest.
- Temporal data analysis using trajectories, applied for video shot boundary detection and gesture recognition.

In Chapter 9, the book crystallizes the main findings of this work and offers some recommendations of avenues for future research.

CHAPTER 2

Unsupervised Learning

2.1 INTRODUCTION

The goal of Unsupervised Learning is to essentially formulate or discover significant patterns or features in a given set of data, without the guidance of a teacher. The patterns are usually stored as a set of exemplars (prototypes)—representations of natural groupings of similar data or clusters, present within an input pattern space. In describing an unknown set of data, such techniques find much application across a wide range of industries, particularly in bioinformatics (clustering of genetic data [7], protein structure analysis [8]); image processing (feature extraction [9], image segmentation [10–12], and information retrieval [13, 14]); signal compression and coding [15]; and other applications that warrant a significant need for data mining [16].

In this chapter, a general review of Unsupervised Learning is conducted. In Sections 2.2 and 2.3, generic clustering issues are first defined and explained. A survey of traditional approaches to Unsupervised Learning is then presented in Section 2.4, and the chapter concludes in Section 2.5, with a discussion of assessment measures and limitations in the evaluation of clustering solutions.

2.2 UNSUPERVISED CLUSTERING

The concept of clustering is invariably tied to an adequate definition of what constitutes a *cluster*. This is the subject of much debate and often depends on problem domain. Nevertheless, the concept of a cluster is inherently related to the concept of *similarity* between samples from an input data space. In the majority of cases, the distinct lack of a priori information in an Unsupervised Learning problem warrants the need for a generalized framework. As such, the process of clustering can be broadly defined as one that seeks to *group together similar or related entities*. Each entity or sample is often taken to be some n-dimensional vector (defined on an input space $\Re^n$)—this is represented as a two-dimensional (2D) space in Figure 2.1 for clarity. Ultimately, any given clustering solution, is then necessarily based on

Unsupervised Learning: A Dynamic Approach, First Edition.
Matthew Kyan, Paisarn Muneesawang, Kambiz Jarrah, and Ling Guan.

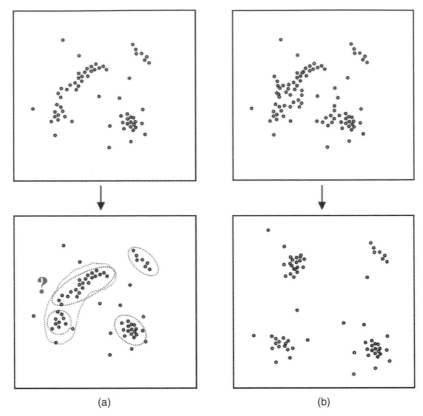

(a)   (b)

FIGURE 2.1 The problem of defining a cluster—portrayal of the ill-posed nature of clustering. (a) Ambiguity in grouping illustrates the difficulty inherent in distinguishing between what may be deemed alternative options for the notion of similar groups. (b) Enhancement/sparsity promotion via feature space ideally should work to reduce the ambiguity in distinguishing between possible groupings.

how we choose to quantify relative dissimilarities between individual samples. For instance, in Figure 2.1a, when considering data points that are similar, there appears to be differing notions of what constitutes an appropriate group. What is evident is that there seems to be interplay amongst the similarities between individual sets of points, and similarities within the broader context—with respect to the other points in the data.

Generally, the ability of an algorithm to extract natural groupings from the data is linked to a choice of distance metric used to assess similarity (e.g., a standard Euclidean metric would tend to favor more spherical groupings). Even with spherical clusters, however, it is unlikely that they will all be of similar densities and sizes. One can see that the nature of clustering or mining characteristic relationships from unlabeled data is thus, an ill-posed problem. In such cases, it is often the sparsity between apparently dense regions that provides equally important cues as to where groupings tend to occur. Often, in light of this, a transformation into a higher dimensional feature space is often made in the hope of promoting such sparsity, and the enhancement of well-separated regions, as depicted in Figure 2.1b. Alternatively, techniques such as Principal Component Analysis (PCA) [17] can be applied to redefine the space in terms of a new coordinate system so as to promote linear separability between samples, or methods such as Independent Components Analysis (ICA) [18] can be used to decompose data into mixtures based on information-theoretic criteria such as mutual information, with the objective as before to promote separability.

Assuming a number of clustered regions can be found, the next difficulty is in evaluating the solution. How do we know whether or not a reasonable clustering solution has been found? Moreover, how do we know how many groups to look for? These issues are as yet unresolved and remain at the heart of unsupervised data mining research.

Typically, the *quality* of a given clustering solution obtained after application to unlabeled data is considered in a subjective light. This being said, research into both quality and validity *indicators* have yielded some useful evaluation measures. Intuitively, such techniques attempt to exploit Local versus Global relationships between samples. Evaluation, for example, may consider the relationship between the size of discovered clusters versus their separation from one another.

Needless to say, distance metrics, quality, and validity are each vast topics unto themselves and become essential, yet difficult considerations in the evaluation of a clustering solution within unsupervised contexts. These will be expanded upon in the following two sections.

2.3 DISTANCE METRICS FOR UNSUPERVISED CLUSTERING

There is a wide range of possible distance metrics that may be used in a clustering solution, some more common than others; however, the basic requirement is that a given distance metric: $d(\mathbf{x}, \mathbf{y})$, where $\mathbf{x} \in \mathfrak{R}^n$, $y \in \mathfrak{R}^n$ satisfy the following conditions [19].

- Symmetry: $d(\mathbf{x}, \mathbf{y}) = d(\mathbf{y}, \mathbf{x})$;
- Non-negativity: $d(\mathbf{x}, \mathbf{y}) > 0$;
- Identity of indiscernibles: $d(\mathbf{x}, \mathbf{y}) = 0$, if and only if $\mathbf{x} = \mathbf{y}$;
- Triangle inequality: $d(\mathbf{x}, \mathbf{y}) < d(\mathbf{x}, \mathbf{z}) + d(\mathbf{z}, \mathbf{y})$.

A range of choices for distance metrics is summarized in Table 2.1. By far, the most used metric is the Euclidean distance (ED), which considers the locus of points (y) sitting on a hyper-spheroid from (x) to be of equal similarity and is invariant under both translation and rotation. In its weighted form (WED), the hyper-spheroid may be warped into a hyper-ellipsoid, thus favoring one dimension over another, which may help in identifying elongated rather than spherical clusters. An example of this is the Standardized or Gaussian normalized Euclidean distance (SED), where

TABLE 2.1   A Summary of Distance Metrics Commonly Used in Clustering

Distance metric	Formulation
Euclidean (ED)	$d_{ED}(\mathbf{x}, \mathbf{y}) = \sqrt{\sum_{i=1}^{n} (x_i - y_i)^2}$
Euclidean Squared (ED2)	$d_{ED2}(\mathbf{x}, \mathbf{y}) = \sum_{i=1}^{n} (x_i - y_i)^2$
Weighted Euclidean (WED)	$d_{WED}(\mathbf{x}, \mathbf{y}, \mathbf{w}) = \sqrt{\sum_{i=1}^{n} w_i \cdot (x_i - y_i)^2}$ *where:* $\mathbf{w}$ = *vector of weights* w_i *per dimension i.*
Standardized Euclidean (SED)	$d_{SED}(\mathbf{x}, \mathbf{y}) = d_{WED}\left(\mathbf{x}, \mathbf{y}, \dfrac{1}{\mathbf{s}}\right)$ *where:* s_i = *sample variance per dimension i.*
Mahalanobis (MhD)	$d_{MhD}(\mathbf{x}, \mathbf{y}) = \sqrt{(\mathbf{x} - \mathbf{y})^T S^{-1} (\mathbf{x} - \mathbf{y})}$ *where:* *S is any n × n positive definite matrix.* *If S = I, then this reduces to ED.* *If S = Σ is diagonal, then this reduces to SED* *(using sample variances).*
Manhattan/city block (MD)	$d_{MD}(\mathbf{x}, \mathbf{y}) = \sum_{i=1}^{n} |x_i - y_i|$
Chebychev (ChD)	$d_{ChD}(\mathbf{x}, \mathbf{y}) = \max_i |x_i - y_i|$
Minkowski (MkD)	$d_{MkD}(\mathbf{x}, \mathbf{y}) = \left(\sum_{i=1}^{n} |x_i - y_i|^m\right)^{\frac{1}{m}}$
Cosine (CD)	$d_{CD}(\mathbf{x}, \mathbf{y}) = \dfrac{\mathbf{x} \cdot \mathbf{y}}{\|\mathbf{x}\|\|\mathbf{y}\|} = \cos(\theta)$ *where:* θ *is the angle between vectors* $\mathbf{x}$ *and* $\mathbf{y}$.
Pearson correlation (PCD)	$d_{PCD}(\mathbf{x}, \mathbf{y}) = 1 - r_{\mathbf{xy}}$ *where:* $r_{\mathbf{xy}} = \dfrac{\sum_i^n (x_i - \mathbf{x})(y_i - \mathbf{y})}{\sqrt{\sum_i^n (x_i - \mathbf{x})}\sqrt{\sum_i^n (y_i - \mathbf{y})}}$ *is the Pearson Correlation Coefficient between* *vectors* $\mathbf{x}$ *and* $\mathbf{y}$.

each dimension is normalized by the variance in the data that occurs along that dimension—highly variable dimensions in the space are thus shrunk with respect to low variance dimensions. Mahalanobis distance (MhD) [20] is a more generalized extension of this principle, wherein a space warping matrix S (e.g., covariance) is used such that weightings are imposed along more arbitrary axes within the space. The variance along such axes is used to stretch or shrink the space.

Manhattan distance (MD) [21], on the other hand, represents a simple metric that evaluates distance as the sum of orthogonal distances it would take if movement from x to y was restricted to be along the direction of one dimension at a time. Such a distance measure tends to exaggerate outliers and is much like traveling along the paths defined by city blocks in a grid-based city-street layout (hence the term Manhattan or City-Block distance). Incidentally, if ED is left in its squared form (ED2), then even more emphasis is placed on outliers than with MD.

Chebychev distance (ChD) [22] summarizes MD by considering only the dimension with the largest distance, thereby focusing on the dimension with the most important difference, while Minkowski distance (MkD) [23] generalizes between ED and MD and is inherently related to the concept of fractal dimension.

Cosine distance (CD) takes a different approach. Used frequently in such tasks as assessing similarity in document clustering [24], CD considers the angle between the two vectors x and y (i.e., vectors are sought with similar alignment rather than separation). Pearson's Correlation Distance (PCD) focuses more on the shape of the pattern vector, that is, assesses whether or not the variations along an entire vector follow a similar trend to the variations along another vector. Such measures have been used in applications such as gene expression clustering and also in collaborative filtering based internet recommender systems [25]. The latter example has received much attention of late in the field of machine learning. A recent application is for users who have a tendency to rate items in a similar way on a website, for instance, movies seen (e.g., NETFLIX.com [26]) or products bought (e.g., Amazon.com [27]), are grouped into clusters exploited for the prediction of whether or not a specific individual will enjoy a particular movie or product that they have not yet experienced.

In the context of this book, distance metrics are restricted to Euclidean-based approaches and weighted forms thereof. However, it should be noted that the techniques developed are of a general form, and as such, other distance metrics may be integrated into the models proposed, and although not investigated explicitly, situations will be highlighted in later chapters where such integration may apply.

2.4 UNSUPERVISED LEARNING APPROACHES

Unsupervised Learning can be loosely classified into both parametric and nonparametric approaches, the latter of which typically constitutes most forms of cluster analysis. Figure 2.2 shows a rough breakdown of the main families of current techniques. This section begins with a definition of cluster membership, before outlining some of the more popular clustering approaches from the literature.

2.4.1 Partitioning and Cluster Membership

A given clustering solution for a set of data is described both in terms of the set of cluster prototypes (e.g., centroids) representing the input space and a class membership function, which represents the resultant mapping of the input space onto these prototypes. In addition, the partition may be defined as either a hard partition, where

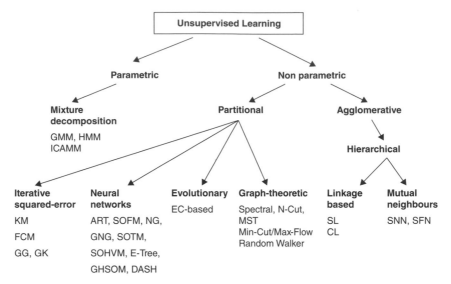

FIGURE 2.2 Unsupervised Learning approaches. All acronyms are explained in Table 2.2.

TABLE 2.2 Full Names of the Acronyms in Figure 2.2

Acronym	Full name
GMM	Gaussian Mixture Model
HMM	Hidden Markov Model
ICA	Independent Component Analysis
KM	K-Means
FCM	Fuzzy C-Means
GG	Gath–Geva
GK	Gustafson–Kessel
ART	Adaptive Resonance Theory
SOFM	Self-Organizing Feature Maps
NG	Neural Gas
GNG	Growing Neural Gas
SOTM	Self-Organizing Tree Maps
SOHVM	Self-Organizing Hierarchical Variance Maps
E-Tree	Evolving Tree
GHSOM	Growing Hierarchical Self-Organizing Maps
DASH	Dynamic Adaptive Self-Organizing Hybrid
EC	Evolutionary Computation
MST	Minimum Spanning Trees
SL	Single Linkage
CL	Complete Linkage
SNN	Shared Nearest Neighbor
SFN	Shared Farthest Neighbor

samples may only belong to one cluster at a time; or as a soft/fuzzy partition, where samples are allowed to belong to multiple or all clusters, according to some probability. To illustrate, let X represent an n-dimensional input data space containing N samples:

$$X = [x_1, x_2, x_3, \dots, x_i, \dots, x_N]; \text{ where } x_i \in \mathfrak{R}^n; \tag{2.1}$$

now let C represent the set of Nc cluster prototypes:

$$C = [C_1, C_2, C_3, \dots, C_k, \dots, C_{Nc}]. \tag{2.2}$$

The mapping from input space X to cluster space C may be described by virtue of a partition matrix $U = [\mu_{ik}]$, where μ_{ik} reflects the degree of membership of the ith sample x_i to the kth cluster C_k.

A hard partition then requires that $\mu_{ik} = 1$ iff $x_i \in C_k$, otherwise $\mu_{ik} = 0$; formally,

$$P_{\text{hard}} = \left\{ U \in \mathfrak{R}^{N \times Nc} \mid \mu_{ik} \in 0,1, \forall i,k; \sum_{k=1}^{Nc} \mu_{ik} = 1, \forall i; 0 < \sum_{i=1}^{N} \mu_{ik} < N, \forall k \right\}. \tag{2.3}$$

While for a fuzzy/soft partition, this constraint is relaxed such that any given x_i can exhibit membership to many clusters, provided its total membership across all possible C_k sums to 1:

$$P_{\text{fuzzy}} = \left\{ U \in \mathfrak{R}^{N \times Nc} \mid \mu_{ik} \in [0,1], \forall i,k; \sum_{k=1}^{Nc} \mu_{ik} = 1, \forall i; 0 < \sum_{i=1}^{N} \mu_{ik} < N, \forall k \right\}. \tag{2.4}$$

2.4.2 Iterative Mean-Squared Error Approaches

Perhaps one of the most fundamental and widely adopted approaches to clustering, the K-Means (KM) clustering algorithm [28] has found application across a broad range of data mining problems. This approach essentially involves the partitioning of a data space into K prototypes. Initially, arbitrary positions of the K-prototypes are assigned before pooling all data into K groups using nearest neighborhood allocation. Each group's prototype is then refined by adjusting it to the mean of samples assigned to that particular group. This process is repeated until no significant change in the prototypes is observed. In effect, the process seeks to reduce the mean square error between all samples and their representative prototypes (represented as cluster centroids). The algorithm is summarized in Figure 2.3.

One simple modification of this algorithm is K-medoids [29], which represents each cluster using the median sample as opposed to the centroid. Other variants such as Spherical K-Means (SPKM) incorporate a cosine distance (Section 2.3) to cluster documents [30]. While widely used, KM methods are extremely sensitive

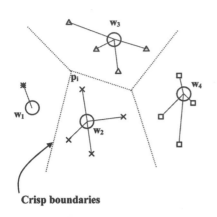

Crisp boundaries

Fuzzy boundaries

U_{hard}

	w_1	w_2	w_3	w_4
p_1	1	0	0	0
p_2	0	0	1	0
...	...			
...	0	0	1	0
p_i	0	1	0	0
...	0	1	0	0
...	0	0	1	0
p_{13}	...			

U_{soft}

	w_1	w_2	w_3	w_4
p_1	0.58	0.3	0.1	0.02
p_2	0.07	0.33	0.4	0.2
...	...			
...				
p_i	0.25	0.4	0.3	0.05
...				
...				
p_{13}	...			

Partition matrix U_{hard}

Fuzzy Partition matrix U_{soft}

FIGURE 2.3 Hard vs. fuzzy decision boundaries in iterative mean-squared-error-based clustering: (left) Hard Clustering with K-Means vs. (right) Fuzzy Clustering; fuzzy membership *blurs* the line between clusters allowing for a certain degree of overlap in boundary regions. While mixture models build *uncertainty* into a solution through incorporating specific probabilities, fuzzy partitions attempt to yield a similar effect by factoring into the result, a certain level of *imprecision*.

to initialization [31]. Both fuzzy and adaptive versions of the KM algorithm have been proposed [32–35]. Fuzzy C-Means (FCM), for instance, relaxes the membership function imposed on individual samples in KM from hard to soft membership (as described in Section 2.4.1) via a fuzzification factor (m). This is achieved by minimizing over a fuzzy means functional $J(X; U, W)$—redistributing the mean-squared error of each sample across all clusters according to its respective degrees of membership:

$$J(X; U, W) = \sum_{k=1}^{N_c} \sum_{i=1}^{N} (\mu_{ik})^m D_{ikS}^2 \qquad (2.5)$$

where

$$D^2_{ikS} = \|x_i w_k\|^2_S = (x_i w_k)^T S (x_i w_k). \qquad (2.6)$$

The algorithm proceeds by pooling samples into respective clusters as with KM, then calculating a fuzzy partition according to

$$\mu_{ik} = \frac{1}{\sum_{j=1}^{Nc} \left(\frac{D_{ikS}}{D_{ijS}}\right)^{\frac{2}{(m-1)}}}; \quad 1 \leq k \leq Nc, 1 \leq i \leq N. \qquad (2.7)$$

This essentially normalizes the inverse of the distances of each sample to every cluster such that they sum to 1. The updated U is then utilized to refine cluster centroids for the next iteration, where the process repeats until convergence. This fuzzification of class membership allows for some level of overlap between clusters and, in some way, improved decision level for samples occurring at cluster boundaries. Moreover, the use of a Standardized Euclidean norm (see Table 2.1) will allow the algorithm to seek elongated hyper-ellipsoid clusters; however this will be restricted to finding clusters in a single orientation only.

Other modifications of these approaches include Gustafson–Kessel (GK) [33] and Gath–Geva (GG) [35], which attempt to incorporate adaptive distance norm that influence the local vicinity of each cluster (i.e., each cluster includes its own space-warping/norm-inducing matrix S_k). Specifically, GK requires that the determinant of each S_k be fixed, thus constraining the volume of each cluster. GG, on the other hand, employs a distance norms based on fuzzy maximum likelihood estimates. With both, fuzzy partitions are calculated per cluster (over all samples) in order to infer individual S_k matrices. These new norms are then individually applied to each cluster during the subsequent pooling step in order to calculate the nearest neighbor to each sample. Such algorithms impact boundaries and offer greater flexibility in locating clusters of different shape and orientation.

2.4.3 Mixture Decomposition Approaches

Mixture models such as the Gaussian mixture model (GMM) [36] assume that the data is generated by a finite mixture of probability distributions (each representing a different cluster). These typically utilize learning algorithms such as Expectation Maximization (EM) [37] to estimate parameters defining possible Gaussian mixtures present in the data. Samples are essentially treated as individual observations of an n-dimensional random vector:

$$f(x \mid \theta) = \sum_{k=1}^{Nc} \alpha_k \phi \left(x \mid \mu_k, \Sigma_k\right) \qquad (2.8)$$

where ϕ is a Gaussian function describing the kth Gaussian mixture component; α_k is the probability or density associated with the kth Gaussian mixture, and

$\theta = \left(\alpha_k, \mu_k, \Sigma_k \right)$ for $k = 1, \ldots, \mathrm{Nc}$ is the set of parameters describing the complete mixture.

The EM algorithm offers a tractable mechanism for estimating a new set of model parameters $\theta = \theta_n$ by starting with an initial value for each of the parameters θ_0 and then iteratively processing two steps: an expectation step that estimates the posterior (probability of cluster C_k given the data), according to the previous state of the model θ_{n-1}; next, a maximization step uses this posterior to update estimates of each of the model parameters such that the log-likelihood of X is progressively maximized.

E-step:

$$p_{\theta_{n-1}}(C_k \mid x_i) = \frac{\alpha_k \phi \left(x_i \mid \mu_k, \Sigma_k \right)}{\sum_{l=1}^{\mathrm{Nc}} \alpha_l \phi \left(x_i \mid \mu_l, \Sigma_l \right)}. \tag{2.9}$$

M-step:

$$\alpha_k' = \frac{1}{Ns} \sum_{i=1}^{Ns} p_{\theta_{n-1}} \left(C_k \mid x_i \right). \tag{2.10}$$

$$\mu_k' = \frac{\sum_{i=1}^{Ns} x_i p_{\theta_{n-1}} \left(C_k \mid x_i \right)}{\sum_{i=1}^{Ns} p_{\theta_{n-1}} \left(C_k \mid x_i \right)}. \tag{2.11}$$

$$\Sigma_k' = \frac{\sum_{i=1}^{Ns} p_{\theta_{n-1}} \left(C_k \mid x_i \right) \left(x_i - \mu_k' \right) \left(x_i - \mu_k' \right)^T}{\sum_{i=1}^{Ns} p_{\theta_{n-1}} \left(C_k \mid x_i \right)}. \tag{2.12}$$

Alternative functions may be considered in order to parameterize mixtures; however, each will involve the derivation of new EM algorithmic steps. Such approaches are beneficial when there is some a priori information available about the data being mined. This group includes Hidden Markov Models (HMM) and Independent Component Analysis Mixture Models (ICAMM) [38], where the latter techniques utilize information-theoretic criteria to separate possible mixtures based on mutual information or other entropy-based considerations. ICAMM has the potential to model class distributions that have non-Gaussian structure.

2.4.4   Agglomerative Hierarchical Approaches

In the field of bioinformatics and the interpretation of gene expression from microarray DNA testing, with the exception of squared error–based approaches, hierarchical clustering techniques typically form the bulk of research work performed [39]. Such approaches begin by treating every individual sample as its own cluster, before progressively connecting pairs of related clusters together to form new clusters. This merging process is achieved by assessing a proximity matrix (which may, for example, denote pair-wise distances between clusters), based on the current clusters in the

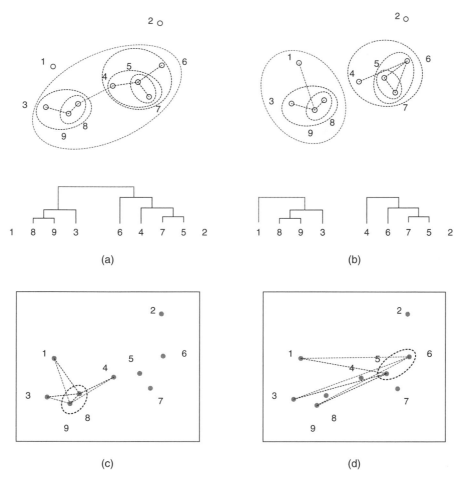

FIGURE 2.4 Examples of agglomerative based clustering approaches: in (a) Single Linkage and (b) Complete Linkage, linkage decisions are shown for the sixth agglomerative step; in (c) Shared Nearest Neighbors and (d) Shared Farthest Neighbors, the distances considered when two candidate samples are considered for grouping are indicated.

solution. The hierarchy of connections formed in the final result must then be cut using an appropriate heuristic in order to separate into cluster groups. A dendrogram is often used for the purpose of visualizing the clusters and represents the hierarchy of connected elements and relative distances between clusters and subclusters (see Fig. 2.4).

Single-linkage (SL) variants merge clusters/sample pairs based on the minimum distances between any two samples from each cluster, while Complete-linkage (CL) variants merge based on the minimum of the greatest distance of any two samples from each cluster [40]. Other more statistical based linkage functions have also been employed, for example, Average-linkage (AL) and Ward's algorithm [41].

A corollary to such approaches has seen the development of similar techniques that attempt to group clusters/sample pairs based on mutual neighborhood information: shared nearest (SNN) [42, 43] or shared farthest neighbors (SFN) [39], which each relate to SL and CL, respectively. In these approaches, grouping is based on whether two samples share similarity not just with one another, but also with a minimal set of other samples. As agglomerative methods need to consider pair-wise similarities across all samples, they are typically computationally exhaustive for large datasets and either take copious amounts of memory to run, or an extremely long time. Sensitivity to noise and inconsistency in clustering is quite common but is alleviated somewhat through SNN and SFN.

2.4.5 Graph-Theoretic Approaches

Graph-theoretic approaches tend to treat the samples as nodes on a graph, connected with edges, to which popular algorithms from graph theory can apply. Minimum spanning trees (MST) belong to this group, as do the recent methods such as Graphcut and Grabcut [44], which have found recent favor for use in semi-supervised (user-seeded) foreground/background selection in image and video data. In such methods, clusters are typically inferred based on the removal of the largest edges as in MST or finding optimal cuts through the edges that minimize some energy function to identify regions of lower density separating samples. In a related spectral-based approach, N-Cut [45] infers a way to sever such connections based on the spectral properties (eigen properties) of the pair-wise distance/similarity matrix.

2.4.6 Evolutionary Approaches

Evolutionary computation-based methods have also been applied to the problem of unsupervised clustering. In general, approaches in this category evolve or modify a population of solutions toward a more optimal set, or rather, a set in which certain members of the population achieve an optimal clustering solution (in terms of a chosen performance criterion).

In Reference 46, the concept of using hyperboxes to cluster spatial data was first considered. In this approach, the hyperbox is treated as a fuzzy cluster/set. Samples to be clustered are assigned a fuzzy membership based on whether or not they fall inside or nearby the region enclosed by the hyperbox (using fuzzy membership rules). Beginning with an initial hyperbox, enclosing a subset of samples, the hyperbox was either grown or new hyperboxes were added, as new samples were considered. This concept was then reframed using evolutionary programming [47, 48], wherein a *population* of hyperboxes is considered as a potential clustering solution. An element of random perturbation is then introduced, such that hyperboxes can be maintained, grown, or repositioned to form clusters that are more optimal in terms of the minimum description length criterion [49]. The MDL criterion quantifies the trade-off between goodness-of-fit to the data, with degrees of freedom defining the solution (e.g., number of parameters, number of clusters). In later efforts, this work was extended [50] to allow hyperboxes to be oriented (normally aligned) to feature axes. In addition, self-adaptive parameters were introduced to control the degree of perturbation in generating new hyperbox configurations.

These early evolutionary approaches proved quite effective for unsupervised clustering, motivating further efforts in the field. The Genetic Algorithm (GA), for instance, has been used in a similar manner for clustering [51]. In this case, parameters defining a set of clusters are each encoded by a single *chromosome* (e.g., a string denoting membership of samples belonging to one of a set of possible clusters). A fixed-size population of chromosomes (possible solutions) are maintained and evolved over a series of generations. At each generation, chromosomes are evaluated in terms of their fitness as a likely solution (e.g., validity measure outlined in Section 2). More fit solutions then become subject to processes rooted in natural selection, where their genetic material is shared and passed onto future generations, for instance, through reproduced offspring and/or random mutations. The result is a directed, parallel search strategy for more optimal populations of solutions.

By contrast, particle swarm (PS) approaches to clustering [52], offer an alternative notion of an evolving population, framed not in terms of the modification of genetic properties, but rather, one based around the social dynamics (swarming, hive, or flocking behaviors) commonly exhibited by different species within the animal kingdom. Examples of such dynamics can be seen in ant or insect colonies, or flocks of birds. In essence, a series of mobile agents exhibit swarm intelligence by being able to sense and change their local environment in the data space, while foraging for clustered regions. Behaviors exhibited and changes made by individuals have the ability to in turn modify the behavior of others, thereby influencing group dynamics. This works to redirect or dispatch local agents toward areas of interest for further investigation. PS represents an emerging area of research into data mining.

2.4.7   Neural Network Approaches

Neural network approaches offer the ability to identify and generalize across highly nonlinear relationships mined from the data. Neural Network methods typically fall into two groups: those based on competitive learning or learning vector quantization; and those born out of principles of PCA, factor analysis, and the more recent ICA [53].

Much of the research conducted, however, has focused on the former—competitive learning–based approaches. In unsupervised contexts, such approaches are primarily dominated by models rooted in Self-Organization. The methods developed and introduced in this monograph are focused in this direction. Principles governing self-organization and its relationship to the general concepts of Unsupervised Learning and clustering are reviewed in depth in Chapter 3.

We first digress, however, to a brief survey of the issues that need to be considered in assessing the validity of unsupervised clustering results.

2.5   ASSESSING CLUSTER QUALITY AND VALIDITY

In the context of Unsupervised Learning tasks, the role of cluster validity becomes twofold: namely, both to estimate an optimal number of cluster groups existing in the data, and to assess or evaluate the quality of any given clustering solution. This becomes especially important when the data space to be clustered is beyond a dimensionality that can be visually or subjectively assessed, or as an additional confidence indicator that may be used in conjunction with subjective evaluation.

As indicated previously, the absence of a priori information leads to much uncertainty in knowing what makes a valid cluster. As such, certain assumptions about the nature of a cluster, as well as the mechanism used to discover clusters, are what generally lead to the definition of cluster validity indices and ultimately their performance or value. With this in mind, we make a loose assumption that, for our purposes, by transforming our data vectors into a feature space, wherein we assess the relative similarity between data vectors, we expect our clusters to be somewhat Gaussian in nature, although different groupings are likely to each have differing densities.

According to Lam et al. [54], cluster validity measures fall into three classes: cost-function-based indices, density-based indices, and geometric-based indices, as well as those that exhibit hybrid properties. A vast number of validity indicators have been proposed over recent years; however, relatively few demonstrate promising and consistent performance. As such, attention is restricted to some of the more successful indices that have emerged from the recent literature.

2.5.1 Cost Function–Based Cluster Validity Indices

Cost-function-based indices attempt to minimize some error or heuristic criterion and include measures such as Figure of Merit [55], Akaike information criterion [56], and Bayes Information Criterion [57].

2.5.1.1 *Figure of Merit*   Figure of Merit (FOM), for instance, attempts to choose as its optimum the number of clusters that minimizes the cost function of the KM algorithm. This amounts to computing the root-mean-square of the distance between each data vector and the center of the cluster to which it is deemed a member.

$$\text{FOM}\left(N_c\right) = \sqrt{\left(\frac{1}{N_s}\right) \sum_{k=1}^{N_c} \sum_{x \in C_k} \|x - w_k\|^2} \qquad (2.13)$$

where N_c is the number of clusters in the solution; N_s is the total number of samples; C_k is the kth cluster; x is a sample vector belonging to the kth cluster, and w_k is the prototype vector representing the center of C_k. Typically, FOM will become smaller to indicate more desirable clustering solutions. The problem with this index is that as the number of clusters increases indefinitely, so too will the FOM decrease, as would be the case if one particular cluster was subdivided indefinitely, or until every data point is its own cluster, in which case FOM becomes zero.

2.5.1.2 *Bayes Information Criterion*   Bayes Information Criterion (BIC), on the other hand, avoids this problem by attempting to balance a likelihood criterion for model selection, with a term that penalizes increasing complexity.

$$\text{BIC}\left(N_c\right) = -2 \cdot \ln\left(L\right) + N_c \ln\left(N_s\right) \qquad (2.14)$$

where L is a maximized likelihood function for the estimated model. In a clustering context, a simple model might resemble a residual sum of squares from samples to their respective cluster centers, as in FOM. The second term penalizes complexity based on the number of clusters; however, if a model with more parameters is assumed (for instance, multivariate Gaussians with sample means w_k and covariances Σ_k), then both the likelihood and penalty terms may take on added complexity, as in Reference 58.

2.5.1.3 *I-index*   The I-index [59] takes an interesting deviation in that it is somewhat of a hybrid between a cost-function and geometric-based index and works through the combination of three factors:

$$I\left(N_c\right) = \left(\frac{1}{N_c} \cdot \frac{E_1}{E_{N_c}} \cdot D_{N_c}\right)^p. \tag{2.15}$$

$$E_{N_c} = \sum_{k=1}^{N_c} \sum_{j=1}^{N_s} u_{kj} \|x_j - z_k\|. \tag{2.16}$$

$$D_{N_c} = \max_{i,j=1}^{N_c} \|z_i - z_j\|. \tag{2.17}$$

The first factor in Equation 2.15 obviously attempts to reduce I as the number of clusters grows. By contrast, the second factor tends to decrease, promoting the formation of an increased number of compact clusters. The last factor measures maximum separation between all pairs of clusters and increases with N_c, while p acts as a contrast control between different cluster configurations [59]. Typically, an optimal N_c would be expected to maximize I.

2.5.2 Density-Based Cluster Validity Indices

Density-based indices attempt to capture information regarding the degree of overlap or mixing between clusters in a given clustering solution. As such, they are often related to fuzzy-based methods, although they are nott necessarily limited to such. As per Equation 2.7, a solution that defines crisp clusters may be interpreted in fuzzy terms, wherein such indices may be applied.

2.5.2.1 *Partition Coefficient*   PC is essentially a measure of how much overlap occurs between clusters when the partitioning is considered in a fuzzy sense. This is achieved by applying Equation 2.7 to estimate a fuzzy partition based on the state of the cluster centroids. The index is defined in Reference 60 as, for which N_c the maximum is expected to be optimal.

$$PC\left(N_c\right) = \frac{1}{N_s} \sum_{i=1}^{N_s} \sum_{j=1}^{N_c} \left(u_{ij}\right)^2. \tag{2.18}$$

Unfortunately, PC often exhibits monotonic growth as with FOM and thus tends to continue increasing with N_c, without penalty.

2.5.2.2 *Classification Entropy*
Like PC, CE too is related to an inferred fuzzy partition. This index takes the form:

$$\text{CE}\left(N_c\right) = -\frac{1}{N_s} \sum_{i=1}^{N_s} \sum_{j=1}^{N_c} u_{ij} \log\left(u_{ij}\right) \tag{2.19}$$

and measures the degree of fuzziness inherent. It mimics PC, in that a maximal value indicates more optimal clustering solutions.

2.5.2.3 *Xie Beni Index*
Essentially a hybrid between density- and geometric-based indices, XB [61] estimates the ratio of compactness π of a fuzzy K-partition of a dataset to its separation. As with PC and CE, the fuzzy partition can be estimated from a hard partition. XB has been mathematically shown to relate to Dunn's index, outlined in Section 2.5.3.1.

$$\text{XB}\left(N_c\right) = \frac{\sum_{i=1}^{N_s} \sum_{j=1}^{N_c} u_{ik} \|x_i - w_k\|}{N_s \min_{i,j} \|w_i - w_j\|}. \tag{2.20}$$

2.5.3   Geometric-Based Cluster Validity Indices

Geometric-based cluster validity indices form the bulk of measures proposed in the literature, due to their practicality in attempting to exploit the geometrical properties of clusters formed. Essentially, they all consider to some degree, the intuitive relationship between within- and between-cluster relationships, often working to maximize the within-cluster scatter with respect to between-cluster separation.

2.5.3.1 *Dunn's Index*
Dunn's index (DI) was also originally proposed for use in the identification of compact and well-separated clusters [62, 63] and is based on geometrical considerations. There are many variations and modifications of this index in the literature, primarily attempts at overcoming some inherent computational complexity. The index, in its original form, is

$$\text{DI}\left(U\right) = \min_{1 \leq i \leq N_c} \left\{ \min_{1 \leq j \leq N_c} \left\{ \frac{\delta\left(X_i, X_j\right)}{\max_{1 \leq k \leq N_c}\left(\Delta\left(X_k\right)\right)} \right\} \right\} \tag{2.21}$$

where δ denotes some form of linkage functional between two clusters (e.g., SL: the minimum distance between any two samples X_i in the two clusters); while Δ denotes the diameter of a cluster—maximum distance between any two points within. δ is analogous to the MkD of Section 2.3 and is used as a measure of class separation. δ is a point-by-point assessment on the data within the clusters. Similarly, Δ assesses the volume of scatter in a cluster. The goal then, is to maximize intercluster distances, while minimizing intra-cluster distances; therefore, large values of DI indicate favorable clustering solutions—choose N_c for which DI is maximized. One main limitation of the DI is that the computational complexity increases dramatically as N_c and N_s increase.

2.5.3.2 Calinski–Harabasz Index

The CH index [64] is currently one of the more successful indices, outperforming most others as reported in recent surveys [59, 65]. Again, as with other geometric-based indices, CH attempts to model the within-cluster scatter versus between-cluster separation via the respective traces of the between B, and within W cluster scatter matrices. Unlike other indices, however, CH binds explicit reference of all clusters to a global centroid z of the data space:

$$\text{CH}\left(N_c\right) = \frac{\text{Tr}\left(B\right) \cdot \left(N_c - 1\right)}{\text{Tr}\left(W\right) \cdot \left(N_s - N_c\right)}. \tag{2.22}$$

$$\text{Tr}\left(B\right) = \sum_{k=1}^{N_c} |C_k| \cdot \|w_k - z\|^2. \tag{2.23}$$

$$\text{Tr}\left(W\right) = \sum_{k=1}^{N_c} \sum_{i=1}^{|C_k|} \|x_i - w_k\|^2. \tag{2.24}$$

2.5.3.3 Geometric Index

A fairly recent index, proposed in Reference 66, again attempts to relate within-cluster scatter to between-class separation. Only, in this index, within-cluster scatter is instead estimated as the sum of the square roots of its eigenvalues (as estimated from the samples allocated to the cluster).

The underlying principle in this index is that each eigenvector λ_{jk}, from the largest to the smallest, represents an orthogonal set of axes through the kth cluster along its d most variant orientations. As such, the square roots of each eigenvalue are akin to a set of radii defining an enclosing hypersphere over the dense region of the cluster. The numerator then estimates the volume of the enclosing region as the square of the sum of set of diameters along each eigenvector. In two dimensions, this is easier to visualize, namely, that the square of two radii of an enclosing ellipse amounts to the area of an enclosing box. Taken to three dimensions, this becomes an enclosing volume, and so on. The formula for this index is given as follows.

$$\text{GI}\left(N_c\right) = \max_{1 \le k \le N_c} \frac{\left(2 \sum_{j=1}^{d} \sqrt{\lambda_{jk}}\right)^2}{\min_{1 \le q \le N_c} \|v_k - v_q\|_2} \tag{2.25}$$

where v_i represents the ith cluster centroid.

As reported in many surveys in the literature, DI, I-index, and CH show superior performance in assessing unsupervised clustering solutions on labeled data. GI also shows equal promise (although is relatively new to the field).

In the majority of cases in the literature, such indices are used to highlight suitable choices of an optimal number of clusters, after solutions have been found, that is, a clustering algorithm must be run to completion, for a number of choices of N_c, before validity criteria may be applied. Obviously, this is a time-consuming task, and it might be difficult to estimate an appropriate range over which to select K values with which to cluster. However, such is the current state of the art.

In this book, particular attention is paid to these indices, both on account of their reported success, and the fact that dynamic self-organizing models for clustering have the unique opportunity to embed such considerations on-the-fly, as they attempt to build an appropriate number of clusters into a viable solution. As such, they are uniquely poised to implement cluster validation simultaneously, while inferring likely candidates for new clusters. In a new model for dynamic self-organization, proposed in Chapter 7, we show how the I-index, GI, and CH-related indices may in fact be estimated through the natural course of learning, due to properties that are inherent in the new model.

CHAPTER 3

Self-Organization

3.1 INTRODUCTION

In this chapter, the principles of Self-Organization will be presented. Special focus will be given to Adaptive Resonance Theory and Self-Organizing Map neural networks. The chapter begins with the investigation of the theoretic basis of formulations of these neural networks and ends with illustrations of a few examples. The structures of these networks and their learning algorithms are also thoroughly explored.

3.2 PRINCIPLES OF SELF-ORGANIZATION

Unsupervised Learning and Self-Organization are inherently related. In general, self-organizing systems are typified by the union of Local interactions and competition over some limited resource. In his book [2], Haykin identifies four major principles of Self-Organization.

- Synaptic Self-Amplification;
- Synaptic Competition;
- Cooperation;
- Knowledge through Redundancy.

3.2.1 Synaptic Self-Amplification and Competition

The first principle of Self-Organization (self-amplification) is expressed through Hebb's postulate of learning [67], which is supported by neurobiological evidence. This states that (on the cellular level), when two cells are within significant proximity enabling one to excite another, and furthermore, do so persistently, some form of physiological/metabolic growth process results. This process works to enhance the

Unsupervised Learning: A Dynamic Approach, First Edition.
Matthew Kyan, Paisarn Muneesawang, Kambiz Jarrah, and Ling Guan.
© 2014 by The Institute of Electrical and Electronics Engineers, Inc. Published by John Wiley & Sons, Inc.

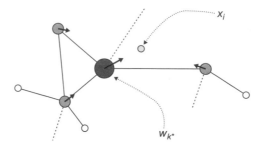

FIGURE 3.1   Self-amplification, competition, and cooperation in learning: wk* represents the synaptic vector of the winning neuron (competition), which adapts (self-amplifies) toward the input, thereby strengthening its correlation with future inputs in this region. At the same time, associative memory is imparted to neighboring neurons (cooperation)—related to the winner through some defined or inferred topology.

firing cell's efficiency in triggering the second cell. In other words (in neural network terms), a synaptic path evolves and strengthens between the two neurons (memory cells), so that future associations occur much more readily. This action of strengthening the association between two nodes, functions as a correlation between their two states.

Typically, the Hebbian learning rule that ensues from this principle would eventually drive synapses into saturation were it not for the second principle, wherein some competition occurs for limited resources. These properties combined, have led to the modified Hebbian adaptive rule, as proposed by Kohonen [68]:

$$\Delta w_{k*} = \alpha \varphi \left(k^*, x_i \right) \left[x_i w_{k*} \right] \tag{3.1}$$

where w_{k*} is the synaptic weight vector of the winning neuron k^* (see Figure 3.1), α is the learning rate, and some scalar response $\varphi \left(\cdot \right)$ to the firing of neuron k^* (activation).

The activation function $\varphi \left(\cdot \right)$ is the result of the second principle (synaptic competition). Neurons generally compete to see which is most representative of a given input pattern presented to the network. Some form of discriminative function oversees this process (e.g., choosing a neuron as a winner if its synaptic vector minimizes Euclidean distance over the set of all neurons). This process is often termed *Competitive Learning*.

3.2.2   Cooperation

Hebb's postulate is also suggestive of the lateral or associative aspect to the way knowledge is then captured in the network, that is, not just through the winner, but also through nearby neurons in the output layer. This property is generally implemented in self-organizing architectures by virtue of the way in which nodes are interconnected. Often the strength of connection is not considered, but rather, a simple link functions as an indicator of which other nodes in the network will more readily be associated with a winning node. Thus, a Local neighborhood is defined, and it is through this that knowledge may be imparted. Local adaptation usually follows the simple Kohonen update rule (Equation 3.1), whereby a portion of information is learned by the winning node, with neighboring nodes extracting lesser portions from the same input.

3.2.3 Knowledge Through Redundancy

Although not explicitly encoded, the final principle of Self-Organization implicitly results from the action of the first three. When exposed, any order or structure inherent within a series of activation patterns represents redundant information that is ultimately encoded by the network as knowledge. In other words, the network will evolve such that similar patterns will be captured and encoded by similar output nodes, while neighboring nodes organize themselves around these dominant redundancies, each in turn focusing on and encoding lesser redundant patterns across the input space.

3.3 FUNDAMENTAL ARCHITECTURES

3.3.1 Adaptive Resonance Theory

A common attribute of biological systems is the ability to extract and act on regularities within their natural environment without the the help of a teacher. The goal of self-organizing neural networks is to discover significant regularities within the input data without external supervision. Simulating the behavior of human beings, self-organizing systems attempt to discover the structure, patterns, or features directly from their environment [69–74]. The ability to learn about the environment without a teacher has been considered an important characteristic of intelligent systems. For example, if we want to classify the vectors within a certain input environment, at a certain point in time we may train a backpropagation neural network using N vectors to do the task. When training is completed these N vectors will be correctly classified. However, as the input environment changes in time the accuracy of the backpropagation network will rapidly decrease because the weights are fixed, thus preventing the network from adapting to the changing environment. Therefore, this algorithm is not plastic. Algorithms can only be plastic if they retain the potential to adapt to new input vectors. To overcome this problem the network can be retrained on the new input vectors. The network will adapt to any changes in the input environment, but this will cause a rapid decrease in the accuracy because old classification in formation is lost. Thus, when the network adapts to the new input (becoming plastic), it becomes unstable. It can only retain its stability if it preserves previously learned knowledge.

Taken together, the problems can be posed as follows. How can a learning system be designed to remain plastic, or adaptive, in response to significant events and yet remain stable in response to irrelevant events? How does the system know how to switch between its stable modes and its plastic modes to achieve stability without rigidity and plasticity without chaos? How can it preserve its previously learned knowledge while continuing to learn new things? And what prevents the new learning from washing away the memories of prior learning?

The Adaptive Resonance Theory (ART), developed by Carpenter and Grossberg, suggests a solution to the problems faced by all intelligent systems that are capable of autonomous learning and skillful performance within complex environments [75,76].

The ART architecture is a specifically designed neural network to overcome the stability–plasticity dilemma. It is described using nonlinear differential equations and has been shown to be stable [77, 78]. It also carries out Self-Organization of recognition codes for arbitrary sequences of input patterns.

3.3.1.1 *The ART Architecture*   The ART architecture consists of two layers of neurons called the comparison (input) layer and the recognition (output) layer. The basic features of the ART architecture are shown in Figure 3.2. It has feedforward connections from the input layer to the output layer and feedback connections from the output layer to the input layer. In the recognition layer, there are lateral inhibitory connections that allow competition. For each layer, there are gain control signals that control the data that flow through the layers at each stage of the operating cycle. Between the input and output layers there is a reset element. This plays a vital role in the network. It is responsible for comparing the input patterns to a vigilance threshold that determines whether a new cluster should be created for an input pattern.

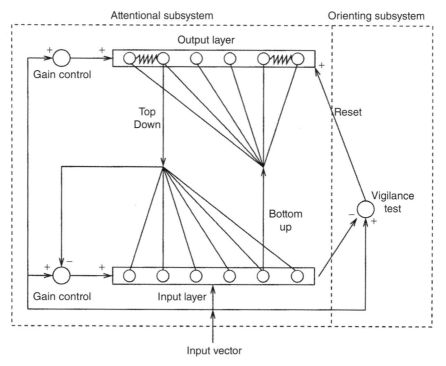

FIGURE 3.2   The ART architecture.

3.3.1.2 *Equations and Algorithms*   The dynamic equations for the activities of any neuron on both input and output layers have the form:

$$\frac{d}{dt}x_k = -x_k + (1 - Ax_k)J_k^+ - (B + Cx_k)J_k^-, \tag{3.2}$$

where J_k^+ is an excitatory input to the kth unit and J_k^- is an inhibitory input, and all the parameters A, B, and C are nonnegative.

Each neuron i in the input layer receives three inputs.

1. An input value I_i.
2. A gain control G.
3. The top-down prototype from output layer neuron v_j to input layer neuron v_i.

The top-down prototype input:

$$V_i = \sum_j f(x_j)z_{ji}, \tag{3.3}$$

where $f(x_j)$ is the signal generated by activity x_j of v_j and z_{ji} is the top-down weight from v_j to v_i. The total excitatory input J_i^+ to the ith unit v_i of input layer is

$$J_i^+ = I_i + DV_i + BG, \tag{3.4}$$

where D and B are constants.

The inhibitory term:

$$J_i^- = \sum_j f(x_j). \tag{3.5}$$

Thus $J_i^- = 0$ if and only if output layer is inactive. When output layer is active, only the winning neuron has a nonzero output:

$$f(x_j) = \begin{cases} 1 & \text{the winner} \\ 0 & \text{otherwise} \end{cases}. \tag{3.6}$$

Since $J_i^- = -1$, substituting Equations 3.3, 3.4, 3.5, and 3.6 into Equation 3.2, the equation for the ith neuron in the input layer becomes

$$\frac{d}{dt}x_i = -x_i + (1 - Ax_i)(I_i + Dz_{ji} + BG) - (B + Cxi), \tag{3.7}$$

where the gain control:

$$G = \begin{cases} 1 & \text{if input vector is not zero and output layer is inactive} \\ 0 & \text{otherwise} \end{cases}. \tag{3.8}$$

The equilibrium activities of x_i are as follows. If there is no input vector and output layer is inactive, then

$$x_i = -\frac{B}{1+C}.$$ (3.9)

If an input vector is applied, while keeping the output layer inactive for the moment, then

$$x_i = \frac{I_i}{1 + A(I_i + B) + C}.$$ (3.10)

If the input vector is active and the output layer is active, then

$$x_i = \frac{I_i + Dz_{ij} - B}{1 + A(I_i + Dz_{ij}) + C}.$$ (3.11)

Whether x_i is greater than, equal to, or less then zero depends on the quantities in the numerator in Equation 3.11. There are three cases of interest, which are determined by application of the $\frac{2}{3}$ *Rule*.

The $\frac{2}{3}$ Rule requires that x_i be positive when the input layer neuron v_i has a positive input value I_i and a large value from top-down weight z_{ij}. Thus, in the most extreme case with $z_{ij} = 1$ and $I_i = 1$, the numerator in Equation 3.11 becomes $1 + D - B > 0$, or

$$B < D + 1.$$ (3.12)

The $\frac{2}{3}$ *Rule* requires that x_i be negative if any input layer neuron does not receive a top-down signal from the output layer. In this case, $I_i + Dz_{ij} - B = 1 - B < 0$, or

$$B > 1.$$ (3.13)

Finally, the $\frac{2}{3}$ *Rule* also requires that x_i be negative if the output layer is producing a top-down output, but there is not yet an input vector. $I_i + Dz_{ij} - B = 0 + D - B < 0$, or

$$D < B.$$ (3.14)

Combining Equations 3.12, 3.13, and 3.14 to give the overall $\frac{2}{3}$ *Rule* inequality:

$$\max\{D, 1\} < B < D + 1.$$ (3.15)

The top-down weight obeys a learning equation of the form:

$$\frac{d}{dt}z_{ji} = f(x_j)[-z_{ji} + h(x_i)].$$ (3.16)

If the output layer neuron v_j is active and the input layer neuron v_i is inactive, then $h(x_i) = 0$ and $f(x_j) = 1$, so

$$\frac{d}{dt}z_{ji} = -z_{ji}. \tag{3.17}$$

Thus, z_{ij} decays exponentially toward zero.

On the other hand, if both v_j and v_i are active, then $f(x_j) = h(x_i) = 1$, so

$$\frac{d}{dt}z_{ji} = -z_{ji} + 1. \tag{3.18}$$

Thus z_{ij} increases exponentially toward zero.

Combining Equations 3.16–3.18 leads to the learning rule governing the top-down weights:

$$\frac{d}{dt}z_{ji} = \begin{cases} -z_{ji} + 1 & \text{if } v_j \text{ and } v_i \text{ are active} \\ -z_{ji} & \text{if } v_j \text{ is active and } v_i \text{ is inactive.} \\ 0 & \text{if } v_j \text{ is inactive} \end{cases} \tag{3.19}$$

Recall from Equation 3.11 that the condition of the numerator giving a positive value is

$$I_i + Dz_{ij} - B > 0. \tag{3.20}$$

Since $I_i = 1$, this relation defines a condition on z_{ji}:

$$z_{ji} > \frac{B-1}{D}. \tag{3.21}$$

The bottom-up weight from v_i on input layer to v_j on output layer is determined by

$$\frac{d}{dt}z_{ij} = Kf(x_j)\left[(1 - z_{ij})Lh(x_i) - z_{ij}\sum_{k\neq i}h(x_k)\right], \tag{3.22}$$

where K and L are constants, $f(x_j)$ is the output of v_j, and $h(x_i)$ is the output of v_i.

If v_i is active then $h(x_i) = 1$, otherwise $h(x_i) = 0$. When v_j is active, $f(x_j) = 1$. Thus Equation 3.22 reduces to

$$\frac{d}{dt}z_{ij} = -Kz_{ij}\sum_{k\neq i}h(x_k). \tag{3.23}$$

If both v_i and v_j are active, so

$$\frac{d}{dt}z_{ij} = K\left[(1 - z_{ij})L - z_{ij}\sum_{k\neq i} h(x_k)\right].$$

(3.24)

If the input pattern is **I**, then the magnitude of **I** is defined as $|\mathbf{I}| = \sum_i I_i$. Since I_i is either 0 or 1, the magnitude of **I** is equal to the number of nonzero inputs. The output of the input layer is the pattern **S**. Its magnitude is $|\mathbf{S}| = \sum_i h(x_i)$.

$$\mathbf{S} = \begin{cases} \mathbf{I} & \text{the output layer is inactive} \\ \mathbf{I} \cap \mathbf{V}^J & \text{the output layer is active} \end{cases},$$

(3.25)

where the superscript on $\mathbf{V}^J$ means that v_J is the winning neuron on output layer.

Since $|\mathbf{S}| = \sum_i h(x_i)$, then $\sum_{k\neq i} h(x_k) = \sum_k h(x_k) - h(x_i)$, which will be equal to either $|\mathbf{S}| - 1$ or $|\mathbf{S}|$.

By combining Equations 3.22, 3.23, and 3.25:

$$\frac{d}{dt}z_{ij} = \begin{cases} K\left[(1 - z_{ij})L - z_{ij}(|\mathbf{S}| - 1)\right] & \text{if } v_i \text{ and } v_j \text{ are active} \\ -K|\mathbf{S}|z_{ij} & \text{if } v_i \text{ is inactive and } v_j \text{ is active.} \\ 0 & \text{if } v_i \text{ is inactive} \end{cases}$$

(3.26)

The weights on the winning neuron in output layer v_J take on the asymptotic values given by

$$z_{iJ} = \begin{cases} \dfrac{L}{L-1+|\mathbf{S}|} & \text{if } v_i \text{ is active} \\ 0 & \text{if } v_i \text{ is active} \end{cases},$$

(3.27)

where $L > 1$ in order to keep $L - 1 > 0$.

Since all patterns are a subset of the pattern containing all 1s, the initial weight values are set within the range:

$$0 \le z_{ij}(0) \le \frac{L}{L-1+M},$$

(3.28)

where M is the number of neurons on the input layer. This condition ensures that some uncommitted neuron does not accidentally win over a neuron that has learned a particular input pattern.

The ART algorithm is summarized as follows.

Let M be the number of neurons on the input layer and N be the number of neurons on the output layer. Other parameters are chosen in terms of the following constraints.

$$A \geq 0$$
$$C \geq 0$$
$$D \geq 0$$
$$\max\{D, 1\} < B < D + 1$$
$$L > 1$$
$$0 < \rho \leq 1$$

Top-down weights $(v_j \rightarrow v_i)$ are initialized according to

$$z_{ji}(0) > \frac{B-1}{D}$$

and bottom-up weights $(v_i \rightarrow v_j)$ are initialized according to

$$0 < z_{ij}(0) < \frac{L}{L-1+M}.$$

The activities on output layer are initialized to zero and the input layer activities are initialized to

$$x_i(0) = -\frac{B}{1+C}.$$

After the initialization, the procedures are as follows.

1. Apply an input vector $\mathbf{I}$ to the input layer. The activities are calculated in terms of

$$x_i = \frac{I_i}{1+A(I_i+B)+C}.$$

2. Calculate the output vector for the input layer,

$$s_i = h(x_i) = \begin{cases} 1 & x_i > 0 \\ 0 & x_i \leq 0 \end{cases}.$$

3. Propagate S forward to the output layer and calculate the activities according to

$$T_j = \sum_{i=1}^{M} s_i z_{ij}.$$

4. Only the winning neuron has a nonzero output

$$f(x_j) = \begin{cases} 1 & T_j = \max\{T_k\}\forall k \\ 0 & \text{otherwise} \end{cases}.$$

5. Backpropagate the output to the input layer,

$$V_i = \sum_{j=1}^{N} f(x_j) z_{ji}.$$

6. Calculate the new activities according to

$$x_i = \frac{I_i + D z_{ji} - B}{1 + A(I_i + D z_{ji}) + C}.$$

7. Perform the vigilance test,

$$\frac{|\mathbf{S}|}{|\mathbf{I}|} = \frac{\sum_{i=1}^{M} s_i}{\sum_{i=1}^{M} I_i}.$$

8. If $|\mathbf{S}|/|\mathbf{I}| < \rho$ mask the current winner and go to Step 1 to select another winner; otherwise go to Step 10.

9. If no neuron passes the vigilance test, create a new neuron to accommodate the new pattern.

10. Adjust the bottom-up weights,

$$z_{i,J} = \begin{cases} \dfrac{L}{L-1+|\mathbf{S}|} & \text{if } v_i \text{ is active} \\ 0 & \text{if } v_i \text{ is inactive} \end{cases}.$$

11. Update the top-down weights,

$$z_{J,i} = \begin{cases} 1 & \text{if } v_i \text{ is active} \\ 0 & \text{if } v_i \text{ is inactive} \end{cases}.$$

3.3.1.3 *An Experimental Example*   The behavior of the ART neural network is illustrated in Figure 3.3. It is assumed that the patterns to be classified are the six patterns of the letters $S, I, Y, I, N,$ and G. These patterns have 5×7 pixels that are presented to the ART with 35 input neurons. The vigilance threshold is set to 0.9.

The left side of Figure 3.3 shows the input to the network. The right side presents prototype patterns formed after each iteration. After the network is initialized, the first pattern is presented. Since no stored prototypes exist at this stage, the first unallocated neuron in the recognition layer wins. The internal connection weights are altered to form an internal prototype that is identical to the "S." When the second pattern is applied, it is sufficiently different from the previously stored pattern; thus, a new "I" prototype is added. Similar behaviors for the letters "Y," "N," and "G" lead to three stored prototypes. The fourth input pattern matches the second prototype "I." As a result, no additional prototype is formed; only weights are updated. When a pattern "S" with a missing black pixel in the upper edge is applied, it is accepted as being similar to the "S" prototype. But the "S" input degrades this prototype during the updating of the top-down weights. Similar behavior occurs in the last pattern.

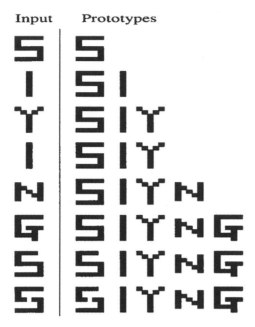

FIGURE 3.3   Prototypes formation.

The results of the experiment have shown that the ART network can perform well with perfect input patterns. The disadvantage of the ART is that it is sensitive to the order of input patterns and even a small amount of noise will cause problems. Another problem can be caused by the vigilance value that is uniform across both features and categories. For example, a vigilance setting that separates "O" from "Q" may impose intolerance to noise for other characters. As the input patterns increase, it is very hard to set the Global threshold value to distinguish various prototypes. Modifications are necessary to enhance the performance of the ART algorithm, allowing a dynamic setting of the vigilance parameter.

3.3.2   Self-Organizing Map

The Self-Organizing Map (SOM) is another unsupervised neural network model and algorithm that implements a characteristic nonlinear projection from the high dimensional space of the input signal onto a low dimensional array of neurons. It was proposed by Kohonen [79]. The principle of the network is based on a similar model developed earlier by Willshaw and Malsburg [80], explaining the formation of direct topographic projections between two laminar structures known as retinotectal mappings.

Kohonen discovered an astounding new phenomenon—there exist adaptive systems that can automatically form one- or two-dimensional maps of features that are present in the input signals. The input signals can be presented in a random order. If they are metrically similar in some structured way, then the same structure, in

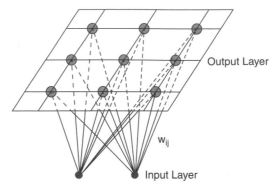

FIGURE 3.4 The SOM architecture.

a topologically correct form, will be reflected in the spatial relations of the output responses. This phenomenon follows closely the observations of biological systems in which different sensory inputs are known to be mapped onto neighboring areas of the brain in an orderly fashion.

3.3.2.1 *The SOM Architecture* The SOM architecture consists of two layers, an input layer and an output (competitive) layer. Typically, the neurons in the output layer are organized as a two-dimensional (2D) grid as shown in Figure 3.4. These two layers are fully connected. Each neuron in the output layer is associated with a set of weight vectors $\mathbf{w}_j = (\omega_{1j}, \omega_{2j}, \ldots, \omega_{nj}) \in R^n$.

When an input vector $\mathbf{x} = (x_1, x_2, \ldots, x_n) \in R^n$ is presented, each neuron in the input layer takes on the value of the corresponding entry in the input vector. The output layer computes a matching value for each neuron and competes to find a winning neuron. Then, the best matching $\mathbf{w}_j$ is updated to comply better with $\mathbf{x}$. The overall operation of the SOM is similar to the ART's winner-take-all competitive learning paradigm. However, the SOM differs in the details of its equations and the choice of the weights to be updated on each training cycle.

3.3.2.2 *SOM Learning* According to the *Euclidean* distance, the most matching neuron, or the winner c, is defined as

$$c(t) = \arg \min_j \{||\mathbf{x}(t) - \mathbf{w}_j(t)||\}, t = 1, 2, \ldots, \tag{3.29}$$

which is the same as

$$||\mathbf{x}(t) - \mathbf{w}_c(t)|| = \min_j \{||\mathbf{x}(t) - \mathbf{w}_j(t)||\}. \tag{3.30}$$

The objective is to define the $\mathbf{w}_j$ in such a way that the mapping is ordered and descriptive of the distribution of $\mathbf{x}$.

Traditional vector quantization techniques attempt to optimally determine the $\mathbf{w}_j$ by minimizing the average expected quantization error:

$$E = \int f[d(\mathbf{x}, \mathbf{w}_c)]p(\mathbf{x})d\mathbf{x}, \tag{3.31}$$

where f is a monotonically increasing function of the distance d and $p(\mathbf{x})$ is the probability density function of $\mathbf{x}$ and $\mathbf{w}_c$ is the codebook vector that is closest to $\mathbf{x}$ in the input space.

Since, in general, the probabilistic information about the pattern vector such as $p(\mathbf{x})$ is unknown and the index c is also a function of $\mathbf{x}$ and all the $\mathbf{w}_j$, the exact optimization of Equation 3.31 is still an unsolved theoretical problem. Even though some suboptimal solutions for the set of values $\{\mathbf{w}_j\}$ have been found, the indexing of these values can be made in an arbitrary way. Therefore, the mapping from input space onto the set of codebook vectors is still unordered.

In view of these problems, Kohonen has shown that if E is modified in such a way that the quantization error is *smoothed locally* and the smoothing kernel h_{cj} is a particular type of function of the distance between neurons c and j, then minimization of the new objective function:

$$E' = \int \sum_j h_{cj} f[d(\mathbf{x}, \mathbf{w}_j)]p(\mathbf{x})d\mathbf{x} \tag{3.32}$$

defines *ordered* values of the $\mathbf{w}_j$. The best solution for Equation 3.32 is based on the Robbins–Monro stochastic approximation. Based on this idea, the stochastic sample function $E''(t)$ of E' is considered:

$$E'' = \sum_j h_{cj} f(d[\mathbf{x}(t), \mathbf{w}_j(t)]). \tag{3.33}$$

Let $d(\mathbf{x}, \mathbf{w}_j) = ||\mathbf{x} - \mathbf{w}_j||$; then the approximate optimization algorithm is

$$\mathbf{w}_j(t+1) = \mathbf{w}_j(t) + \alpha(t)h_{cj}(t)[\mathbf{x}(t) - \mathbf{w}_j(t)], \tag{3.34}$$

where $h_{cj}(t)$ is the neighborhood function and $\alpha(t)$ is the learning rate coefficient. During the course of the ordering, both the neighborhood function and the adaptation rate decrease monotonically with time. The neighborhood function $h_{cj}(t)$ is a central function in the SOM, which describes the interaction of reference vector $\mathbf{w}_j$ and $\mathbf{w}_c$ during adaptation. If a step function is used, namely:

$$h_{cj}(t) = \begin{cases} 1 & \text{if } c \in N_c(t) \\ 0 & \text{if } c \notin N_c(t) \end{cases}, \tag{3.35}$$

where $N_c(t)$ is the neighborhood set centered on the winner. Alternatively, as depicted in Figure 3.5, a Gaussian neighborhood may be used to concentrate the learning more

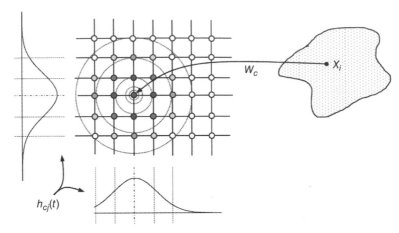

FIGURE 3.5   Local neighborhood smoothing in the SOM.

locally about the winning neuron:

$$h_{cj}(t) = \begin{cases} e^{-\frac{\|\mathbf{r}_c - \mathbf{r}_j\|}{2\sigma}} & \text{if } c \in N_c(t) \\ 0 & \text{if } c \notin N_c(t) \end{cases}, \tag{3.36}$$

where $\mathbf{r}_c$ and $\mathbf{r}_j$ each represent position vectors on the output layer for the winning neuron and current neuron, respectively, and σ represents the radius of the neighborhood set $N_c(t)$. With an appropriate neighborhood function chosen, the SOM equations can then be expressed as

$$\mathbf{w}_j(t+1) = \mathbf{w}_j(t) + \alpha(t)[\mathbf{x}(t) - \mathbf{w}_j(t)], \forall j \in N_c(t) \tag{3.37}$$

$$\mathbf{w}_j(t+1) = \mathbf{w}_j(t), \forall j \notin N_c(t).$$

3.3.2.3   The SOM Algorithm   The SOM learning algorithm can be summarized as follows.

1. *Initialize the MAP.* Given a MAP of size (M, N), where M is the number of neurons and N the dimensions of each input vector, define the weights $w_{ij}(t)$ between input i and output neuron j at time t. Initialize weights from the n inputs to the output neurons to small random values. Set the initial radius of the neighborhood function around neuron j, $N_j(0)$, to be large. Let $\mathbf{x}(t), t = 0, 1, \ldots$, $n - 1$ represent the training vector sequence.
2. *Present input vector* $\mathbf{x}(t)$. Place the sensory stimulus input vector $x_0 t, x_1(t), \ldots$, $x_{n-1}(t)$, where $x_i(t)$ is the input neuron i at time t, onto the input layer.
3. Calculate distances d_j between the input and each output neuron j:

$$d_j = \sum_{i=0}^{n-1} (x_i(t) - w_{ij}(t))^2. \tag{3.38}$$

4. *Similarity matching*. Select the output neuron whose weight vector best matches input vector $\mathbf{x}(t)$, that is, with minimum d_j, as the winning neuron. Designate the winning neuron to be j^*.

5. *Update weights*. Adaptively modify weights for neuron j^* and its neighbors $N_{j^*}(t)$ such that neurons within the activity bubble are moved toward the input vector as follows.

$$w_{ij}(t+1) = w_{ij}(t+1) + alpha_{ij}(t)(x_i(t) - w_{ij}(t))$$

for $j \in N_{j^*}(t)$, $(0 < \alpha(t) < 1)$ and $0 \le i \le n - 1$. The learning rate $\alpha(t)$ decreases with time, which slows the weight adaptation. The neighborhood $N_{j^*}(t)$ decreases in size as time goes on, thus localizing the area of maximum activity.

6. *Check condition for termination*. Exit when no noticeable change to the feature map has occurred. Otherwise repeat by going to Step 2.

3.3.2.4 *Experimental Examples*   The following experimental results explain the SOM clustering phenomenon using probability density functions. The probability density function is a statistical measure that describes the data distribution in the pattern space. Given a pattern space with a certain probability density function, it can be shown that the map will order itself so that the point density of the neurons in the map tends to approximate the probability density function of the pattern space. To visualize the ordering processes, examples with intermediate self-organizing phases are given.

Figures 3.6 and 3.7 show an example of mapping 2D vectors onto a 13×13 square array. The training patterns are uniformly distributed on a square region $(0 \le x_1 \le 6, 0 \le x_2 \le 6)$ shown in Figure 3.6.

The weights start from random values as shown in Figure 3.7a. As learning progresses, indicated by the snapshots in Figure 3.7(b and c), the weights are pulled apart by the input patterns and organized into a square grid, that is, to represent the

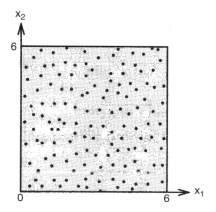

FIGURE 3.6   A square 2D vector.

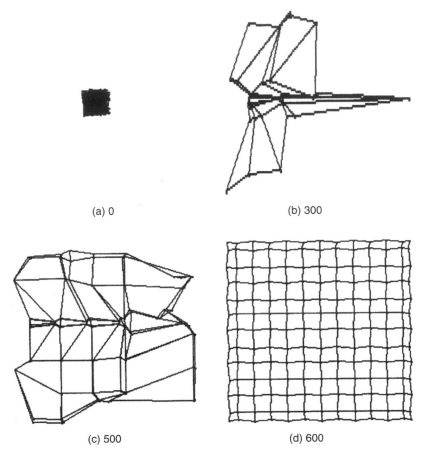

(a) 0

(b) 300

(c) 500

(d) 600

FIGURE 3.7   SOM mapping of the 2D vector in Figure 3.6 onto a square array.

distribution of the pattern space. The final state of the network in Figure 3.7d shows that the neurons have been optimally ordered to span the pattern space as accurately as possible.

Figure 3.8 shows another example of mapping from 2D inputs to a square array. The input probability distribution is chosen uniformly from a 2D triangular region. Figure 3.8(a–c) shows the development of the spatial ordering of the weight vectors. The final map, Figure 3.8d, shows that the square shape of the output array makes the point density somewhat nonuniform (structure dependent).

It is also worthwhile to try maps from two dimensions onto one dimension, despite the impossibility of preserving all the topology. Figure 3.9 shows the development of the map from the same 2D square region as Figure 3.7 to a 1D line of 88 neurons. The initial weights start from random values in a small square as shown Figure 3.9a. They evolve rather quickly to regular curves in Figure 3.9(b and c), and then gradually develop a finer structure to cover the space as best as they can, as shown in Figure 3.9d.

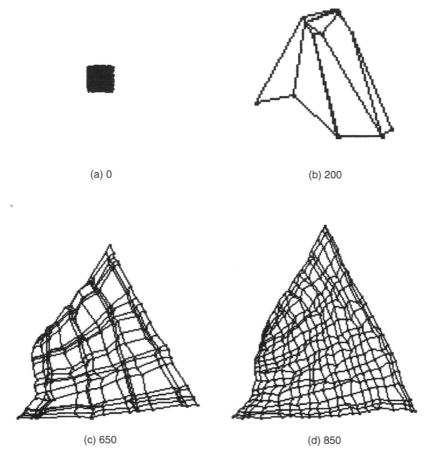

(a) 0   (b) 200

(c) 650   (d) 850

FIGURE 3.8   SOM mapping of a triangular 2D vector onto a square array.

Figure 3.10 illustrates a case in which the uniform distribution is over a triangular area. With enough neurons, it is possible to get a good approximation of a space-filling curve. The linear neurons tend to approximate a higher dimensional distribution by the space-filling curve (Peano curve).

3.4   OTHER FIXED ARCHITECTURES FOR SELF-ORGANIZATION

In addition to ART and SOM, there are two other fixed approaches that could be considered fundamental, namely, Neural Gas and the Hierarchical Feature Map. While both are strongly related to the SOM in terms of the learning mechanism, they each have spawned a range of newer architectures and thus warrant a brief introduction in this section. Their relationship to newer architectures will be expanded upon in Section 3.5.

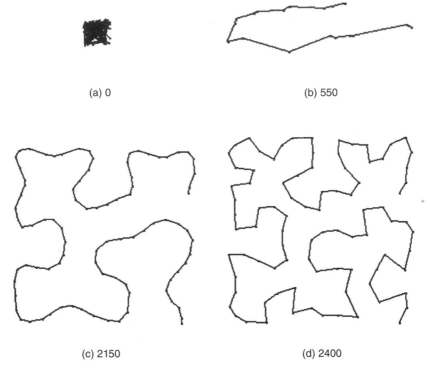

(a) 0   (b) 550

(c) 2150   (d) 2400

FIGURE 3.9   SOM mapping of the square 2D vector into a 1D representation.

3.4.1 Neural Gas

In typical SOM-based approaches, topology is *imposed* rather than inferred (via a fixed predefined lattice of nodes). Neural Gas (NG) [81], on the other hand, does not attempt to impose any topology, instead, the k-nearest neighbors at every stage in learning are evaluated and utilized in order to refine winning and neighboring prototypes. The k-nearest neighbors approach in effect attempts to achieve the associative sharing of information that is exhibited through the Gaussian neighborhood in the SOM.

Unlike the SOM, however, the neighborhood function is generally realized as an exponential over the *rank* R_j of each of the k neighbors (with the winner having a rank value of $R_{k*} = 0$ and the remaining nodes having values $R_j = [1, 2, 3, \ldots, k-1]$. From here, the neighborhood function of Equation 3.36 is replaced with Equation 3.39 and applied as in the SOM. The progression of the NG algorithm is shown pictorially in Figure 3.11b.

$$h_{cj}(t) = \begin{cases} e^{\left(\frac{-R_j}{2\sigma}\right)} & \text{if } c \in N_c(t) \\ 0 & \text{if } c \notin N_c(t) \end{cases}. \tag{3.39}$$

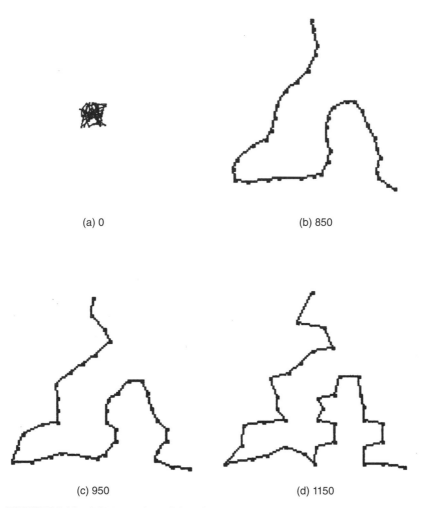

(a) 0   (b) 850

(c) 950   (d) 1150

FIGURE 3.10   SOM mapping of the triangular 2D vector into a 1D representation.

3.4.2   Hierarchical Feature Map

In the Hierarchical Feature Map (HFM) [82], a pyramidal hierarchy of SOMs are trained in a top-down manner. Each unit in the SOM of an upper layer is connected to its own SOM map in a lower layer, as depicted in Figure 3.11c, where the data space for training lower level maps results from individual portions of the original data space, as partitioned by higher level SOMs.

An appropriate choice of network parameters that can handle different datasets remains elusive; thus, any classification is inherently bound to the network structure rather than the underlying data distribution.

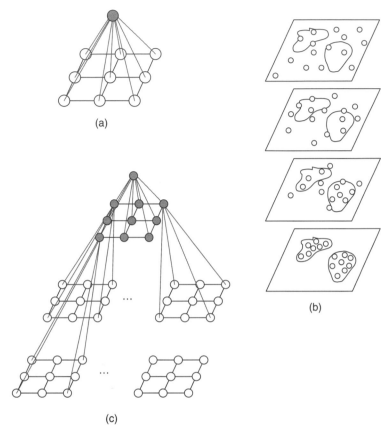

(a)

(b)

(c)

FIGURE 3.11 Classic stationary Competitive Learning architectures: (a) Kohonen's SOM; (b) Neural Gas; (c) Hierarchical Feature Map.

3.5 EMERGING ARCHITECTURES FOR SELF-ORGANIZATION

As alluded to in Chapter 2, Unsupervised Learning is ill-posed—the nature of the underlying data is unknown; thus, it is difficult to infer what an appropriate number of classes might be or how they should be topologically related. In this regard, there is a trade-off between the SOM/HFM and NG. Imposing a rigid topology allows for the output space to be easily visualized (e.g., on a 2D lattice). This is, however, at the expense of some topological distortion and inefficiency in allocating nodes to key patterns in the data. NG allows for more flexibility, at the expense of visualization or the extraction of any topological information.

In the end, fixed architectures are limited as their choice of an appropriate number of nodes (to capture cluster prototypes) must be guessed at runtime or before the data is seen, making them relatively inflexible to handling different input spaces. Dynamically generating self-organizing networks attempt to address this issue by formulating a set of dynamic prototypes and associations as they grow to represent the data space.

Among the many proposed dynamic extensions to the classic SOM algorithm, there exist two principal approaches: hierarchical and nonstationary, as well as hybrids of any of these two. Many of these structures have foundations in various stationary methods including the SOM itself, Competitive Learning (CL) [74], NG, or the HFM. Although they form a basis for many of the dynamic architectures highlighted in this section, stationary models of themselves are limited as SOM is, in terms of the number of possible classes being constrained at runtime. Nevertheless, they serve as important precursors to the following.

3.5.1 Dynamic Hierarchical Architectures

This class of approaches attempts to foster the extraction of hierarchical relationships—groupings based on differing levels of granularity within the data to be clustered. Such models are based on principles similar to the HFM, yet rather than imposing a fixed SOM at each new level, SOMs of different sizes are allowed. In addition, the hierarchy can continue to grow to an adaptive depth level.

In the Growing Hierarchical SOM (GHSOM) [83–86], an initial SOM is grown until a map quality criterion is satisfied, after which SOFMs are branched according to quality measures achieved at higher levels, where the process is continued. Growth thus proceeds in a layered fashion (see Fig. 3.12a).

Efficient computation is achieved when utilizing relatively smaller maps in upper levels of the hierarchy (where training data is large), and larger maps in lower levels of the hierarchy. This allows for finer resolution of detail in the more confined regions of the original data space. Such approaches have been used for tasks such as the mining and archiving of text documents, where small maps in higher levels of the hierarchy form reference to coarse grain topics, while lower level maps more readily specialize [86].

The Tree Structured SOM [87] offers a computational boost by building a binary tree hierarchy for efficient fast winner search. Similar principles are adopted in the Evolving Tree algorithm [88], wherein the frequency with which a given node is fired accumulates, acting as an indicator for subdivision of the network. Subdivision itself is controlled by a threshold, which decays over time to hinder the growth of the tree according to a fixed regularization parameter. New nodes (a predefined number) then form children at the location of the original winner, which is subsequently retired from competition, retaining its memory for use in a top-down search for future winning nodes.

One of the problems with these approaches, however, is that nodes from differing branches (lower in the hierarchy) may in fact move closer to one another during later iterations. In doing so, higher resolution clusters that are initially targeted may lead to errors in matching winners with the current input. One option is to subdivide the input space along with the tree network. This would resolve the search dilemma; however, errors in coarse segmentations at higher levels of the hierarchy, may result in parts of natural clusters in the data at higher resolutions being disassociated from one another

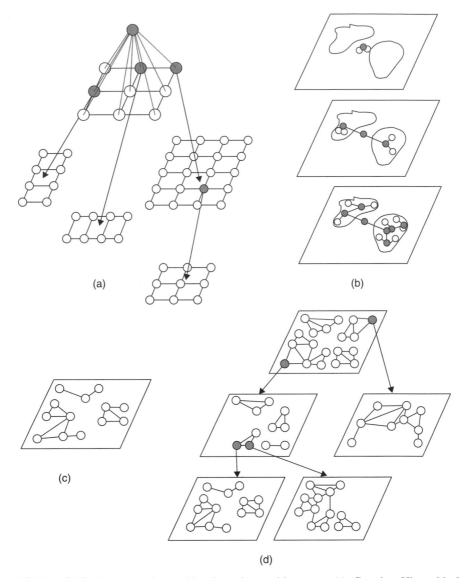

FIGURE 3.12 Dynamic Competitive Learning architectures: (a) Growing Hierarchical SOM; (b) Evolving Tree; (c) Growing Neural Gas; (d) Dynamic Adaptive Self-Organizing Hybrid.

within the hierarchy. Clearly, such approaches need a mechanism to redistribute data (and/or nodes) between sub-trees within the overall hierarchy as needed.

3.5.2 Nonstationary Architectures

The well-known NG mechanism has spawned a family of dynamically network variants: Growing Cell Structures (GCS) [89], Growing Grid (GG) [90] and Growing

Neural Gas (GNG) [91]. Each of these algorithms follow a subdivision strategy based on the consideration of accumulated error measures evaluated at regular intervals during network evolution.

In the GNG for instance, topological information is simultaneously captured through a Competitive Hebbian Learning (CHL) mechanism [92]. In this process, the Hebbian principle of associative memory is extended for the formation of associative connections in the network, which allows for the dynamic adaptation of neighborhood topologies themselves. We defer a detailed description of this mechanism until Chapter 7, wherein its relationship to a new model for Self-Organization is explored. Adaptive topology is exploited along with accumulated error information for the selective insertion of new nodes into the network. Existing nodes possessing the highest accumulation of error at the time of evaluation are split, until a maximum error criterion is satisfied by all nodes within the network. GNG also may implement a strategy to drop nodes formed, should they ever become completely disassociated (have no connection with any other node).

Due to the online nature of measuring error statistics, these methods simulate *average* distortion error within each node, by accumulating, then redistributing error between the original error-prone nodes, and their inserted offspring. Error values throughout the network are "relaxed," or decayed over time to emphasize the accumulation of more recent errors as opposed to those accumulated due to past network states.

An alternative mechanism for deducing *average* distortion errors might be to incorporate the Conscience Learning mechanism [93], as a relative measure of probability density (more akin to an online measure of frequency with which a neuron wins the competition in the network). In addition, conscience learning may yield a better estimate of candidates for node removal than edge information alone (particularly in GNG variants).

Error-based mechanisms for partitioning the input data space seem more intuitive than those based on density alone, as some consideration of the similarity between data points associated with a given node, directly impacts the formation of new cluster prototypes. By inserting nodes to reduce such error, the network naturally works to reduce the mean square error between cluster prototypes and the original data. This process can be allowed to continue unchecked, of course, causing unlimited growth of the network—limited in size only by the original data space itself. Such growth is obviously undesired; thus, the relaxation of error statistics serves a secondary purpose—that of hindering the growth of the network.

When considering error alone as a trigger for node insertion, there is the implication that desired clusters are of a similar size (i.e., degree of similarity). To an extent, similar density is also implied, as error is evaluated as an accumulation. In other words, it is anticipated that different groupings of data within some feature space, group to within the same degree of similarity. For many applications this may be a valid assumption to make, for others it may not (e.g., locating two spatial Gaussian distributions of differing standard deviation).

Error-driven processes may also lead to the premature assignment of dead nodes (nodes that become trapped in low density regions such as outliers or noise), as a blind insertion mechanism attempts to force a node between two existing nodes with significant error. This problem is alleviated somewhat by restricting the insertion such that it only occurs between connected nodes of high error, under the assumption that connections only form when some underlying density has been detected in the region between the nodes.

It is anticipated that nodes so inserted, will track back to regions of higher density in due course, as a result of Kohonen learning. The ability of a node to be pulled out of Local minima, however, becomes more difficult as the network grows, and more nodes compete for dense regions of the data space. In GNG and its variants, the distortion resulting from the proliferation of dead nodes is very sensitive to the regularity (some interval of iterations, λ) with which the network is evaluated and node insertion enforced.

3.5.3 Hybrid Architectures

Error-driven methods also do not necessarily work to capture Global topology at all levels of network evolution but rather unfold or unravel through the data space to approach a more Global description of the topology. Thus, little to no hierarchical information eventuates.

One hybrid mechanism that has been proposed that attempts to blend hierarchical information of GHSOM with dynamic growth properties of GNG is the Dynamic Adaptive Self-Organizing Hybrid (DASH) model [94]. With nonstationary properties of GNG, this model features some level of tolerance to maintaining hierarchical relationships yet is able to adjust to new information while forgetting old information that has become no longer relevant. In this model, layers of GNGs are essentially formed; however, within each, traditional limitations of the GNG are still evident.

In the following chapters, the self-organizing tee map (SOTM) [95] newer extension to, and a new model arising thereof, is explored. In principle, SOTM-based methods would typically be grouped in the nonstationary family; however, since they grow and encode hierarchical information naturally, they can be considered as belonging to both.

3.6 CONCLUSION

In this chapter, the algorithms of the ART and the SOM are presented in some detail. Specifically, the ART network overcomes the stability–plasticity dilemma by using nonlinear differential equations. The input and stored prototypes are said to resonate when they are sufficiently similar. A new category is formed when the input pattern is not sufficiently similar to any existing prototype. The sufficiency of the similarity between the input and prototypes depends on a vigilance threshold ρ. If ρ is large, the similarity condition becomes very stringent; therefore many finely divided categories are formed. On the other hand, a small ρ gives a coarse categorization. The experimental result has shown that the ART network suffers from the difficulty of setting the vigilance value.

The SOM is one of the most powerful unsupervised networks. It fulfills a characteristic nonlinear projection from the high dimensional space of input signals onto a low dimensional array of neurons. It can automatically form 1D or 2D maps of features that are present in the input signals. Experiment results have shown that the results of the best-match computations tend to be concentrated on a fraction of neurons in the map when the input signal distribution has a prominent shape. This will be explored further in the next chapter.

In order to provide an appropriate context for the work to be presented in the remainder of this book, the chapter then concludes with a brief survey of other popular architectures to have emerged based on similar principles of Self-Organization, drawing a distinction between static (fixed) and dynamic (growing or nonstationary) architectures.

CHAPTER 4

Self-Organizing Tree Map

4.1 INTRODUCTION

As mentioned in Chapter 3, the Adaptive Resonance Theory (ART) network can perform well with a fewer number of perfect input patterns. But a small amount of noise will cause problems as illustrated in Figure 3.3. As the number of input patterns increases, it is difficult to set the Global threshold value to distinguish different prototypes.

For the self-organizing map (SOM) network, the linear and planar topologies of the networks are shown in Chapter 3. If the input pattern distribution is uniform, the neuron set neatly adapts to the input data. When the input pattern distribution has a prominent shape, as shown in Figure 4.1(a and b), the result of the best-match computations tends to be concentrated on a fraction of neurons in the map. Due to successive applications of Equation 3.37, it may easily happen that the neurons lying in zero-density areas are affected by input patterns from all the surrounding parts of the nonzero distribution [96]. Although the SOM's topology exhibits the distribution of the structured input vectors, it also introduces false representations outside the distribution of the input space as shown in Figure 4.1(c and d) from our experiments. In Figure 4.1c, there are grid points in the regions with zero probability of information, and it is difficult to find a better solution without clustering a lot of points near each inside corner. The outlying neurons are pulled toward the wining neuron. As this happens repeatedly, the window size shrinks and the fluctuation ceases. As a result, the outlying points remain outliers since they have no stable places to go.

In view of the above observation of the ART and the SOM, a new mechanism named the self-organizing tree map (SOTM) is proposed. The motivation of the new method is twofold: (a) to keep the ART's ability to create new output neurons dynamically while overcoming the Global threshold setting problem; (b) to keep the SOM's property of topology preservation while strengthening the flexibility of adapting to changes in the input distribution and maximally reflecting the distribution of the input patterns. In the SOTM, relationships between the output neurons can be dynamically defined during learning. This allows the learning of not only the weights

Unsupervised Learning: A Dynamic Approach, First Edition.
Matthew Kyan, Paisarn Muneesawang, Kambiz Jarrah, and Ling Guan.
© 2014 by The Institute of Electrical and Electronics Engineers, Inc. Published by John Wiley & Sons, Inc.

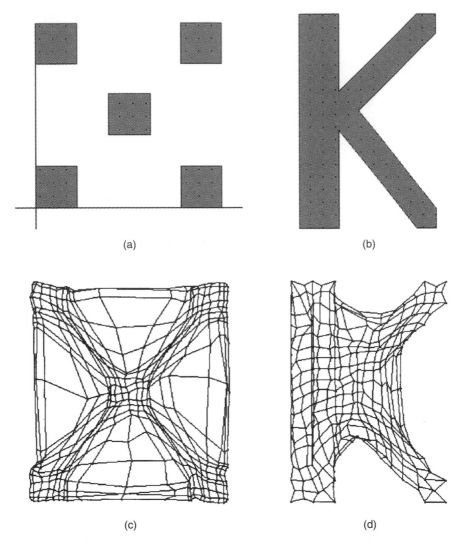

FIGURE 4.1 (a) Uniformly distributed input vectors in five squares; (b) K-shape distribution of the input vectors; (c) final representation of the SOM for input vectors uniformly distributed in five squares; (d) final representation of the SOM for K-shape distribution of the input vectors.

of the connections, but also the structure of the network including the number of neurons, the number of levels, and the interconnections among the neurons.

4.2 ARCHITECTURE

The SOTM is basically a competitive neural network in which the neurons are organized as a multilayer tree structure. It can be thought of as somewhat of a hybrid between the traditional Kohonen SOM and ART architectures. Like ART, a set of prototype nodes are gradually formed as the input space is parsed. This process is overseen by a vigilance test, which is essentially a test that watches out for an input pattern that is contrary to what is known about the input space seen thus far. If any given input pattern passes the vigilance test, resonance is said to occur, resulting in the refinement of the winning prototype. Otherwise, while there is still capacity, a new prototype is formed.

Following the statistics of the input patterns, the output layer of the SOTM grows from an isolated neuron (root node) to form a self-organizing tree, capturing the Local context of the pattern space and mapping it onto the structure of the tree.

Aside from the natural resonance experienced by the existing neurons in the network, network growth (insertion) is driven by a top-down process that effectively explores the input data space from the outside-in, governed by a dynamic hierarchical control function $H(t)$. At any one snapshot in time during learning, $H(t)$ acts as a dynamic vigilance threshold, evaluating the proximity of each new input sample against the closest existing prototype (winning neuron or best matching unit (BMU)) currently in the network. Samples encountered outside the scope of the current network's prototypes will thus result in the generation of new neurons (leaf nodes) in the network model. There are thus, two different levels of adaptation in the SOTM.

- **Weight adaptation:** If the input vector is close to one of the neurons in the network and the distance between them is within the hierarchy control function range, the winner's weight vector can be adjusted toward the incoming vector.
- **Structure adaptation:** Adapt the structure of the network by changing the number of neurons and the structural relationship between neurons in the network. If the distance between the incoming vector and the winner neuron is outside the hierarchy control function range, the input vector becomes the winner's child, forming a sub-node in the tree.

The clustering algorithm works to coalesce nearby patterns into the tree-like map, where the resulting interconnections allow the parsing process to maintain some level of topology preservation. As is the case in the SOM, the refinement of existing prototypes (weight-level adaptation) is governed by Kohonen style learning rules. By forcing $H(t)$ to decay from a large initial value, the SOTM exhibits the property of hierarchical partitioning—initially identifying coarse, well-separated clusters early, only partitioning into higher resolution clusters at later stages. This property is depicted in Figure 4.2.

4.3 COMPETITIVE LEARNING

The basic principle underlying competitive learning is vector quantization. Competitive learning neural networks adaptively quantize the pattern space R^N. Neurons compete for the activation induced by randomly sampled pattern vectors $\mathbf{x} \in R^N$. The

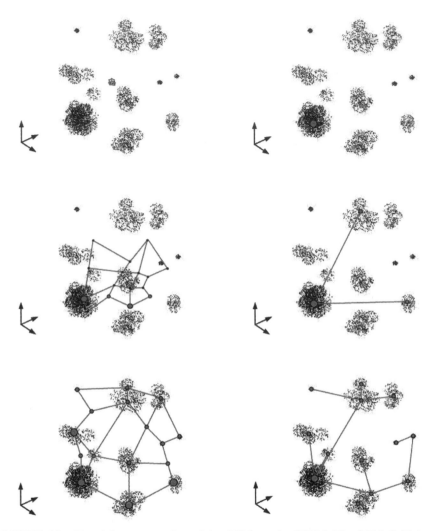

FIGURE 4.2   Pictorial representation of the SOM vs. the SOTM. The SOM (left) has a predefined lattice of neurons that unfold to span the input space by progressively relating input samples to their closest prototypes in the lattice—information from each sample is imparted to the "winning" neuron and its immediate neighbors. The SOTM (right), by contrast, explores the input space by randomly parsing and cultivating the growth of characteristic prototypes, in a top-down vigilant (outside-in) manner.

corresponding random weight vectors $\mathbf{w}_j$ represent the Voronoi regions[1] about $\mathbf{w}_j$. Each weight vector $\mathbf{w}_j$ behaves as a quantization vector or reference vector. Competitive learning distributes the reference vectors to approximate the unknown probability

---

[1]Voronoi tessellation partitions the pattern space into regions around reference vectors; such regions are called Voronoi regions.

ALGORITHM   **57**

density function $p(x)$. The network learns as weight vectors $\mathbf{w}_j$ change in response to random training data.

In the SOTM, each input pattern vector $\mathbf{x} = \{x_1, \ldots, x_n\} \in R^N$ is projected onto a tree node. With every node j, a weight vector $\mathbf{w}_j = [w_{1j} \ldots w_{Nj}] \in R^N$ is associated. When an input vector is presented to the network, it is compared with each of the $\mathbf{w}_j$, and the best matching node is defined as the winner. The input vector is thus mapped onto this location. The best matching node is defined using the smallest of the Euclidean distances $\|\mathbf{x} - \mathbf{w}_j\|$. We modify the closest weight vector or the "winning" weight vector $\mathbf{w}_{j*}$ with a simple difference learning law, which is similar to Kohonen's SOM algorithm. A scaling factor of $\mathbf{x}(t) - \mathbf{w}_{j*}(t)$ is added to $\mathbf{w}_{j*}(t)$ to form $\mathbf{w}_j(t + 1)$. The "losers" are not modified: $\mathbf{w}_j(t + 1) = \mathbf{w}_j(t)$.

$$\mathbf{w}_j(t + 1) = \mathbf{w}_{j*}(t) + \alpha(t)[\mathbf{x}(t) - \mathbf{w}_{j*}(t)],$$

$$\mathbf{w}_j(t + 1) = \mathbf{w}_j(t) \qquad \text{if } j \neq j^*, \tag{4.1}$$

where $\alpha(t)$ denotes a monotonically deceasing sequence of learning coefficients. We can also update the nearest neighbors of the winning node. However, in this work, we modify only one weight vector at a time.

A hierarchy control function is proposed to control the growth of the tree. At the initial stage, there is only one neuron whose weight vector is randomly chosen from the input pattern space to become the root of the tree. The stimulus that activates the neurons has a wide dynamic range, that is, the hierarchy control function is set large enough to enable all the neurons to be activated by the input stimulus. Then the hierarchy control function shrinks monotonically with time. The decreasing speed can be linear or exponential depending on the applications. During each decreasing stage, the input vector is checked to see if it is within the range of the hierarchy control value. If the input vector falls into the range, the weight vector is adjusted to the input vector. Otherwise, a new node (sub-node) is formed in the tree. The formation of the tree map is shown in Figure 4.3.

Within a given period of the hierarchy control function, the learning tends to be a stochastic process; the weight vectors will eventually converge in the mean-square sense to the probabilistic mean of their corresponding input vectors as the learning rate decreases. The hierarchical classification organizes the samples such that each node represents a subset of samples that share some similar features. Such hierarchical classification can be quickly searched to find a matching pattern for a new input.

4.4 ALGORITHM

The SOTM algorithm is summarized as follows.

- **Step 1.** Initialize the weight vector with a random value (randomly take a training vector as the representative of the root node).

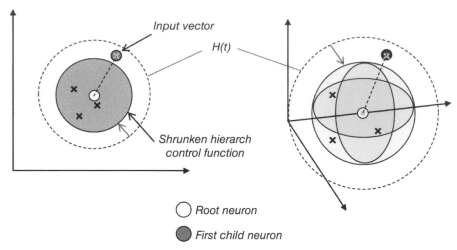

Root neuron

First child neuron

FIGURE 4.3 Decision boundary used to trigger map growth in the SOTM—shown for 2D (left) and 3D (right) feature spaces. Xs represent initial stimuli falling within the radius/ellipsoid of significant similarity (assumed Euclidean metric). Decay of this boundary inspires hierarchical growth of neurons (prototypes).

- **Step 2.** Get a new input vector and compute the distances d_j between the input vector and all the nodes using

$$d_j = \sqrt{\sum_{i=1}^{N}(x_i(t) - w_{ij}(t))^2} \qquad (j = 1, \dots, J) \qquad (4.2)$$

where J is the number of nodes.

- **Step 3.** Select the wining node j^* with minimum d_j.

$$d_{j^*}(\mathbf{x}, \mathbf{w}_j) = \min_j d_j(\mathbf{x}, \mathbf{w}_j) \qquad (4.3)$$

- **Step 4. If** $d_{j^*}(\mathbf{x}, \mathbf{w}_j) \leq H(t)$,
  where $H(t)$ is the hierarchy control function, which decreases with time. $H(t)$ controls the level of the tree.
  Then assign $\mathbf{x}$ to the jth cluster, and update the weight vector $\mathbf{w}_j$ according to the following learning rule.

$$\mathbf{w}_j(t + 1) = \mathbf{w}_j(t) + \alpha(t)[\mathbf{x}(t) - \mathbf{w}_j(t)], \qquad (4.4)$$

where $\alpha(t)$ is the learning rate, which decreases with time, $0 < \alpha(t) < 1$.
Else form a new sub-node starting with $\mathbf{x}$.

ALGORITHM **59**

- **Step 5.** Check condition for termination: exit if one of the following three conditions is fulfilled.
  - The specified number of iterations is reached.
  - The specified number of clusters is reached.
  - No significant change to the tree map has occurred.

  Otherwise, repeat by going back to Step 2.

Learning in the SOTM takes place in two phases: the locating phase and the convergence phase. The adaptation parameter $\alpha(t)$ controls the learning rate, which decreases with time as weight vectors approach the cluster centers. It is given by either a linear function $\alpha(t) = (1 - t/T_1)$ or an exponential function $\alpha(t) = e^{(-t/T_2)}$. T_1 and T_2 are constants that determine the decreasing rate. During the locating phase, the Global topological adjustment of the weight vectors $\mathbf{w}_j$ takes place. $\alpha(t)$ stays relatively large during this phase. Initially, $\alpha(t)$ can be set as 0.8, and it decreases with time. After the locating phase, a small $\alpha(t)$ for the convergence phase is needed for the fine tuning of the map.

The hierarchy control function $H(t)$ controls the levels of the tree. It begins with a large value and decreases with time. It adaptively partitions the input vector space into smaller subspaces. In our experiments, $H(t)$ is defined as $H(t) = (1 - t/T_3)$ or $H(t) = e^{-t/T_4}$. T_3 and T_4 are also constants that control the decreasing rate.

With the decreasing of the hierarchy control function $H(t)$, a sub-node comes out to form a new branch. The evolution process progresses recursively until it reaches the leaf node. The entire tree structure preserves topological relations from the root node to the leaf nodes.

Learning in SOTM follows the stochastic competitive learning law, which is expressed as a stochastic differential equation [97–100].

$$\dot{\mathbf{w}}_j = \mathbf{I}_{D_j}[\mathbf{x}_j - \mathbf{w}_j], \tag{4.5}$$

where $\mathbf{w}$ is the weight vector and $\mathbf{x}$ is the input vector. I_{D_j} denotes the zero–one indicator function of decision class D_j.

$$I_{D_j} = \begin{cases} 1 & \text{if } \mathbf{x} \in D_j \\ 0 & \text{if } \mathbf{x} \notin D_j \end{cases}. \tag{4.6}$$

I_{D_j} indicates whether pattern x belongs to decision class D_j.

The stochastic differential equation describes how weight random processes change as a function of input random processes. According to the centroid theorem [101], the competitive learning converges to the centroid of the sampled decision class. The probability of $\mathbf{w}_j = \mathbf{x}_j$ at equilibrium is

$$Prob(\mathbf{w}_j = \overline{\mathbf{x}}_j) = 1, \tag{4.7}$$

where the centroid $\overline{\mathbf{x}}_j$ of decision class D_j equals its probabilistic center of mass, given by

$$\overline{\mathbf{x}}_j = \frac{\int_{D_j} \mathbf{x}p(\mathbf{x})\mathbf{dx}}{\int_{D_j} p(\mathbf{x})\mathbf{dx}}$$

$$= E[\mathbf{x}|\mathbf{x} \in D_j]. \tag{4.8}$$

The centroid theorem concludes that the average weight vector $E[\mathbf{w}_j]$ equals the jth centroid $\overline{\mathbf{x}}_j$ at equilibrium:

$$E[\mathbf{w}_j] = \overline{\mathbf{x}}_j. \tag{4.9}$$

The weight vector $\mathbf{w}_j$ vibrates in a Brownian motion about the constant centroid $\overline{\mathbf{x}}_j$. Our simulated competitive weight vectors have exhibited such Brownian wandering about centroids. This progression is illustrated in Figure 4.4.

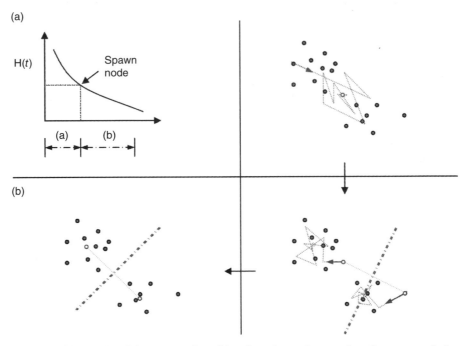

FIGURE 4.4   A pictorial representation of the adaptation and generation of prototypes during SOTM parsing of an input space: (a) each node in the map performs a random walk about the center of mass of the underlying distribution until such time as $H(t)$ spawns a new node; (b) new nodes then each perform a random walk within their Local contexts, converging to more regional densities.

4.5   EVOLUTION

The evolution processes of the SOTM and the convergence of the stochastic competitive learning are illustrated in this section by some snapshots. Dynamic topology and classification capability are two prominent characteristics of the SOTM, which will be demonstrated by an application.

4.5.1   Dynamic Topology

The dynamic SOTM topology is demonstrated in the following examples. In Figure 4.1a, the learning of the tree map is driven by sample vectors uniformly distributed in the five squares. The tree mapping starts from the root node and gradually generates its sub-nodes as $H(t)$ decreases. The waveform of $H(t)$ function and learning rate $\alpha(t)$ is shown in Figure 4.5. Each time $H(t)$ decreases, $\alpha(t)$ starts from the initial state again. For every $H(t)$, α decreases with time. By properly controlling the decreasing speed of $\alpha(t)$, the SOTM finds the cluster center. For example, in the beginning of learning, the initial $H(t)$ is set large; it covers the whole space of the input patterns. As $\alpha(t)$ decreases with time, the SOTM converges to the root node shown in Figure 4.6a. When $H(t)$ shrinks with time, the sub-nodes are formed at each

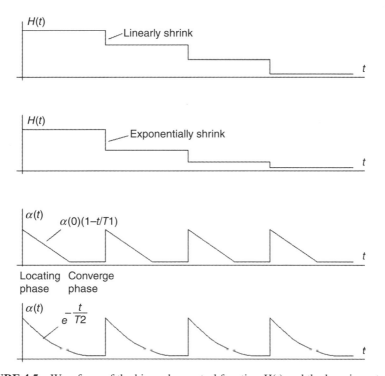

FIGURE 4.5   Waveform of the hierarchy control function $H(t)$ and the learning rate $\alpha(t)$.

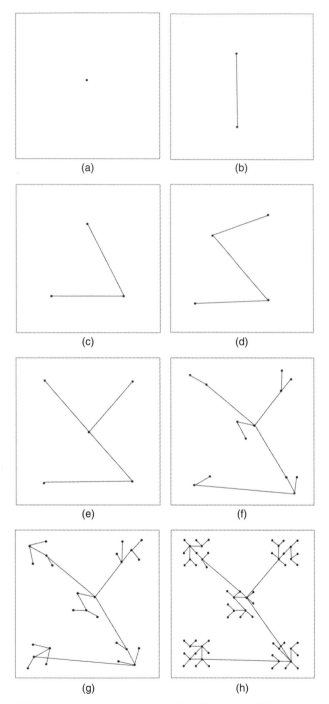

FIGURE 4.6 Different quantizers produced by the SOTM with different $H(t)$ for Figure 4.1a: (a) root node representing the mean of all the input vectors; (b–g) evolution of the Self-Organizing Tree; (h) final SOTM representation.

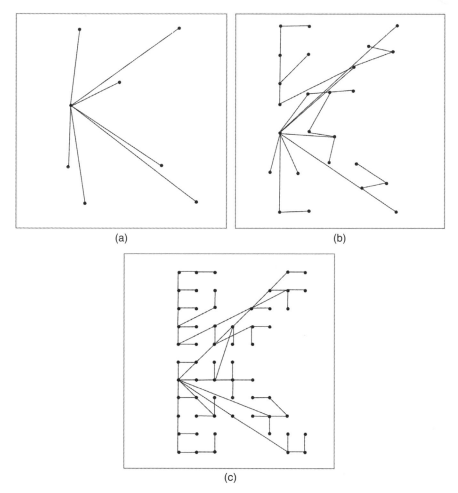

FIGURE 4.7 The representation of SOTM for K-shape distribution of the input vectors: (a and b) evolution of the tree map; (c) final representation.

stage shown in Figure 4.6(b–h). In the node organizing process, the optimal number of the output nodes can be obtained from visualizing the tree map evolution.

Another merit of the SOTM topology is shown in Figure 4.7. The input space is the same as Figure 4.1b. From Figure 4.7, it can be seen that all the tree nodes are situated within the area of the distribution. The entire tree truthfully reflects the distribution of the input space. Using these nodes as code vectors, the distortion of vector quantization can be kept to a minimum.

As a means of understanding the important properties of the SOTM, we also highlight its potential for hierarchical-based partitioning, and speculate as to the significance of such, through comparison against popular clustering techniques selected from the literature: namely, K-Means (KM) [31], Fuzzy-C-Means (FCM) [32], Gaussian Mixture Model (GMM) [36].

In Figures 4.8 and 4.9, we show two different test runs (left and right columns) for each of the 3 models (KM, FCM, and GMM) in comparison with SOTM, for a synthetically generated dataset (containing 9 visible clusters of different sizes). Each cluster includes N_s samples, which have $33 < N_s < 128$, and are Gaussian distributed with variance $0.0345 < \sigma < 0.0901$. In Figure 4.8, the total number of nodes in the network is restricted to four, while in Figure 4.9, the network is expanded to six nodes.

We note that the SOTM provides a more consistent solution, and one that is more inline with a hierarchical partitioning of the data, based on the limitation placed on the number of nodes. Essentially, in the SOTM solution, clusters within one grouping are never closer to clusters from different groupings, as is the case in the other solutions. The hierarchical partitioning is not in terms of dividing larger clustered groups *per se*, rather, the subdivision of more scattered, less compact groups. As such, the SOTM can be seen to prioritize isolation of each of the more separated groups around the extremities of the data space, particularly evident in Figure 4.9, where division of the more fuzzy, potentially touching or overlapping groups is delayed until the clearly separated, less proximal clusters are first resolved.

4.5.2 Classification Capability

To demonstrate the classification ability of the SOTM, an application of the SOTM algorithm to perform pattern classification of document images is presented. The document image captured by a digital camera is shown in Figure 4.10. The document image is chosen because it is easy to compare the pattern classification ability of the SOTM in contrast to that of the ART. However, in practice, the SOTM algorithm can be used as an effective substitute for the ART algorithm in any pattern classification application, such as English characters, Chinese characters, and Japanese characters.

The characters in the image are first segmented into isolated patterns. The segmentation is completed by scanning the image vertically from top-to-bottom, left-to-right. Due to the distortion and noise introduced by digitization, characters that appear similar to the human eyes are not pixel-identical to the computer. They may be broken into parts or connected to the other characters. In this case, they are treated as different patterns.

After the segmentation of the document image, a feature extract operator is applied onto the isolated patterns to obtain useful features, such as the width and height of the pattern, the gravity and the first or second order moment of the patterns. These features are formed as input vectors to the SOTM system. The first input vector that is chosen randomly from the feature space is placed in a library as a prototype and is assigned a label code. Each new pattern in the image is compared with the prototype. If the comparison is within a tolerance range, the library prototype label code is marked along with the pattern location coordinates. Otherwise, the new pattern is placed in the library. With the increasing of the prototypes in the library, the competitive mechanism becomes effective in ensuring the incoming pattern is matched to the beset prototype in the library. The final pattern prototypes in the library are shown in

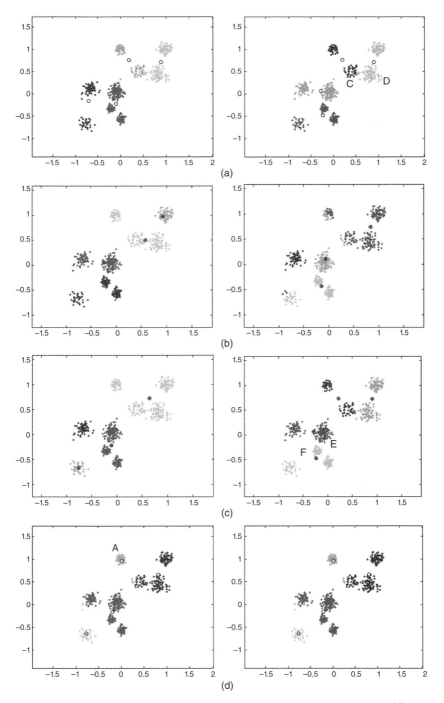

FIGURE 4.8 Clustering performance of SOTM vs. common algorithms—classification of synthetic 2D data into 4 classes, with run 1 (left), run 2 (right): (a) K-Means; (b) Fuzzy C-Means; (c) Gaussian Mixture Model; (d) SOTM. SOTM demonstrates more consistent, hierarchical sense of grouping, prioritizing isolation of the most detached clusters A and B. In the other methods, close clusters C, D and E, F are often grouped with clusters that are further away (e.g., clusters E, F are separated in (a) run 2, (b) runs 1 and 2, and (c) run 2).

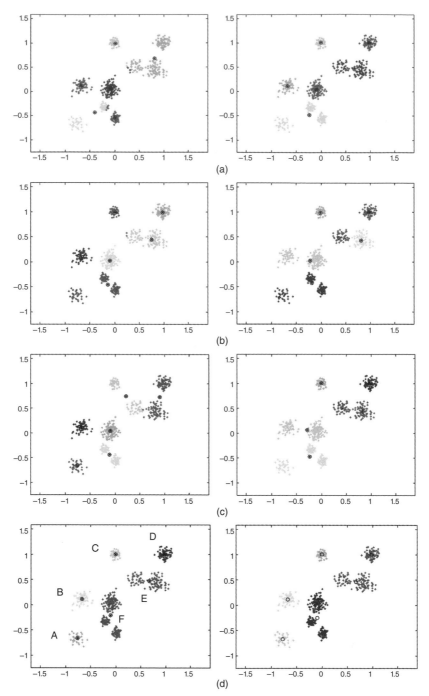

FIGURE 4.9 Clustering performance of SOTM vs. common algorithms—classification of synthetic 2D data into six classes, with run 1 (left), run 2 (right): (a) K-Means; (b) Fuzzy C-Means; (c) Gaussian Mixture Model; (d) SOTM. Again, SOTM demonstrates a consistent and hierarchical partitioning, where the more fuzzy, proximal clusters (E, F) are grouped together, while the clearly distinct clusters on the outskirts (A, B, C, D) have been isolated. The other solutions exhibit increased variability across different runs.

Servers

What types of servers will this brave new world ne
answer is probably not known at this time. Mankin
best use of a technology. A few categories have al
in this section.

Remember that a server is defined as a program th:
the resources that the server owns. By definition, a
home is not. To use a restaurant, you make functio
the other hand, just sits there when you give it orde
so it is not a server.

(a)

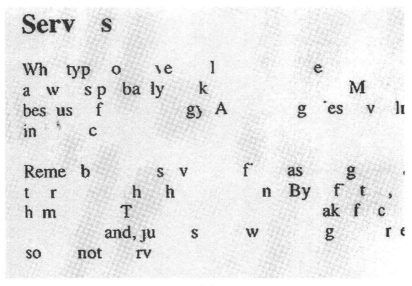

(b)

FIGURE 4.10   Application of the SOTM algorithm to perform pattern classification of document images. (a) Document image captured by a digital camera. (b) Final pattern prototypes
in the library.

Figure 4.10b. Comparing it with the result in Figure 3.3, it is obvious that the SOTM system is more robust against distortion and noise than the ART.

This application has great potential in document image compression. This pattern classification system can be used for efficient facsimile data transmission or storage of document images. When adaptive Huffman coding is applied to the library, the compression ratio for Figure 4.10a is about 48:1. With the document file getting longer and longer, as the same characters in the document repeat more often, only the index numbers need to be stored, which means the library size will not increase very much. Therefore, even higher compression ratios can be achieved.

4.6 PRACTICAL CONSIDERATIONS, EXTENSIONS, AND REFINEMENTS

In this section, a number of operational modalities and refinements are explored and justified toward the construction of more robust and scalable versions of the SOTM algorithm of Section 4.4. In this way, the refined SOTM is expected to be able to handle different datasets with little to no tuning. Specifically, functions and scheduling for $H(t)$, learning rates, normalization, and stop criteria are considered.

4.6.1 The Hierarchical Control Function

In general, under the assumption that data is presented to the network in a random or stochastic fashion, the only constraint imposed on $H(t)$ is that it be a monotonically decreasing function with the number of sample presentations (a.k.a. iterations). In addition, $H(t)$ ideally should decay from a large enough value—presumably one that encompasses the span of the data. This is such that the largest differences in the data may be encoded early in the network, deferring the segregation of more subtle differences until later stages.

As such, two standard functions are proposed for the SOTM: linear and exponential decay. We formalize both here through the incorporation of a time constant τ_H, which is bound to the projected size of the input data X, and an initial value $H(0)$ that is bound to properties of the random sub-sample X_T, where $X_T \subset X$, used in training an SOTM map:

$$H(t) = H(0) \left[\left(1 - e^{-\frac{\xi}{\tau_H}} \right) \frac{H(0)}{\xi} \right] \cdot t \tag{4.10}$$

$$H(t) = H(0)e^{-\frac{t}{\tau_H}} \tag{4.11}$$

where t is the number of iterations (or sample presentations) and ξ is the number of iterations over which the linear version of $H(t)$ would decay to the same level as the exponential version of $H(t)$.

Decaying from a fixed value $H(0)$ greater than the maximum possible range across the input space offers a mechanism by which all levels of resolution across the space may be systematically explored. We propose two natural choices for this parameter.

1. **Range-based** $H(0)$: $\sum$ (all ranges across each dimension of X_T).
2. **Standard Deviation-based** $H(0)$: $> 2(3\sigma_{X_T})$: a distance beyond twice the maximum deviation (radius $r = 3\sigma_{X_T}$) of 99% of samples from the mean/centroid of X_T.

In addition, it is envisaged that $H(t)$ may operate in a number of modalities. We propose a number of alternative strategies for $H(t)$, each of which is depicted in the timing diagrams of Figure 4.11 and justified as follows.

1. **Pure $H(t)$ decay:** This is the typical approach; however, in transitioning to a new $H(t)$ with each new iteration, only a single random sample is considered at each resolution. Thus a rather limited search is conducted at each level of the hierarchy. In fact, the slowing of the decay in lower levels of resolution means that they are assessed more thoroughly.

2. **Stepped $H(t)$ with regular period** τ_{Hstep}**:** By introducing a stepped form of decay, $H(t)$ switches down progressively, thereby allowing at least τ_{Hstep} samples to be explored for possible node insertion before narrowing the search to a finer resolution of data space. The random nature of samples implies that at least some samples from all parts of the data space should be encountered in this period.

3. **Stepped $H(t)$ with irregular period:** This extends mode 2, by resetting a counter every time a new node is generated, such that the search in a given hierarchical level will continue for at least another τ_{Hstep} samples. This is to allow a node spawned near the end of a level in mode 2 to have a chance to adjust itself so that the search for other candidates, given the newly formed network state, may be exhausted before stepping down $H(t)$.

4. **Stepped $H(t)$ with irregular period and node inhibition:** This additional constraint extends mode 3 by forcing network adaptations only for a fixed period of τ_{Hstep} before considering the insertion of new nodes; thus, nodes have sufficient time to reorganize and learn Local information before new (possibly unnecessary nodes are prematurely allocated). This process repeats after the generation of each new node and acts as a settling period for the network.

Intuitively, modes 2–4 are preferred as they each restrict the hierarchical function from decaying for a period of time, while the current network is allowed to evolve. As can be seen from Figure 4.11d, node production is more forcibly spread over the duration of $H(t)$; however, as noted in Figure 4.11c, there is sufficient spread in the input space to warrant production of nodes 2 and 3 at a higher level of $H(t)$. In Figure 4.11d, the spread between nodes 2 and 3 is not discovered until a lower resolution of $H(t)$. This can be explained by the fact that, under mode 4, nodes 1 and 2 are allowed to see more of the input space and thus more readily converge to

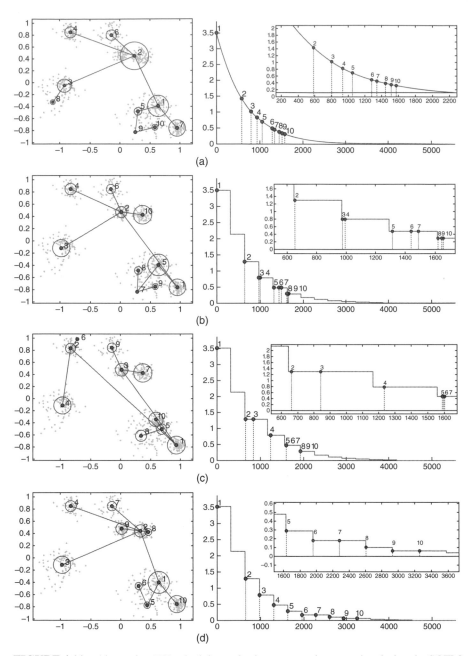

FIGURE 4.11   Alternative $H(t)$ schedules and subsequent node generation during the SOTM clustering of a synthetic 2D data space: (a) pure $H(t)$ decay; (b) stepped $H(t)$ with regular period; (c) stepped $H(t)$ with irregular period (recommended); (d) stepped $H(t)$ with irregular period and node inhibition.

between-cluster centroids before being allowed to spawn a new node (which, as a result, would now not occur until a lower $H(t)$). In Figure 4.11c, the attempt is made to search more thoroughly at a given resolution before continuing with the decay since $H(t)$ will remain at a level until there is no node production for a period of at least τ_{Hstep}. Empirically, we find this approach to be the most suitable, combined with an SD-based initialization of $H(t)$.

4.6.2 Learning, Timing, and Convergence

The learning rate $\alpha(t)$ can also operate in a number of different modes in both a Global or in a Local context (where, respectively, a single rate operates for all, or a set of individual rates operate for each node). Specifically, we propose 3 new modalities (items 2–4 listed below) over the periodic reset strategy on which the original SOTM was based. Timing diagrams in Figure 4.12 illustrate these modalities, for example, clustering runs of the SOTM on the two-dimensional (2D) dataset used in Figure 4.11, each used in conjunction with stepped $H(t)$ decay with irregular period. Original and proposed modalities for learning rate adaptation thus include

1. **Global periodic reset:** traditional approach that allows the network to constantly refresh its memory with regard to the underlying density.
2. **Global reset upon node generation:** a modification based on the intuition that the network need only reorganize its memory when the map is grown.
3. **Local reset of winner and child upon node generation:** this modification restricts renewed plasticity to the region of the map in which new information has caused map growth based on the assumption that adjustment of more distant nodes is unlikely to be impacted greatly by adjustments in the region where map growth is occurring.
4. **Local reset of winner, child, and siblings upon node generation:** similar to mode 3; however, in this modification, any children previously spawned from the winning node are also considered to be plastic within the newly mined region.

While intuitively, one might expect modes 3 and 4 to perform better, we in fact find that modes 1 and 2 are preferred options for an SOTM process. This is primarily due to the fact that while the SOTM is topologically aware in the sense of where the next node will be inserted, the relationships or connections formed at earlier phases of learning begin to lose significance in later phases, as evidenced by nodes that compete over adjacent regions in the data (e.g., nodes 2, 10, and 3 in Fig. 4.12a; nodes 1 and 8 in Fig. 4.12b; and nodes 3, 4, and 9 in Fig. 4.12c). With the Global reset of alpha in modes 1 and 2, all such nodes are able to recompete locally and adapt accordingly. Empirically, we find mode 2 to be preferred, as the reset is typically only justified when new information must be blended into the network after node production. By contrast, a regular reset schedule may potentially gravitate nodes to lower regions of density (e.g., node 7 in Fig. 4.12a).

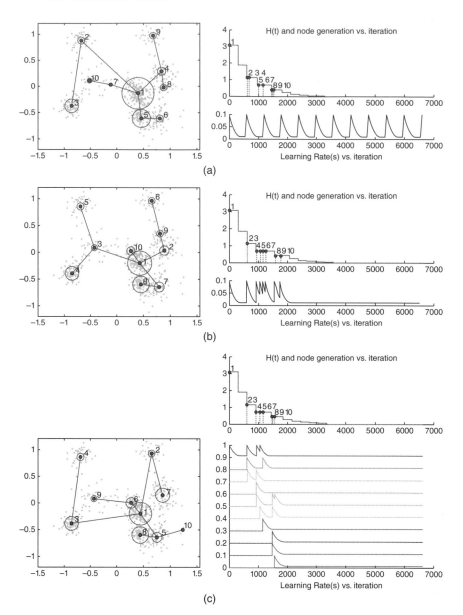

FIGURE 4.12 Example timing diagrams of learning rate(s) for different learning modalities for the SOTM clustering of a synthetic 2D data space: (a) mode 1; (b) mode 2; (c) mode 3. Mode 4 has an alpha pattern similar to mode 3 shown above; however, more than 2 nodes may be triggered for refresh at the same time.

4.6.3 Feature Normalization

Another issue to consider when performing clustering on a feature space is how to fuse unrelated features. If the dynamic range of any one feature far exceeds that of another feature, then the partitioning will be favored along the dimension with greater variance. For instance, when the two features are related (such as in the 2D sample of Fig. 4.11), the aspect ratio between the x and y features should be maintained regardless of the distributions in each dimension; however, if the features are unrelated, then those with a small dynamic range will contribute little influence over the clustering solution. For example, consider clustering image pixel samples of dimension 2, where the first dimension represents a gray scale value on [0, 255], while a second dimension represents a localized statistic, say standard deviation of gray scale within a 3 × 3 neighborhood on [0, 20]. In order to have each feature contribute equally in a Euclidean-based clustering, they should be normalized such that their dynamic ranges are similar, for example, to [0,1], otherwise distances in gray scale alone will dominate node generation. Of course, the corollary is that this can be exploited, such that we favor one feature over another. This, however, is more easily managed after normalization has been performed, after which it becomes possible to apply a set of systematic weights to signify the importance of one feature over another.

Typical choices for normalization include a simple scaling of the dynamic range, or Gaussian normalization. The Gaussian approach attempts to scale the data according to its standard deviation such that large outliers do not impact the useful dynamic range (e.g., if most of the information of a gray scale distribution is concentrated in the interval [10, 40], with outliers at [230], the scaling based on the range will cause [10, 40] to be squeezed into a smaller interval on [0,1], leaving most of the interval unused. The methods for normalization of the jth feature of the ith sample are

$$x'_{ij} = A' + \frac{(x_{ij} - A)(B' - A')}{(B - A)} \tag{4.12}$$

$$x'_{ij} = \frac{x_{ij}\mu_{X_j}}{\eta\sigma_{X_j}} \tag{4.13}$$

where x'_{ij} is the normalized version of x_{ij}. In Equation 4.12, $[A, B]$ represents the interval on which x_{ij} exists, with $A = \min(X_j)$ and $B = \max(X_j)$, while $[A', B']$ represents the new normalized interval (e.g., $[-1, 1]$ or $[0, 1]$). For Gaussian normalization in Equation 4.12, μ_{X_j} represents the mean value across jth feature for all X, while σ_{X_j} represents the standard deviation. An additional factor η controls the scaling factor— $\eta = 3$, for instance, will squeeze 99% of the samples from the jth feature into the interval $[-1, 1]$, while $\eta = 1$ will only squeeze 60% of the samples onto $[-1, 1]$.

4.6.4 Stop Criteria

If $H(t)$ is allowed to decay indefinitely and there is no limitation on the number of neurons that may be allocated to the network, then it follows that the network will continue to grow indefinitely. Intuitively, this growth should be limited by the smallest resolution of feature points (i.e., the Euclidean sum of the smallest resolutions of all feature sets included in the feature space). Beyond this limit, it makes no sense to generate new cluster centers—yet, at this limit, the purpose of clustering to provide a compact representation of the dominant patterns or redundancies in the data also becomes meaningless, since the network will continue to grow until the number of classes equals the number of feature data points (or greater).

We suggest an additional constraint to the stop criterion of the SOTM algorithm— namely, to impose a lower limit $H(\infty)$ on the decay of $H(t)$, as a factor of the Global statistical properties of the training set X_T. This amounts to modifications to both Steps 4 and 5 in the SOTM algorithm of Section 4.4.

1. **Step 4.** Change Else condition to only add a new node if $H(t) > H(\infty)$.
2. **Step 5.** Require that $H(t) = H(\infty)$ alongside previous conditions to enable termination.

In this way, $H(t)$ may decay from different initial values that are dependent on the natural ranges found in the data. Different centers will be spawned during this process according to how the data are distributed across this range. The SOTM will then essentially parse the feature space, allowing the natural distribution of data to trigger the partitioning process.

4.7 CONCLUSIONS

In this chapter, an SOTM is presented. This model not only enhanced the ART's autonomous category classification and the SOM's topology preservation, but also overcame their weaknesses. Based on the competitive learning algorithm, the SOTM adaptively estimates the probability density function $p(x)$ from sample realizations in the most faithful fashion and tries to preserve the structure of $p(x)$. Since weight vectors during learning tend to be stochastic processes, the centroid theorem is used to demonstrate its convergence. In conclusion, the weight vectors converge in the mean-square sense to the probabilistic centers of input subsets to form a quantization mapping with a minimum mean squared distortion. A number of examples were used to illustrated the dynamic topology of the SOTM and its classification ability, which will be further exemplified in the following chapters.

CHAPTER 5

Self-Organization in Impulse Noise Removal

5.1 INTRODUCTION

Removal of noise from images while preserving as much fine detail as possible is an essential issue in image processing. A variety of linear and nonlinear filtering techniques have been proposed for improving the quality of images degraded by noise [102–105]. In the early stages of signal and image processing, linear filters were the primary tools for noise cleaning. However, linear filtering reduces noise at the expense of degrading signals. It tends to blur the edges and does not remove impulse noise effectively. The drawbacks of linear filters spurred the development of nonlinear filtering techniques for signal and image processing [106].

In 1971, the best known and most widely used nonlinear filter, the median filter, was introduced by Tukey as a time series analysis tool for robust noise suppression [107]. Later, this filter came into use in image processing. Median filtering has the advantages of preserving sharp changes in signals and of being effective for removing impulse noise when the error rate is relatively small. This is performed by moving a window over the image and replacing the pixel at the center of the window with the median value inside of the window. Due to the computational simplicity and easy hardware implementation, it is recognized as an effective alternative to the linear smoothing filter for the removal of impulse noise.

One problem with the median filter is that it removes very fine details in the images and changes signal structures. In many applications, the median filter not only smooths the noise in homogeneous image regions, but also tends to produce regions of constant or nearly constant intensity. These regions are usually linear patches (streaks) or amorphous blotches. These side effects of the median filter are highly undesirable since they are perceived as either lines or contours that do not exist in the original image. To improve the performance of the median filter, many generalized median filters, and alternatives to the median filter have been

Unsupervised Learning: A Dynamic Approach, First Edition.
Matthew Kyan, Paisarn Muneesawang, Kambiz Jarrah, and Ling Guan.
© 2014 by The Institute of Electrical and Electronics Engineers, Inc. Published by John Wiley & Sons, Inc.

proposed. These include the weighted median (WM) filter [108], center-weighted median (CWM) filter [109], weighted order statistic (WOS) filter [110], max/median filter [111], multistage median filter [112, 113], nonlinear mean filters [114, 115], etc. The generalized median filters tend to have better detail-preserving characteristics than the median filter, but they preserve more details at the expense of poor noise suppression. Their performance depends strongly on the noise model and the error rate. Nonlinear mean filters exhibit better impulse suppression ability than the regular median filter when only positive or negative impulse noise exists. The results of nonlinear mean filters are unsatisfactory for mixed impulse noise [105, 116].

In this chapter, we propose a novel approach for suppressing impulse noise in digital images while effectively preserving more details than previously proposed methods. The method presented is based on impulse noise detection and noise-exclusive restoration. Our motivation is that if impulses can be detected and their positions can be located in the image, then it is possible to replace the impulses with the best estimates by using only the uncorrupted neighbors. The noise removing procedure consists of two steps: the detection of the noise and the reconstruction of the image. As the self-organizing tree map (SOTM) network possesses the capability of classifying image pixels, it is employed to detect the impulses. A noise-exclusive median (NEM) filtering algorithm and a noise-exclusive arithmetic mean (NEAM) filtering algorithm are proposed to restore the image. By noise-exclusive, it is meant that all the impulses in the window do not participate in the operation of order sorting or do not contribute to the operation of mean calculation. The new filtering scheme is different from the traditional median-type filtering because for the median-type filters, all the noise pixels inside the window are involved in the operation of ordering. This is the fundamental difference between the new filtering techniques and the traditional ones. According to the distribution of the remaining pixels in the window. the point estimation can be adaptively chosen either from the NEM filter or the NEAM filter. As the method is able to detect noise locations accurately, the best possible restorations of images corrupted by impulses noise are achieved. This filtering scheme also has the characteristic that it can be generalized to incorporate any median-type filtering techniques into the second step after noise detection.

5.2   REVIEW OF TRADITIONAL MEDIAN-TYPE FILTERS

When an image is coded and transmitted over a noisy channel, or degraded by electrical sensor noise, as in a vidicon TV camera, degradation appears as salt-and-pepper noise (i.e., positive and negative impulses) [117, 118]. Two models have been proposed for the description of such impulse noise [119]. The first model assumes fixed values for all the impulses. In the literature, corrupted pixels are often replaced with values that are equal to either the minimum or the maximum of the allowable dynamic range. For 8-bit images, this corresponds typically to fixed values equal to 0 or 255. In this chapter, a more general model in which a noisy pixel can take on arbitrary values in the dynamic range is proposed.

Impulse Noise: Model 1.

$$x_{ij} = \begin{cases} d & \text{with probability } p \\ s_{ij} & \text{with probability } 1 - p \end{cases} \tag{5.1}$$

where s_{ij} denotes the pixel values of the original image, d denotes the erroneous point value, x_{ij} denotes the pixel values of the degraded image.

A modified model assumes that both positive and negative impulses are present in the image.

$$x_{ij} = \begin{cases} d_p & \text{with probability } p_p \\ d_n & \text{with probability } p_n \\ s_{ij} & \text{with probability } 1 - (p_p + p_n) \end{cases} \tag{5.2}$$

where d_p and d_n denote positive and negative impulse noise.

The second model allows the impulses to follow a random distribution.

Impulse Noise: Model 2.

$$x_{ij} = \begin{cases} d_p + n_{gu} & \text{with probability } p_p \\ d_n + n_{gu} & \text{with probability } p_n \\ s_{ij} & \text{with probability } 1 - (p_p + p_n) \end{cases} \tag{5.3}$$

where n_{gu} follows a random distribution with zero mean.

As stated previously, the median filter has been widely used in image processing due to its property of removing impulse noise while preserving sharp edges. Because the design of the median filter is based on the theory of order statistics, it possesses the characteristic of robust estimation. However, it is also the ordering process that removes the fine details and changes the signal structure. Thus, the generalized median-type filters have been introduced to retain the advantage of the robustness of the median filter and to take into account the details as well.

The properties of some typical generalized median-type filters are summarized below. The CWM filter puts more emphasis on the central weights aiming to increase the signal preservation.

$$y_i = med(x_{i-v}, \dots, (k + 1) * x_i, \dots, x_{i+v}) \tag{5.4}$$

where $v = (n - 1)/2$, n is the window size, and $(k + 1) * x_i$ denotes $(k + 1)$ duplications of x_i.

The max/median filter emphasizes the preservation of multidimensional structural information based on the fact that the desired features are of lower dimensionality than that of the observation space. The max/median filter traces all possible direction lines through the center pixel and makes a ranked median operation on the pixels lying along each line separately. Combining all one-dimensional (1D) estimates, the multidimensional max estimate is made.

$$z_1 = med(x_{i,j_v}, \ldots, x_{ij}, \ldots, x_{i,j+v}).$$ (5.5)

$$z_2 = med(x_{i-v,j}, \ldots, x_{ij}, \ldots, x_{i+v,j}).$$ (5.6)

$$z_3 = med(x_{i+v,j-v}, \ldots, x_{ij}, \ldots, x_{i-v,j+v}).$$ (5.7)

$$z_4 = med(x_{i-v,j-v}, \ldots, x_{ij}, \ldots, x_{i+v,j+v}).$$ (5.8)

$$y_{ij} = max(z_1, z_2, z_3, z_4).$$ (5.9)

The multistage/median filter further improves the performance of max/median filter by using a median estimate in Equation 5.9 instead of a max estimate because the median filter will be less biased toward large values.

$$y_{ij} = med(med(z_1, z_2, x_{ij}), med(z_3, z_4, x_{ij}), x_{ij}).$$ (5.10)

It preserves details in horizontal, vertical, and diagonal directions by including the four sub-filters Equations 5.5–5.8, which are sensitive to these directions.

However, all these median-type filters obtain the detail preservation at the expense of poor noise suppression. For 2D images, the generalized median-type filtering schemes are based on replacing the central pixel value in a window with a value derived from one of the generalized median filtering criteria. Since the window is sliding over each pixel in the image from left to right and top to bottom, all of the pixels in the image are processed once. This procedure tends to remove fine details, smear thin lines, and causes streak effects more or less similar to the median filter because the ordering process destroys the structural and spatial neighborhood information. This is particularly a problem when the size of the window is large as such filters often use large windows to suppress impulse noise.

Another drawback with median-type filters (including the median filter) is that the image quality degrades as the noise rate increases. This can be seen from Figure 5.1. We will use statistical analysis of the median filter and the CWM filter based on the model in Equation 5.1 to show this fact quantitatively. According to the definition of the impulse noise Model 1 for the median filter, the error occurs with probability p, independent of both the errors at other pixels and all the original pixels. In fact, the number of erroneous points in the window follows a binomial distribution. Let x_i be the input image and y_i be the output image.

$$y_i = median\{ x(i) \in W \}.$$ (5.11)

The output value will be correct if and only if the number of errors within the window W is less than half the number of points in the window, that is, less than or equal to

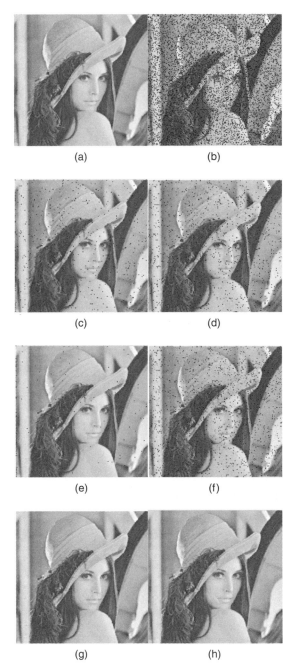

FIGURE 5.1   All filtered images with window size 3 × 3: (a) original lena image; (b) 20% negative impulse corrupted image; (c) median filtered image; (d) center-weighted median filtered image; (e) max/median filtered image; (f) multistage median filtered image; (g) noise-exclusive median filtered image; (h) noise-exclusive arithmetic mean filtered image.

$(n-1)/2$, where n is the size of the window. Therefore, the probability of incorrect reconstruction at the center of the window is

$$P_e = \sum_{l=(n+1)/2}^{n} \binom{n}{l} p^l (1-p)^{n-l}. \tag{5.12}$$

It is obvious that the result will be good only when error rate p is small. For the CWM filter, we will first give a mathematical expression of the error probability after reconstruction and then compare reconstruction error rates given by the median and the CWM filter. For the max/median and multistage median filters, only visual examples are presented.

Theorem: Assume the central pixel has weight $k+1$ in the CWM filter. The probability of erroneous reconstruction based on Model 1 is given by

$$P_e = \sum_{l=(n-1-k)/2}^{n-1} \binom{n-1}{l} p^{l+1}(1-p)^{n-l-1} + \sum_{l=(n+1+k)/2}^{n-1} \binom{n-1}{l} p^l (1-p)^{n-l}. \tag{5.13}$$

Proof: Two cases must be considered. In the corrupted image (a) the central pixel is in error; (b) the central pixel is not in error.

$P_e = P_r\{\text{the central pixel is in error},$

$\quad$ at least $(n-1-k)/2$ out of the other $n-1$ pixels are in error$\}$

$\quad +P_r\{\text{the central pixel is not in error},$

$\quad$ at least $(n+1+k/2)$ out of the other $n-1$ pixels are in error$\}$

$\quad = P_r\{\text{the central pixel is in error}\}$

$\quad * P_r\{\text{at least } (n-1-k)/2 \text{ out of the other } n-1 \text{ pixels are in error}\}$

$\quad +P_r\{\text{the central pixel is not in error}\}$

$\quad * P_r\{\text{at least } (n+1+k/2) \text{ out of the other } n-1 \text{ pixels are in error}\}$

$$= P \sum_{l=(n-1-k)/2}^{n-1} \binom{n-1}{l} p^l (1-p)^{n-l-l}$$

$$+(1-P) \sum_{l=(n+1+k)/2}^{n-1} \binom{n-1}{l} p^l (1-p)^{n-l-l}. \tag{5.14}$$

$\blacksquare$

Corollary: When $k=0$, P_e in Equation 5.13 becomes P_e in Equation 5.12.

Proof: Starting from Equation 5.13

$$P_e = \sum_{l=(n-1)/2}^{n-1} \frac{(n-1)!}{l!(n-1-l)!} p^{l+1}(1-p)^{n-1-l} + \sum_{l=(n+1)/2}^{n-1} \frac{(n-1)!}{l!(n-1-l)!} p^{l}(1-p)^{n-l}$$

$$= \frac{(n-1)!}{(n-1)!(n-n)!} p^{n}(1-p)^{n-n}$$

$$+ \sum_{l=(n+1)/2}^{n-1} \left[\frac{(n-1)!}{(l-1)!(n-l)!} p^{l}(1-p)^{n-l} + \frac{(n-1)!}{l!(n-1-l)!} p^{l}(1-p)^{n-l} \right]$$

$$= p^{n} + \sum_{l=(n+1)/2}^{n-1} \frac{(n-1)!}{(l-1)!(n-1-l)!} p^{l}(1-p)^{n-l} \left(\frac{1}{l} + \frac{1}{n-l} \right)$$

$$= p^{n} + \sum_{l=(n+1)/2}^{n-1} \frac{(n-1)!}{(l-1)!(n-1-l)!} \frac{n-l+l}{(n-l)l} p^{l}(1-p)^{n-l}$$

$$= p^{n} + \sum_{l=(n+1)/2}^{n-1} \frac{(n)!}{(l)!(n-l)!} p^{l}(1-p)^{n-l}$$

$$= \sum_{l=(n+1)/2}^{n} \binom{n}{l} p^{l}(1-p)^{n-l}.$$

∎

The result shown in the corollary is conceptually intuitive, since when $k = 0$, the CWM filter becomes the median filter.

It is shown in Table 5.1 that the probability of erroneous reconstruction increases drastically as error rate increases. From Figure 5.1, it can be seen that using the CWM and multistage median filters, noise suppression is worse than that of the median filter. Although the max/median filter has better noise suppression in this negative impulse case (the entire image tends to have higher intensity, because of the biased estimation), it produces worse results than that of the median filter when both positive and negative noise exist. In summary, the generalized median-type filters improve the detail preservation but decrease noise suppression. To obtain the same

TABLE 5.1   The Erroneous Reconstruction Probabilities of the Median and the CWM filters with Window Size $n = 9$

Error rate	Median	$CWM_{k+1=3}$
0.10	0.00089	0.00345
0.15	0.00563	0.01359
0.20	0.01960	0.03328
0.30	0.09900	0.09966

noise suppression effect as that of the median filter, larger windows must be applied. But this causes even more blur effect than that of the median filter as shown in Figure 5.2. This leads to the conclusion that the generalized median-type filters do not overcome the drawbacks of the median filter fundamentally. To overcome these problems, we have developed a new filtering scheme that produces images with good quality irrespective of the increase of impulse noise to certain degrees. The visual results generated by the method are shown in Figure 5.1(g and h).

5.3   THE NOISE-EXCLUSIVE ADAPTIVE FILTERING

The problems with the median-type filters are the following: (a) all pixels in the image are processed irrespective of whether they are impulses or normal pixels; (b) impulse noise pixels are included in the ordering and filtering. The net effect is the degradation of the originally correct pixels and biased estimation due to the inclusion of the impulses in the filtering. In order to avoid unnecessary processing on pixels that are not corrupted by impulse noise and to improve the correct reconstruction rate, the impulse noise suppression is divided into two steps in our proposed approach. In the first step, we focus on noise detection and aim at locating noise pixels in the image. In the second step, to make full use of the robust estimation of order statistics and to take into account the simplicity of computing the sample mean, two noise-exclusive filtering algorithms are introduced. By performing these operations, the fine details can be preserved and proper estimations for the corrupted pixels can be derived. Experimental results will be given in the following section.

5.3.1   Feature Selection and Impulse Detection

People usually attempt to use the Local statistical characteristics to remove the impulse noise. The Local statistics can help characterize the impulse noise to a certain degree, but the impulse noise can not be completely determined by the Local information, as sometimes the Local information does not represent the characteristics of the impulse noise very well. For instance, in Equations 5.15 and 5.16, both pixels in the center of the window represent positive impulses. It is hard to say that the central pixel in Equation 5.16 is due to impulse noise.

$$
\begin{matrix} 69 & 99 & 120 \\ 241 & 238 & 121 \\ 244 & 56 & 241 \end{matrix} \quad md = \text{pixel value} - \text{median} = 238 - 121 = 117. \quad (5.15)
$$

$$
\begin{matrix} 235 & 19 & 21 \\ 236 & 241 & 237 \\ 249 & 17 & 237 \end{matrix} \quad md = \text{pixel value} - \text{median} = 241 - 236 = 5. \quad (5.16)
$$

In order to effectively detect the impulse noise, the Local statistics are used as feature vectors. Impulse noise detection is, in fact, a special application of the

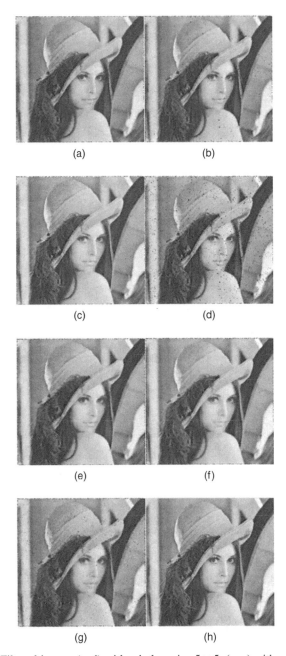

FIGURE 5.2   Filtered image: (a–d) with window size 5×5, (e–g) with window size 7×7; (a) median filtered image; (b) center-weighted median filtered image; (c) max/median filtered image; (d) multistage median filtered image; (e) center-weighted median filtered image; (f) max/median filtered image; (g) multistage median filtered image; (h) noise-exclusive median filtered image with window size 3×3.

vector quantization. From a statistical point of view, the impulse noise should be characterized by its distribution of the probability density function. Our goal is to find the reference vectors that represent the impulse noise instead of using Local statistics to compare each pixel with a threshold [114]. To extract features from Local statistics, a 3×3 square window is used to pass through the entire noise-degraded image. The size and shape of the window are not restricted to 3×3 and a square. It may vary, for example, 5×5 or even as large as 7×7 and any shape, cross or circle. The consideration for choosing a 3×3 square window is twofold. (a) The square window can best reflect the correlations between the pixel at the center and the neighbors. As the central pixel has neighbors in each direction, it contains sufficient information for the statistical analysis. (b) Working within a smaller window is computationally efficient. From the pixel values within a sliding window, many useful Local features, such as mean, median, variance, range, and extreme range can be gathered. Using these features, the concept of noise detection is expressed as feature extraction and pattern classification.

Suppose that N features are to be measured from each input pattern. Each set of the N features can be considered as a vector $\mathbf{x}$ in the N-dimensional feature space. The problem of classification is to assign each possible vector to a proper pattern class. To fulfill the pattern classification, the aforementioned SOTM neural network, which is capable of cluster analysis, is employed. Of the Local features, two are chosen as an input pattern to be fed into the neural network in our experiment. One feature is the pixel value, and the other is termed the median deviation, which is obtained from the difference between the pixel value and the median in the window.

These two features are used to distinguish the impulse noise from the signals, as they can effectively reflect the characteristics of the impulse noise. The image normally has homogeneous regions and the median deviations of the homogeneous regions should have small values. The median deviation has a large value if and only if there is impulse noise or a thin line existing within the window. The first feature helps the neural network to train the weight vectors to represent impulses of both directions (positive impulse and negative impulse) according to the modified impulse noise Model 1. Since the median value is a robust estimate of the original pixel value based on the theory of order statistics, the second feature provides accurate information about the likelihood of whether the current pixel is corrupted. The approach of using SOTM in impulse detection is obviously superior to that of the Local detection approach [114]. The advantage of the SOTM is that it not only considers the Local features, but also takes into account the Global information in the images. In addition, it detects not only fixed value impulse noise, but also impulse noise with a random intensity distribution, as the SOTM can classify input vectors into clusters and find the center of each cluster.

5.3.2 Noise Removal Filters

Since the cluster centers that represent the means of the impulse noise have been detected, recovering of image becomes the process of matching pixels with the cluster centers. If the pixel value lies in the interval of one of the impulse noise cluster centers with the variance, and the pixels median deviation is large enough, then the pixel is determined to be impulse noise. The NEM and the NEAM are two noise-exclusive filters [120, 121] that are introduced to restore the impulse corrupted images. The window size of these filters may vary as the traditional median-type filters. The noise-exclusive scheme is incorporated in filtering by applying the filters to the impulses but without affecting the uncorrupted pixels. The NEM filter only enables uncorrupted pixels inside the window to participate in ordering, while the NEAM filter calculates arithmetic means from these uncorrupted pixels. Since both filters use true information in the window to estimate the corrupted pixels, the quality of the restored image is ensured. For example, in Equations 5.15 and 5.16, the results obtained by the NEM filter and NEAM filter are

$$y_i = med(56, 69, 99, 120, 121) = 99, \tag{5.17}$$

$$y_i = mean(69, 99, 120, 121, 56) = 92, \tag{5.18}$$

and

$$y_i = med(17, 19, 21) = 19, \tag{5.19}$$

$$y_i = mean(19, 21, 17) = 19, \tag{5.20}$$

respectively, while the original pixel values in the center of Equations 5.15 and 5.16 are 104 and 15.

It can be seen that the NEM filter is a natural and logical extension of the median filter. The median filter takes the median value within a window that may contain some contaminated pixels. Its aim is to reduce the probability of taking the extreme values, whereas the NEM filter first eliminates the extreme values in the window, then takes the median. Since the estimation of the NEM filter is based on the reduced original sample space, its estimation accuracy is better than that of the median filter. Therefore, the NEM filter possesses all the good properties that the median filter has, such as edge preservation robust estimation, and also preserves the integrity of the image without changing the structure of the signals.

Combining the NEM and the NEAM filters can even further improve their performance. Among the remainder of the pixels, a comparison of a predefined value V with the range value is performed. If the value is bigger than V, the NEM filter is chosen, otherwise the NEAM filter is chosen. For instance, for Equation 5.17 the range value is equal to 65, which is rather large, so we use the NEM filter. The adaptive procedure further ensures the accuracy of the estimation. If the NEAM filter is applied to the degraded image, the operation can be simplified and computing time can be reduced, because no sorting operation is involved. The α-trimmed mean filter [122] is, in fact, a special case of NEAM filter, when both negative and positive impulses exist.

Proof: We give the general expression of the NEAM filter as

$$y = \frac{1}{n[1 - (p_p + p_n)]} \sum_{i=1}^{n[1-(p_p+p_n)]} x_i.$$

If we do the sorting before eliminating the noise pixels in the window, then calculating the exclusive mean, the above formula becomes

$$y = \frac{1}{n[1 - (p_p + p_n)]} \sum_{i=[np_n]+1}^{n-[np_p]} x_i.$$

Let $p = p_n = p_p$; then

$$y = \frac{1}{[n(1 - 2p)]} \sum_{i=[np]+1}^{n-[np]} x_i.$$

This is the case of α-trimmed mean [122].

$$X_\alpha = \frac{1}{n - 2 * [\alpha n]} \sum_{i=[n\alpha]+1}^{n-[\alpha n]} x_i$$

where $\alpha \le 0.5$ and $[\cdot]$ is the nearest integer to $\cdot$. ∎

The NEAM filter has two merits superior to the α-trimmed mean filter. The first is that it does not require the sorting operation. It simply calculates the mean from the uncorrupted pixels. The second is that it can handle unevenly distributed positive and negative impulses.

5.4 EXPERIMENTAL RESULTS

The noise-exclusive filtering schemes described in Section 5.3 have been extensively tested and compared with several popular median-type filtering techniques, such as the median, the CWM, the max/median, and the multistage median filters. A number of experiments are preformed in the presence of negative, positive, or both negative and positive impulse noise with low and high probabilities. The comparisons of the performance are based on the normalized mean square error (NMSE) and the subjective visual criteria. Quantitative error results are presented and their filtered images are shown for subjective evaluation. The NMSE is given by

$$NMSE = \frac{\sum_{i=0}^{N-1} \sum_{j=0}^{N-1} [f_{ij} - y_{ij}]^2}{\sum_{i=0}^{N-1} \sum_{j=0}^{N-1} [f_{ij}]^2} \tag{5.21}$$

TABLE 5.2   The Performance Comparison of Filters in terms of NMSE with Window Size 3 × 3 and Condition of Even Impulse Noise Distribution

	Lake	Tower	Flower	Lena
Image size	256 × 256	256 × 256	256 × 256	256 × 256
Noise rate	0.13	0.18	0.20	0.40
Median	0.004885	0.006075	0.003854	0.0036475
CWM k+1=3	0.007615	0.00698	0.008749	0.070176
Max	0.088714	0.069088	0.126696	0.395211
Multistage	0.010214	0.007905	0.01685	0.081947
NEM	0.000558	0.001064	0.000161	0.003061
NEAM	0.000566	0.000998	0.000232	0.002928

where f_{ij} is the original image, y_{ij} is the filtered image, and N is the width and height of the image.

The experiments performed include the following.

- An assessment of the proposed filters with respect to the percentage of impulse noise corruption;
- A demonstration of the robustness of the proposed filtering scheme with respect to the model of impulse noise;
- An evaluation of the NEM and the NEAM with respect to the edge preservation, fine details preservation, and signal distortion;
- An overall comparison of the features of both the NEM and the NEAM with the median-type filters;
- A demonstration of the perceptual gains achieved by the filtering scheme.

Experiment 1: The restoration performances of different methods for fixed impulse noise with even distribution are compared in Table 5.2, and subjective evaluations are given in Figures 5.3, 5.4, 5.5, and 5.6. All the filters use 3 × 3 windows. The CWM filter has its central weighted coefficient $k + 1 = 3$. To generate a set of test images, four pictures (256 × 256 pixels, 8 bits/pixel) of different types including a lake, a tower, a flower, and lena are used in the experiment.

The original images are shown in Figures 5.3a, 5.4a, 5.5a, and 5.6a, respectively. Images corrupted by even positive and negative impulse noise with different probabilities are shown in Figures 5.3b, 5.4b, 5.5b, and 5.6b.

From the visual result of the filtered images, one can easily tell that the median filter has the ability of providing robust estimates against impulse noise and the ability to preserve sharp edges. However, it removes fine details and thin lines and causes a slight blur effect as shown in Figures 5.3c , 5.4c, 5.5c, 5.6c. These images also show that as the impulse noise ratio gradually increases, the equalities of the filtered images decreases. When the impulse noise ratio increases to 40%, the filtered image becomes unacceptable as shown in Figure 5.6c. In general, the median filter can only suppress the impulse noise effectively when the noise rate is lower than 20% and

(a)   (b)

(c)   (d)

(e)   (f)

(g)   (h)

FIGURE 5.3 All filtered images with window size 3×3: (a) original image; (b) 13 % impulse corrupted image; (c) median filtered image; (d) center-weighted median filtered image; (e) max/median filtered image; (f) multistage median filtered image; (g) noise-exclusive median filtered image; (h) noise-exclusive arithmetic mean filtered image.

FIGURE 5.4   All filtered images with window size 3 × 3: (a) original image; (b) 18% mixed impulse corrupted image; (c) median filtered image; (d) center-weighted median filtered image; (e) max/median filtered image; (f) multistage median filtered image; (g) noise-exclusive median filtered image; (h) noise-exclusive arithmetic mean filtered image.

FIGURE 5.5   All filtered images with window size 3 × 3: (a) original image; (b) 20% mixed impulse corrupted image; (c) median filtered image; (d) center-weighted median filtered image; (e) max/median filtered image; (f) multistage median filtered image; (g) noise-exclusive median filtered image; (h) noise-exclusive arithmetic mean filtered image.

FIGURE 5.6   All filtered images with window size 3 × 3: (a) original image; (b) 40% mixed impulse corrupted image; (c) median filtered image; (d) center-weighted median filtered image; (e) max/median filtered image; (f) multistage median filtered image; (g) noise-exclusive median filtered image; (h) noise-exclusive arithmetic mean filtered image.

this must be in the case of mixed impulse noise because of the positive and negative impulse noise offset effect.

With the CWM filter, as expected, the ability for signal preservation increases because more emphasis is placed on the central weight. Unfortunately, the noise suppression decreases correspondingly. Compared with the median filter, the CWM filter preserves fine details better, such as the leaves in the "lake," and the detail appearance in the "tower" images. But it produces visually unpleasing effects as shown in Figures 5.3d, 5.4d, 5.5d, and 5.6d.

The max/median filter, as mentioned in the previous section, can be effective in the negative impulse noise case, but it fails in removal of mixed impulse noise, because it tends to enhance positive spikes in the image as shown in Figures 5.3e, 5.4e, 5.5e, and 5.6e.

From the figures, it is not difficult to discover that the multistage median filtered images visually appear very similar to those of the CWM. The multistage median filter has good edge- and detail-preserving capabilities. In fact, during filtering, it not only preserves edges, but also enhances the contrast of the edge effect, which can be seen in Figures 5.3f, 5.4f, 5.5f, and 5.6f. However, its noise suppression characteristic is worse than that of the CWM. Also, it cannot preserve the thin lines. As shown in Figure 5.4f, the thin lines on the bottom part of the tower wall are smeared. All the filters mentioned above have the same problem in that their noise suppression ability decreases as error rate increases. They also tend to produce blur effects, as these approaches are implemented uniformly across the image. The pixels that are undisturbed by impulse noise are most likely modified. The blur is more obvious especially when a large window is applied.

In contrast, the results obtained by the NEM and the NEAM filters are superior to other filters. The results are shown in Figures 5.3g–5.6g and Figures 5.3h–5.6h, respectively. The two filters possess good properties of noise suppression, edge and fine details preservation, and very little signal distortion. The edge and fine detail characteristics of the filters are compared with those of the above filters. The results are shown in Figures 5.7 and 5.8, respectively. The max/median filter is not suitable for mix impulse noise, while the median, the CWM, and the multistage median filters are not good in single type impulse case. However, the proposed filters are not affected by these limitations. In order to clearly see the reconstructed images and compare them with the original image, the 3D plots of the original image and filtered images are shown in Figure 5.9. From the results, it is obvious that the NEM and NEAM filters are superior to the traditional median-type filters. The achieved restorations result in total impulse cleaning, fine detail preservation, and minimum signal distortion. One of the most significant properties of the two filters is their robustness. The qualities of the reconstructed images by the two filters do not deteriorate when the noise ratio is getting higher.

Table 5.2 summarizes the NMSEs for all filters. From the table, it is clear that the proposed two filters are hardly affected by the error rate. Although, the NMSEs of the two filters increase slightly as the error rate increases, visually, the filtered images still have good qualities. The increased error rate is because too few true pixels left in the estimation window after the noise excluding operation, which causes certain

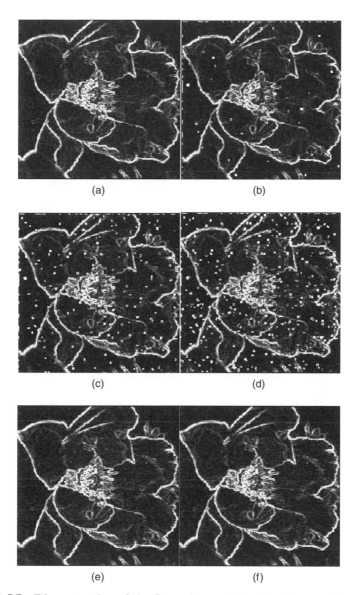

FIGURE 5.7 Edge extraction of the flower image: (a) original image; (b) median filtered image; (c) center-weighted median filtered image; (d) multistage median filtered image; (e) noise-exclusive median filtered image; (f) noise-exclusive arithmetic mean filtered image.

distortion. Although the experiments for other images with varying percentages of impulse noise are not shown, the proposed filtering scheme produces superior results.

Experiment 2: In this experiment, an assessment is made according to the performance of the proposed method with respect to uneven impulse noise. Two images

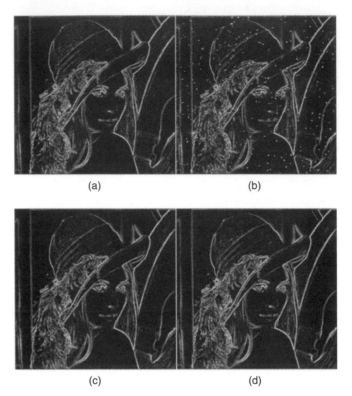

(a)   (b)

(c)   (d)

FIGURE 5.8   Edge extraction of lena image: (a) original image; (b) max/median filtered image; (c) noise-exclusive median filtered image; (d) noise-exclusive arithmetic mean filtered image.

"tower" and "flower" are used to visually illustrate the results of the filters as shown in Figures 5.10 and 5.11, respectively. The "tower" image is corrupted by 25% of uneven impulse noise, of which 19% is negative and 6% is positive. The "flower" image is corrupted by 20% positive impulse noise. The restoration results include the "lena" image in Figure 5.1 and is tabulated in Table 5.3. From the figures, it is shown that the conventional median methods are not effective to remove impulse noise that is unevenly distributed. Because the median, the CWM, and the multistage median filters rely on the negative and positive impulse offset, the max/median filter eliminates negative impulse noise very well. But it is not good for positive impulse noise, whereas the proposed method is unrestricted in this case.

Experiment 3: The proposed method is also robust at eliminating mixed Gaussian random impulse noise expressed in impulse noise Model 2 Equation 5.3. The flower image is used as the test image as shown in Figure 5.12. It is corrupted by 20% random positive and negative impulse noise. In the corrupted image, n_{gu} follows a Gaussian distribution with standard deviation $\sigma = 10$. From the previous results of image and Table 5.4, it is obvious that the proposed method is not only good for

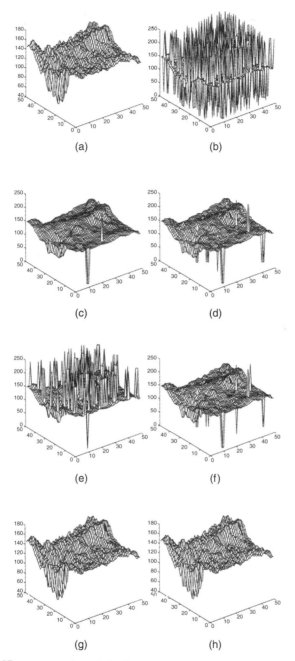

FIGURE 5.9 3D representation of the flower image: (a) original image; (b) 20% impulse noise corrupted image; (c) median filtered image; (d) center-weighted median filtered image; (e) max/median filtered image; (f) multistage median filtered image; (g) noise-exclusive median filtered image; (h) noise-exclusive arithmetic mean filtered image.

(a)   (b)

(c)   (d)

(e)   (f)

(g)   (h)

FIGURE 5.10   All filtered images with window size 3 × 3: (a) original image; (b) 25% uneven impulse noise corrupted image; (c) median filtered image; (d) center-weighted median filtered image; (e) max/median filtered image; (f) multistage median filtered image; (g) noise-exclusive median filtered image; (h) noise-exclusive arithmetic mean filtered image.

(a)   (b)

(c)   (d)

(e)   (f)

(g)   (h)

FIGURE 5.11   All filtered images with window size 3 × 3: (a) original image; (b) 20% uneven impulse noise corrupted image; (c) median filtered image; (d) center-weighted median filtered image; (e) max/median filtered image; (f) multistage median filtered image; (g) noise-exclusive median filtered image; (h) noise-exclusive arithmetic mean filtered image.

FIGURE 5.12   All filtered images with window size 3×3: (a) original image; (b) image corrupted by 20% impulse noise with a Gaussian ($\sigma^2 = 100$ distribution; (c) median filtered image; (d) center-weighted median filtered image; (e) max/median filtered image; (f) multistage median filtered image; (g) noise-exclusive median filtered image; (h) noise-exclusive arithmetic mean filtered image.

TABLE 5.3   The Performance Comparison of Filters in terms of NMSE with Window Size 3×3 and Condition of Uneven Impulse Noise Distribution

	Lena	Lena	Tower	Flower
Image size	480×480	480×480	256×256	256×256
p_n	0.10	0.20	0.19	0.00
p_p	0.00	0.00	0.06	0.20
Median	0.002811	0.014346	0.007720	0.28543
CWM k + 1 = 3	0.005038	0.029565	0.014165	0.055316
Max	0.002242	0.004434	0.011869	0.384172
Multistage	0.005713	0.033056	0.017405	0.065441
NEM	0.001820	0.001924	0.000547	0.000527
NEAM	0.001776	0.001799	0.000551	0.000589

TABLE 5.4   The Performance Comparison of Filters with Window Size 3×3.

Filter	Median	CWM	Max	Multistage	NEM	NEAM
NMSE	0.0058	0.0099	0.1214	0.0152	0.0006	0.0011

removal of fixed impulse noise, but also works extremely well for images corrupted by mixed random impulse noise with Gaussian distribution. This characteristic has practical significance in real applications.

5.5 DETECTION-GUIDED RESTORATION AND REAL-TIME PROCESSING

5.5.1 Introduction

Pictorial information is often made unrecognizable by heavy noise or unwanted distortions. Recovering the desired information from the degraded image is of great importance for the subsequent processing. From the previous sections, it is known that the presence of impulse noise seriously degrades the performance of linear filters, whereas the nonlinear median-type filters do not recover the images very well when the noise ratio is higher than 20%.

One intuitive consideration in improving the noise suppression of the median filter is to iteratively apply the filter to the images [123]. This certainly improves the performance of the median filter to some degree, but the side effect is that it converges to its root very slowly. It usually takes several passes to get a clean picture and introduces severe streak effect on the homogeneous regions and jitter effect on the edges.

Another intuitive modification of the median filters is to introduce recursive structure [124, 125], which uses the previously computed pixels $y_{i-v}, \ldots, y_{i-1}$ for the calculation of y_i.

$$y_i = med(y_{i-v}, \ldots, y_{i-1}, x_i, \ldots, x_{i+v}). \tag{5.22}$$

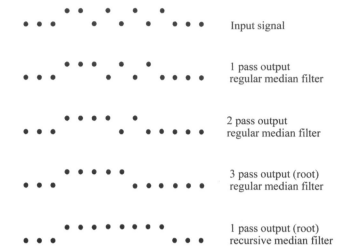

FIGURE 5.13   Recursive vs. regular median filters with window size of 3.

The idea of applying the recursive structure to the median filters for suppressing impulse noise is easily explained by the fact that the output pixels $y_{i-v}, \ldots, y_{i-1}$ contribute directly to the computation of y_i. Indeed, the noise suppression can be improved. However, blurring and jitter become more noticeable because the recursive median filter produces highly correlated signals.

One of the interesting characteristics of the recursive operations is that the root of a signal for a particular recursive can always be found after the first pass of the operation as shown in Figure 5.13. The recursive median filter reduces the signal to a root in a single pass, whereas the regular median filter requires three passes. The property of the recursive median filter also shows that the output of the recursive operation is invariant when the same filter is used repeatedly.

Based on the methods presented in the previous sections in this chapter, an iterative approach is introduced using a recursive NEM filter to restore images corrupted by very strong noise. Since the proposed filtering scheme is nondegrading, iteratively repeated filtering does not further degrade the image. For those images with a percentage of noisy pixels lower than 40%, the desired restoration can be achieved in just one pass. For higher percentages, after only a few rounds of filtering, the image reaches a steady state that remains unmodified by further rounds of restoration. As the restoration acts on the corrupted pixels only, the NEM and the NEAM filters can also be applied to the images recursively. The recursive form of these filters achieves more efficient noise suppression than the nonrecursive form, without producing additional blurring or steak effect. It is shown that image restoration using the proposed method produces very pleasing results, which may be subsequently used in the further processing such as segmentation or region identification.

Another important issue for the proposed filtering scheme is real-time processing [126]. The real-time processing features of the NEM filter for the removal of impulse noise in TV picture transmission is present. In particular, the characteristics of the real impulses are incorporated in the noise identification stage. The suitability of the method in terms of real-time processing for images corrupted by randomly distributed impulse noise and those corrupted by real impulses strokes is analytically and numerically investigated. Impulse corrupted TV picture sequences are used to demonstrate that the proposed method potentially provides a real-time solution to quality TV picture transmission.

5.5.2   Iterative Filtering

As calculated in Table 5.1, the rate of failure of the median filter for impulse noise with window size 3×3 is about 20%. For the images corrupted by a higher noise ratio, it is not expected for the median filter to eliminate all the impulse noise in one pass. Therefore, it is obvious that the best solution is to apply the median filter to the images iteratively. This consideration definitely helps the impulse noise suppression of the median filter as shown in Figure 5.14. From the experiments, when the window of the median filter passes over the image in the first round, the output value for each window position is highly different from the input pixel value occupying the center of the window. When the median filter is used iteratively, the number of pixel changes drops for the next few passes. As the resulting outputs of successive passes approach a root, the number of pixel changes becomes smaller and smaller (this phenomenon can be seen in the 1D case shown in Fig. 5.13). Finally, the image converges to an invariant signal—its root.

According to the experiments, repeated applications of the median filter improve the impulse noise suppression, but the convergence to the image root requires too many passes. On the other hand, when the image reaches its root, only the edges and sharp transitions are retained in the image; areas of gradually varying pixel value become constant and fine details are lost.

In contrast to the median filter, when the NEM and the NEAM filters are applied to the image in Figure 5.14a, only two passes are needed to recover the image. The visual qualities of the recovered images shown in Figure 5.15 are much better than that of the median filter as shown in Figure 5.14. In the proposed filtering scheme presented in the previous sections, only one pass should be enough to recover the image, as all the impulse noise and suspected pixels are detected and their locations are known. However, because the noise ratio is very high, in some windows (3×3) all the pixels are contaminated. The noise-exclusive filters cannot restore the correct value in this case. Therefore, the impulse noise in these windows remains untouched. There are two strategies to solve this problem. One is to increase the filtering window, for example, using a 5×5 window. However, by doing this, the processing speed will be affected because the ordering operation takes longer in the large window, and the distortion will be increased as the correlation in the large window decreases.

The other way to solve the problem is to iteratively use these filters. This way, the good quality of the recovered image can be ensured and the processing time increases very little, in that for the second pass, only a small amount of impulse noise needs to be processed. The iterative filtering process is schematically shown in Figure 5.16.

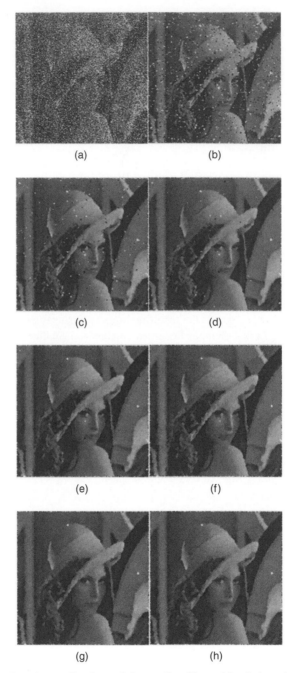

FIGURE 5.14   Iterative applications of the median filter with window size 3×3: (a) 45% mixed impulse noise corrupted image; (b) first iteration; (c) second iteration; (d) third iteration; (e) fourth iteration; (f) fifth iteration; (g) sixth iteration (h); seventh iteration.

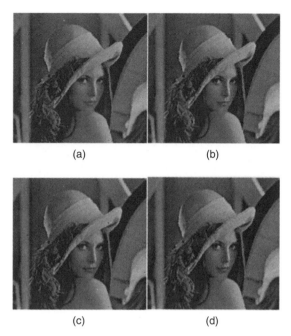

(a)   (b)

(c)   (d)

FIGURE 5.15 Iterative applications of the noise-exclusive median (NEM) and noise-exclusive arithmetic mean (NEAM) filters with window size 3×3: (a) first iteration filtered image by the NEM; (b) second iteration filtered image by the NEM; (c) first iteration filtered image by the NEAM; (d) second iteration filtered image by the NEAM.

The comparison of performances based on the NMSE and processing time is given in Table 5.5.

From the results, it is evident that like the median filter, the NEM and the NEAM filters can also be used iteratively to suppress high ratio impulse noise. But the repeated application, which is exactly the same as one pass filtering, does not affect the quality of the restoration. This is the basic difference between the proposed iterative filtering and the iterative median filtering.

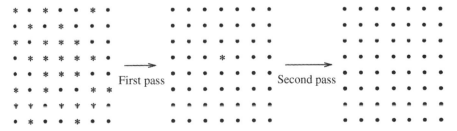

FIGURE 5.16 The iterative filtering process of the NEM and the NEM filters. Dot denotes signal and "*" denotes the impulse.

TABLE 5.5   The Performance Comparison of Filters in terms of NMSE and Processing Time

	NMSE	1st pass	2nd pass	3rd to 7th pass	Total
Median	0.025812	0.095278 min	0.095278 min	0.095278 min	0.666946 min
NEM	0.004789	0.036944 min	0.000583 min		0.037527 min
NEAM	0.004220	0.029683 min	0.000365 min		0.030048 min

5.5.3   Recursive Filtering

According to Equation 5.22, the recursive median filter replaces the center pixel with the median value inside the window and uses this value in the subsequent median calculation. The convergence of the recursive median filter to a root is much faster than that of the nonrecursive one. Figure 5.16 shows the properties of fast convergence and better noise reduction. When the recursive median filter is applied to Figure 5.14a, the amount of impulse noise is rapidly reduced to a very low level. However, in general, when the recursive median filter is used for impulse noise removal, similar problems of blurring and severe jitter as found in regular median filters still exist.

In order to preserve a good quality of restoration while maintaining the speed of filtering processing, the NEM and the NEAM filters are applied recursively. They are performed under a Markov random field model, which is defined by the following expression.

$$p\{x_{i,j}|x^{i,j}\} = p\{x_{i,j}|\text{noise-excluded neighbors at } (i,j) \in W\} \qquad (5.23)$$

where $x_{i,j}$ is the pixel value located at position (i,j) of the image, $x^{i,j}$ are all the uncorrupted pixel values in a 3×3 window W centered at (i,j), $p\{x_{i,j}|x^{i,j}\}$ is the conditional probability density of $x_{i,j}$, given $x^{i,j}$. In this model, an attempt is made to recover the corrupted pixel from its neighbors by means of noise-exclusive estimation. The optimal estimate at each corrupted pixel can be expressed based on the neighboring pixels that are not corrupted by the noise. Although the filtering window moves from left to right in each row and top to bottom for row advances, the operation is not pixel oriented. The filtering window is directly moved to where noise is detected as shown in the left image in Figure 5.17. After the estimation and restoration are made within

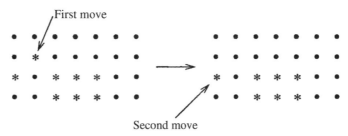

FIGURE 5.17   The recursive filtering process of the noise-exclusive median and the noise-exclusive arithmetic mean filters.

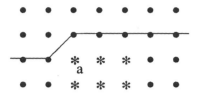

FIGURE 5.18 Recursive restoration. For example, the pixel labeled by "a," its up and left pixels are all recovered in the previous filtering.

the window, the filtering window is moved to the next corrupted pixel as shown in the right image in Figure 5.17. Since the restored pixel is allowed to be involved in the next stage of operation, the corrupted pixel in recursive form always gets a better chance to be recovered than that in the nonrecursive form. Illustration is given in detail in Figure 5.18. If previous restoration is not successful, for example, high noise ratio case, iterative recursive filtering is required.

Figure 5.19 shows the performance of the recursive NEM filter along with a comparison with the nonrecursive NEM filter. Figure 5.19a shows that the test image "lena" is corrupted by mixed impulse noise. The percentage of noise in the image is up to 87%. Iterative restoration strategy is the only solution for such a high noise ratio. The termination of the processing is governed by the following criterion.

$$\|NMSE_{k+1}\| \leq \epsilon \tag{5.24}$$

where ϵ is a predetermined small number. The $NMSE_{k+1}$ is defined as

$$NMSE_{k+1} = \frac{\sum_{i=0}^{M-1} \sum_{i=0}^{N-1} \|\hat{f}_{k+1} - \hat{f}_k\|^2}{\sum_{i=0}^{M-1} \sum_{i=0}^{N-1} \|\hat{f}_k\|^2} \tag{5.25}$$

where $\hat{f}_{k+1}$ and $\hat{f}_k$ denote the $(k+1)$th and (k)th recovered image, M and N denote the image height and width, respectively.

The numerical calculation is given in Table 5.6. It can be seen from the results that recursive filtering is faster than nonrecursive filtering while the qualities of both restored images are similar.

5.5.4 Real-Time Processing of Impulse Corrupted TV Pictures

In the previous sections, the proposed impulse noise filtering method (referred to as basic adaptive method) has been exclusively tested on randomly distributed noisy images. Although it has been shown that the filtering scheme substantially outperforms the median-type filters, two important issues related to applications have not been extensively studied: (a) suitability for real-time processing; and (b) incorporation of special characteristics of impulse noise encountered in real world, such as those in TV picture transmission.

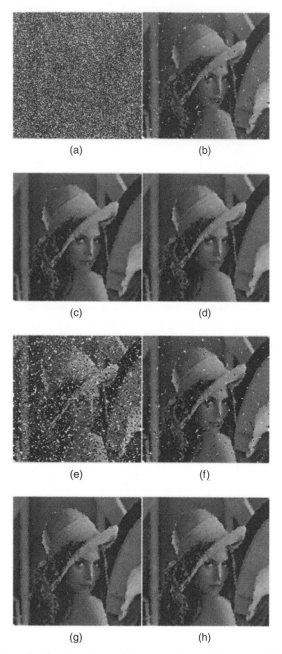

(a) (b)

(c) (d)

(e) (f)

(g) (h)

FIGURE 5.19 Iterative applications of the recursive and nonrecursive noise-exclusive median filter with window size 3×3: (a) 87% mixed impulse corrupted image; (b–d) recursive filtering, (b) first iteration, (c) second iteration, (d) third iteration; (e–h) nonrecursive filtering, (e) first iteration, (f) second iteration, (g) third iteration, (h) fourth iteration.

TABLE 5.6 The Comparison of Recursive and Nonrecursive Filters in Terms of Processing Time

	ε	Iteration 1	Iteration 2	Iteration 3	Iteration 4
Recursive	0.005	0.572049 min	0.042441 min	0.001037 min	
Nonrecursive	0.005	0.605577 min	0.280287 min	0.042393 min	0.001465 min

In this section, the capability of the method to cope with realistic characteristics of impulse noise associated with TV picture transmission is investigated. In particular, the differences between the randomly distributed impulse noise and the real impulse noise are studied, and the special characteristics of the real impulse strokes are incorporated in noise detection.

A TV picture corrupted by impulse noise (Fig. 5.20a) is used for the investigation. Careful observation of the picture reveals that the application of the basic adaptive method to real TV pictures is complicated by the following factors.

- Instead of being randomly distributed, the impulses tend to form short strokes of a single pixel wide in the horizontal direction.
- The intensity distribution of the impulses are not delta functions as suggested in Equation 5.1; it follows a Gaussian distribution as shown in the Equation 5.3. The impulse strokes are fading from high intensity to low intensity.

The explanation for the first point is straightforward when no coding is used in transmission as in cable TV. The impulses in terms of high energy pulses tend to stay relatively stable during the period of corruption and lasts for a sequence of consecutive pixels. Because the image pixels are transmitted row by row in a raster fashion, thus, the impulses are characterized by short strokes of a single pixel wide in the horizontal direction. The basic method with two input features, as in the randomly distributed noise case, does not provide satisfactory results as shown in Figure 5.20b where only one or two pixel/pixels of each impulse stroke is/are suppressed; the rest of the pixels of the strokes still exist after the processing. The reason for this performance is that, only the first one or two pixels of each stroke have a large median deviation, so during the classification, not every pixel in the strokes is classified into the same class. Apparently, the two features used to detect randomly distributed impulses are not adequate enough for the detection of the real impulse strokes. On the other hand, due to the fact that the standard median filter removes thin lines, it can eliminate the short strokes, but it also removes the whole line on the top part of the image and some useful strokes within the characters, so the entire image appears blurred as shown in Figure 5.20c.

In this section, we introduce a strategy that substantially improves the performance of the basic adaptive method in eliminating impulse strokes without increasing much processing time. The strategy is based on the observation that the length of the impulse strokes in TV transmission is normally less than L, $L \leq 20$ pixels in the horizontal

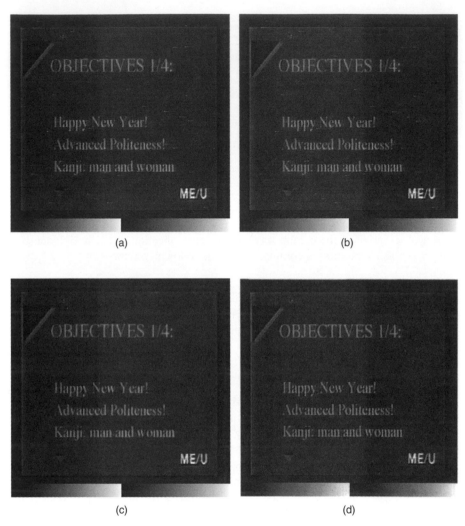

(a)　　　　　　　　　　(b)

(c)　　　　　　　　　　(d)

FIGURE 5.20 Removal of impulse noise from a single frame of a TV sequence. (a) Impulse noise corrupted image (frame 1) from a TV sequence. (b) Image filtered by the basic adaptive method. (c) Image filtered by the median filter. (d) Image filtered by the enhanced adaptive method.

direction, while most meaningful thin lines/edges are longer and the orientations are random. This observation leads to a scheme to improve the quality of processing. The scheme works as follows.

1. Calculate the vertical gradient map of the image by a Laplace filter, and threshold the gradient map into a binary map.
2. Assign a logic "1" to a significant gradient point and a logic "0" otherwise.

3. For any continuous horizontal streams of logic "1"s in the binary map, check their expansion in the vertical direction. If the expansion is one, count horizontally the number of the consecutive logic "1"s, N_1. If

$$N_1 \leq L$$

where L is a predefined positive integer, the stream of "1"s is a stroke. Otherwise it is a thin line/edge.

The advantage of checking the vertical gradient map over checking the original image is that only horizontal strokes/thin lines/edges are possibly converted into logic "1"s in the binary map. From the binary map, a third binary feature $\{0, 1\}$ is generated, which has the power to distinguish pixels belonging to an impulse stroke from those belonging to a thin line/edge. The performance of the enhanced filter is shown in Figure 5.20d, which is significantly better than that processed by the basic adaptive filter (Fig. 5.20b). Careful observation reveals that it also provides a sharper and cleaner image than that by the median filter (Fig. 5.20c).

5.5.5 Analysis of the Processing Time

It will be shown in this section that the processing speed of the adaptive method is faster than that of conventional median-type filters as those given in [109, 111, 112]. The adaptive method is well suited for real-time processing in TV picture transmission. It has been proven to be able to satisfy real-time constraints.

Both the time to process the randomly distributed impulse noise and the time to process the real impulse noise are analyzed. Statistics for the randomly distributed case are based on the image in Figure 5.21a, and statistics for the real impulse noise are based on the TV picture in Figure 5.20a.

Since adaptive filtering requires the training of the SOTM neural network, a number of factors must be considered: (1) processing time; (2) time for preprocessing, training, and detection; (3) robustness of training. These issues are addressed in the following subsections.

Processing time has two components: (a) T_d, time to detect the impulses; (b) T_e, time to eliminate the impulses. Since detection must be performed on all the image pixels, T_d is a fixed factor when the size of the image is known. In other words, T_d is proportional to the size of the image. On the other hand, T_d depends on the percentage of the noisy pixels in the image and the size of the processing window.

In the following, it will be shown that the ratio of T_e and the processing time by the median filter, T_m, can be analytically determined. Since T_d is a fixed factor, the ratio T_d/T_m can be deducted from the difference of the ratio of the calculated processing times and T_e/T_m. Based on the two ratios, the maximum possible ratio can be estimated to justify the processing efficiency of the proposed method.

5.5.5.1 *Eliminating Randomly Distributed Impulse Noise* Assume that the neural network has been properly trained so that it can be used in processing.

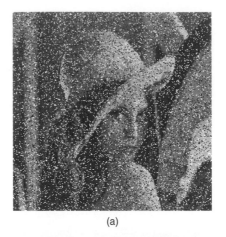

(a)

(b)   (c)

FIGURE 5.21   An image corrupted by randomly distributed impulse noise and the processing by the median and the basic adaptive filters: (a) image corrupted by the impulse noise; (b) image filtered by the median filter; (c) image filtered by the basic adaptive method.

Let the probability that a pixel is corrupted by an impulse be p. Then the average number of pixels corrupted in an image of size $N \times N$ is

$$N_c = pN^2. \tag{5.26}$$

Let the size of the processing window be $n \times n$. Then the average number of uncorrupted pixels in a window is

$$n_c = (1 - p)n^2. \tag{5.27}$$

Apparently, the processing time required by the standard median filter, T_m, is proportional to n^2 and N^2

$$T_m \propto n^2N^2. \tag{5.28}$$

TABLE 5.7   Processing Time for the Basic Adaptive Filter with Window Size equal to 3 × 3

Filter	Median	Adaptive (basic)
Processing time	0.092778	0.040556

and that by the adaptive method, T_e is proportional to n_c and N_c.

$$T_e \propto n_c N_c = (1 - p)n^2 \times pN^2 = (1 - p)pn^2 N^2. \tag{5.29}$$

Combining Equations 5.28 and 5.29 and considering the time required for detecting the noisy pixels, the ratio of the processing time by the adaptive method to that by the median filter is

$$R = \frac{T_e + T_d}{T_m} = \frac{(1 - p)pn^2 N^2 + T_d}{n^2 N^2} = (1 - p)p + \frac{T_d}{T_m} \tag{5.30}$$

where T_d is the time required for detecting the noisy pixels.

Table 5.7 shows the efficiency comparison between the basic adaptive filter and the median filter based on Figure 5.21(b and c). 30% of the pixels in the image in Figure 5.21a are corrupted by randomly distributed impulse noise. Thus $p = 0.3$. The size of the processing window used is 3 × 3. Then the ratio R is

$$R = (1 - p)p + \frac{T_d}{T_m} = (1 - 0.3) \times 0.3 + \frac{T_d}{T_a} = 0.21 + \frac{T_d}{T_a}. \tag{5.31}$$

From Table 5.7, the ratio of the recorded processing time is

$$R_t = 0.040556/0.092778 = 0.437.$$

The ratio of the detection time to the processing time required by the median filter can be estimated as

$$\frac{T_d}{T_m} = R_t - T_e/T_m = 0.437 - 0.21 = 0.227$$

which is a fixed factor in calculating the ratio of the processing times. Therefore, over 50% of the time is spent on impulse detection, which must be performed on all the 256 × 256 pixels in this example.

Since T_d/T_m is a fixed factor, R is maximized when the ratio T_e/T_m is maximized. T_e/T_m is maximized when $p = 0.5$; then

$$T_e/T_m = (1 - 0.5)0.5 = 0.25.$$

Therefore, the maximum possible value for R is estimated at

$$R_{max} = 0.25 + 0.225 = 0.477 < 1.$$

Hence, in the worst case, the adaptive method takes less than half the time required by the median filter to process the same image.

5.5.5.2 *Eliminating Impulse Strokes in TV Pictures*   Let the number of the pixels corrupted in an image of size $N \times N$ be given in Equation 5.31. As mentioned in the previous section, instead of being completely randomly distributed, there exist correlations among the noise pixels. Therefore, the number of corrupted pixels in the processing window must be calculated differently.

Again, let the size of the processing window be $n \times n$. To simplify the analysis, assume that the length of impulse strokes, l, follows a uniform distribution:

$$p(l) = \begin{cases} \dfrac{1}{L_2 - L_1 + 1} & L_1 \leq l \leq L_2 \\ 0 & \text{otherwise} \end{cases}, \tag{5.32}$$

where $L_1 > n$. This is a reasonable assumption since, normally, $n = 3$ or 5 in applications. We also assume that $n < D$, where D is the minimum distance between two impulse strokes on the same row of image pixels. Then, for each l, two cases need to be considered.

- With probability

$$p_{1l} = \frac{l - n + 1}{l}.$$

The number of uncorrupted pixels in a window centered at a noisy pixel is

$$n_{cl} = (n - 1)n \tag{5.33}$$

if the impulse stroke extends beyond both ends of the current window as shown in Figure. 5.22a.

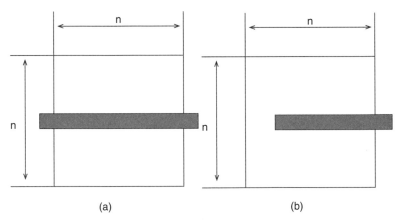

(a)   (b)

FIGURE 5.22   (a) Impulse stroke extends beyond both ends of the processing window. (b) Impulse stroke extends beyond only one end of the processing window.

- Otherwise with probability $p_{2l} = 2/l$, the number of uncorrupted pixels in a window centered at a noisy pixel is

$$n_{cl} = (n-1)n + i, i = 1, 2, \ldots, \frac{n-1}{2} \tag{5.34}$$

as shown in Figure 5.22b.

Therefore, the average number of uncorrupted pixels in a window centered at a noisy pixel is

$$n_{cl} = \sum_{l=L_1}^{L_2} p(l) \left(p_{1l} n_{cl} + p_{2l} \sum_{i=1}^{(n-1)/2} n_{c_i l} \right). \tag{5.35}$$

Similar to the case of randomly distributed impulse noise, the processing time required by the enhanced adaptive method, T_e, is proportional to n_c and N_c.

$$
\begin{aligned}
T_e &= n_c N_c \\
&= \left[\sum_{l=L_1}^{L_2} p(l) \left(p_{1l} n_{cl} + p_{2l} \sum_{i=1}^{(n-1)/2} n_{c_i l} \right) \right] p N^2 \\
&= \frac{p N^2}{L_2 - L_1 + 1} \sum_{l=L_1}^{L_2} \left\{ \frac{l-n+1}{l}(n-1)n + \frac{2}{l} \sum_{i=1}^{(n-1)/2} [(n-1)n+i] \right\} \\
&= \frac{p N^2}{L_2 - L_1 + 1} \sum_{l=L_1}^{L_2} \left\{ \frac{l-n+1}{l}(n-1)n + \frac{2}{l} \left[\frac{n-1}{2}(n-1)n + \frac{l+(n-1)/2}{2}\frac{n-1}{2} \right] \right\} \\
&= \frac{p N^2}{L_2 - L_1 + 1} \sum_{l=L_1}^{L_2} \left[(n-1)n + \frac{n^2-1}{4l} \right] \\
&= p N^2 \left[(n-1)n + \frac{n^2-1}{4(L_2-L_1+1)} \sum_{l=L_1}^{L_2} \frac{1}{l} \right] \\
&= p N^2 \left[n^2 + \frac{(n^2-1)\sum_{l=L_1}^{L_2} 1/l - 4n(L_2-L_1+1)}{4(L_2-L_1+1)} \right].
\end{aligned}
\tag{5.36}
$$

Table 5.8 shows an efficiency comparison between the enhanced adaptive filter and the median filter. The neural network identifies that around 750 of the 512×512

TABLE 5.8   Processing Time of the Two Filters with Window Size equal to 3 × 3

Filter	Median	Adaptive (enhanced)
Filtering time		0.083302
Detection time		0.376420
Total time	0.345000	0.459722

pixels in the image in Figure 5.20a are corrupted by impulse strokes. The probability of impulse corruption, p, is

$$p = \frac{750}{512^2} = 0.00286$$

Let $n = 3$. By counting the lengths of the impulse strokes, $L_1 = 4$ and $L_2 = 12$ are obtained. Then the ratio R is

$$R = \left[1 + \frac{(n^2 - 1)\sum_{l=L_1}^{L_2} 1/l - 4n(L_2 - L_1 + 1)}{4n^2(L_2 - L_1 + 1)} \right] p + \frac{T_d}{T_m}$$

$$= \left[1 + \frac{(3^2 - 1)\sum_{l=L_1}^{L_2} 1/l - 4 \times 3(12 - 4 + 1)}{4 \times 3^2(12 - 4 + 1)} \right] \times 0.00286 + \frac{T_d}{T_m}$$

$$= 0.001815 + \frac{T_d}{T_m}. \tag{5.37}$$

The ratio of the processing time in Table 5.8 is

$$R = 0.083302/0.345000 = 0.291426$$

The ratio of the detection time to the processing time required by the median filter can be estimated as

$$\frac{T_d}{T_m} = 0.291426 - 0.001815 = 0.289611.$$

Therefore, over 99% of the time is spent on impulse detection in this example. The implication is straightforward. Detection must be performed on all the 512×512 pixels, while filtering is only performed on the noisy pixels, which constitute a small fraction (0.286%) of the image.

To estimate the maximum value of T_e/T_m, the value of p is the critical factor since the rest is fixed when L_1, L_2, and n are known. Since T_e/T_m linearly increases with p, a maximum value of p should be determined. A reasonable choice for p is 0.4 since a higher value breaks the assumptions given at the beginning of this subsection. Hence, the estimated maximum value for R in this case is

$$R = \left[1 + \frac{(n^2 - 1) \sum_{l=L_1}^{L_2} 1/l - 4n(L_2 - L_1 + 1)}{4n^2(L_2 - L_1 + 1)} \right] p + \frac{T_d}{T_m}$$

$$= 0.634615 \times 0.4 + 0.289611$$

$$= 0.543457$$

$$< 1.$$

Therefore, the enhanced adaptive method also takes less time to process an image than the median filter.

5.5.5.3 *Robustness of Training*   The combined time (training plus processing) for the enhanced adaptive method is also tabulated in Table 5.8. It can be seen that the combined time is significantly longer than that of median filtering. Therefore, if training was required for every image frame, it would be slower to use the adaptive method.

However, in TV picture transmission, the characteristics of the impulses that affect the quality of transmission are relatively stable [127]. Therefore, the training of the neural network is required only for a few frames in a picture sequence. The trained network can be used to detect impulses in the subsequent image frames. Although the processing of the training frames by the adaptive method is slower than that by the median-type filters, the overall time required for processing the sequence is much shorter. Let us analyze the extreme case—training the neural network for every second frame. Using the statistics in Table 5.8, the combined time for every two consecutive frames by the enhanced adaptive method, T_{2a}, is less than that by the median filter T_{2m}:

$$T_{2a} = 0.083302 + 0.459722 = 0.543024 < 2 \times 0.345000 = 0.690000 = T_{2m}.$$

A visual example is used to support the above analysis. Figure 5.23(a–c) shows frames 2, 3, and 4 in the same video sequence as that in Figure 5.20a. The adaptive filtering parameters obtained by training based on Figure 5.20a were used to process the four images. The results are displayed in Figure 5.24(a–c), respectively. Clearly, this experiment shows that the training method is robust.

5.6 CONCLUSIONS

In this chapter, the two impulse noise models were first introduced. Based on these models, conventional methods using median filtering techniques are often used for suppressing the impulse noise. The median filter has been recognized as a useful image enhancement technique due to its edge-preserving characteristics and the simplicity

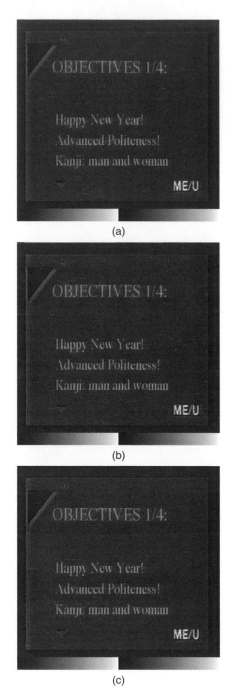

(a)

(b)

(c)

FIGURE 5.23 Removal of impulse noise from frames 2–4 of a TV sequence. (a) Impulse noise corrupted image (frame 2). (b) Impulse noise corrupted image (frame 3). (c) Impulse noise corrupted image (frame 4).

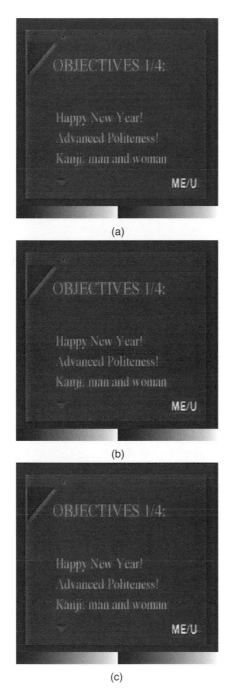

(a)

(b)

(c)

FIGURE 5.24 Removal of impulse noise from frames 2–4 of a TV sequence. (a) Restored image (frame 2). (b) Restored image (frame 3). (c) Impulse noise corrupted image (frame 4).

of implementation. However, the median filter often results in blurring effects in the filtered images. To overcome this problem, many generalized median filters have been developed. The properties of these filters have been statistically analyzed [128] and their strengths and weaknesses discussed in detail. The problem with these filters is that they process every pixel in the image irrespective of whether it is a noise or a signal. This results in blurring for large window size or insufficient noise suppression for small window size. To solve this problem, a new filtering scheme was proposed in this chapter, which aimed to keep the robustness of median-type and nonlinear mean filters while overcoming their disadvantages.

In this new approach, a noise detection step is first introduced. During this step, the Local statistics were used to provide the feature information to form the feature vectors. At the same time, the Global characteristics of impulse noise were considered based on the statistical characteristics of the feature vectors in the entire feature space to determine the impulse noise. The classification of impulse noise was done by the SOTM neural network proposed in the previous chapter. In this second step, two noise-exclusive filters were proposed to restore the corrupted image.

Experiments based on different models and with varying percentage of noise were performed in this chapter. From the results, it can be seen that the proposed filtering scheme thoroughly and fundamentally overcame the drawback of the median filter. The noise-exclusive filters outperformed the traditional median-type filters in the aspects of noise suppression, detail preservation, and minimal signal distortion. The key point is that they keep the integrity of the image (avoid unnecessary processing of pixels that are not corrupted by impulse noise) and use the true information to estimate the contaminated pixel.

The filtering scheme is then further tested on images corrupted by high noise ratio in iterative and recursive fashion. Unlike the median filter, the iterative image restorations of the NEM and the NEAM filters did not affect the qualities of image recovery. Further experiments have shown that the convergence rate of the recursive filtering was faster than that of the nonrecursive filtering and the qualities were almost the same. This is a very useful property for applications where high speed restorations are required.

In the final part of the chapter, the enhancement and real-time processing features of an adaptive filter for the removal of impulse noise in TV picture transmission were presented. Two important issues in the application of impulse noise removal in TV picture transmission were investigated: real-time processing capability and incorporation of special characteristics of impulse noise in detection. The basic method that had been extensively tested on data corrupted by randomly distributed impulses was first enhanced to deal with real TV pictures suffering from impulse noise strokes. In particular, the characteristics of the real impulses were incorporated in the noise-identification stage. Then the suitability of the method in terms of real-time processing for images corrupted by randomly distributed impulse noise and TV pictures corrupted by real impulsive strokes were analytically and numerically studied. Application of the method to TV picture sequences had shown that the proposed method potentially provides a real-time solution for quality TV picture transmission.

CHAPTER 6

Self-Organization in Image Retrieval

Content-based image retrieval (CBIR) is regarded as one of the most effective ways of accessing visual data [129] and has applications in numerous fields, such as distance education, business, entertainment, law enforcement, medicine, and multimedia data management. The objective of this chapter is to provide a comprehensive study on modern approaches in the area of image indexing and retrieval with particular focus on the use of Self-Organization as a core enabling technology. This chapter begins with the development of CBIR systems in Sections 6.1–6.3, which includes the implementation of a radial basis function (RBF) based relevance feedback (RF) method. This is followed by Section 6.4 presenting automatic and semiautomatic methods in multimedia retrieval, using the pseudo-RF for minimizing user interaction in a retrieval process.

Section 6.5 introduces a framework for a novel extension of the self-organizing tree map (SOTM) for hierarchical clustering, the Directed Self-Organizing Tree Map (DSOTM) [130]. This method aims at classifying input patterns while *preserving* the integrity of image clusters relating to the query class. Growth of the DSOTM-structure is directed so as to prevent any unnecessary cluster generation in the low or zero density regions of the feature space, while emphasizing partitions about the known query. As a result, a more plastic map structure is retained in comparison with its two other counterparts, the self-organizing feature map (SOFM) and SOTM. The DSOTM is used to implement pseudo-RF in the CBIR system in order to perform automatic retrieval.

Although DSOTM is seen to be an effective solution for enhancing the performance of image retrieval systems, its performance is highly dependent on the initial query position and the specific combination of features used to characterize the query itself. These issues are addressed in detail in Section 6.6. We demonstrate an optimized architecture for an automatic retrieval system based on a collaboration between the DSOTM and the Genetic Algorithm (GA). This approach enable the discovery of dominant perceptual features in images through the principle of feature weight detection. A study on the feasibility of the proposed feature weight detection scheme in conjunction with the DSOTM, SOTM, and SOFM classifier techniques is presented in Section 6.7.

Unsupervised Learning: A Dynamic Approach, First Edition.
Matthew Kyan, Paisarn Muneesawang, Kambiz Jarrah, and Ling Guan.
© 2014 by The Institute of Electrical and Electronics Engineers, Inc. Published by John Wiley & Sons, Inc.

6.1 RETRIEVAL OF VISUAL INFORMATION

Traditional text-based retrieval systems are not effective for annotating large, unlabeled image and video datasets. CBIR, on the other hand, offers a more intuitive and effective approach in which users are able to browse a database to extract samples based on their resemblance to a known query. Extracted samples are then become candidates for annotation. The term "CBIR" originated after the influential work of David Marr [131]. According to Marr, primitive image features (including edges, angles, color, and spatial proximity), are adequate for a machine to infer sufficient meaning for limited image understanding, pattern recognition, and retrieval. Even though machine-based perception still lags far behind human visual perception, current research in CBIR offers an improved architecture for minimizing the gap between low level image content and the semantics such images represent.

Visual content is generally captured by a multidimensional vector representation of an image (feature space) and can be extracted from images through certain mathematical and statistical analyses. Features describing image content can be classified as either *Standard* or *Specialized*, based in many ways, on their adherence to more generalized and computationally tractable approaches for indexing content, versus more advanced and accurate approaches that incur significant computational burden. Standard features include low level descriptors such as color, texture, and shape that offer a general description of an image. These features may be similar among semantically different images with similar low level feature distributions. Specialized features, on the other hand, refer to more advanced (higher level) descriptors and comprise a more detailed representation of an image. When dealing with large databases, a tradeoff must be made, wherein accuracy is initially sacrificed so that a novel set of variable candidates may first be extracted (whether from a Local or distributed set of databases). With this reduced set (extracted using reference to Standardized features), further refinement may proceed based on use of more Specialized, accurate features.

Figure 6.1 illustrates the standard structure of a CBIR engine. Image indexing and retrieval are two major components in CBIR technology. Features from all images in the database are extracted and stored in the indexing phase. Usually, due to an extensive number of images in a digital library and, thus, exhaustive computational

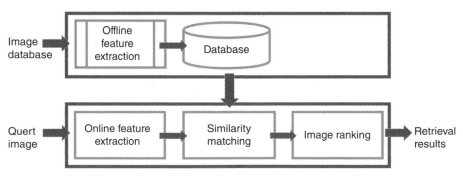

FIGURE 6.1 Rank-based CBIR system.

FIGURE 6.2   A sample query (top left) to demonstrate behavior of the rank-based CBIR system.

demand for extracting their features, Standardized descriptors are precomputed (offline) and stored in a feature database. This reduces retrieval delay significantly. Retrieval is initialized by extracting Standardized query features on the fly, comparing these with all precomputed feature vectors in the database and then ranking database samples based on their degree of resemblance with the query. The top ranked images will be stored and then displayed back to the user.

The CBIR system with the above architecture neglects the deeper semantic resemblance among target samples by searching and retrieving images according to the degree of (statistical) similarities between the query and its neighboring images. Consequently, this system assumes direct association between statistical similarities and semantics of the query image and disregards interrelationships among target images. Figure 6.2 clearly illustrates the limitations of such an approach. In this figure, the query image is located in the top-left corner of the figure and the top 16 images are ranked and retrieved—from left to right and top to bottom—according to the descending degree of similarity to the query. It is evident that target images with high feature similarities may not be semantically similar to the query image due to the gap between low level features used for image indexing and high level concepts used by human observers. This issue is addressed through the introduction of RF-based machine learning (in later sections).

Prior to embanking on such a discussion, we begin by first surveying the major components of all CBIR systems: visual description, vector normalization, and feature subset selection.

6.2   VISUAL FEATURE DESCRIPTOR

Visual content from a machine perspective can be interpreted as a collection of low level descriptors such as color, shape, and texture. In the following, we consider optional descriptors that are appropriate for large scale (low computational complexity) and small scale indexing (higher complexity). The idea is that an initial ranking of database samples against a query should be achieved via a low complexity approach, with further, more accurate refinement using more complex descriptors calculated on the smaller set of retrieved results.

6.2.1   Color Histogram and Color Moment Descriptors

Color is one of the most important visual attributes for human perception and is widely used in computer vision applications. Color features are relatively invariant to spatial translations and scale transformations. Color descriptors are usually defined by three independent distributions in various color spaces including RGB, HSV, and YC_bC_r.

Color histograms are the most conventional way for representing color properties of an image. Color histograms are obtained by discretizing image colors and counting the number of times each color appears in an image array. This method has a number of major advantages that make it attractive for indexing purposes: (1) only those colors that are presented in both images contribute toward the similarity matching process; (2) similarity matching is independent of the number of bins used in the color histograms; (3) histograms are invariant to translations and rotation about the viewing axis and change only slowly under the change of the angle of view, change in scale and occlusion; and (4) histograms, traditionally, do not include spatial information; thus, images with very different layouts may have similar histograms.

According to Swain and Ballard [132], similarity among histograms of two images may be interpreted as the intersection between their two histograms. *Histogram intersection* considers only the overlapping portions of two histograms in establishing a match. Matches are considered between the query and all samples in the database. The higher the match value, the better the fit to query in terms of color content.

In forming histograms, a color space quantization method is required. The decision on the type of quantization process is an important issue as information loss is implied; therefore, quantization should favor the retention of perceptually meaningful color. In general, uniform quantization may be appropriate for the perceptually uniform color spaces (i.e., HSV), whereas, for perceptually nonuniform color spaces (i.e., RGB), a nonuniform quantization method is a better choice.

In the current work, 48-bin color histograms are used to describe the color contents of images in the HSV color space, where H and S are uniformly quantized into 16 and 3 regions, respectively. The V component is discarded due to its sensitivity to the lighting condition as described in [133,134]. In addition, a 9-dimensional (9D) feature vector from mean μ, standard deviation σ, and skewness ς, of the color distribution of each channel in the RGB color space was generated to represent *color moment* descriptors [135].

6.2.2 Wavelet Moment and Gabor Texture Descriptors

Texture refers to the homogeneous or nonhomogeneous property of visual patterns and results from the presence of several colors or intensities in an image. Texture carries information about an object and specifies its relationship with its surroundings. For instance, texture can provide significant information about two overlapping objects by decoding information about their relative orientation and spatial depth.

There are several techniques available to extract textural information from an image. In his book, Manjunath et al. [136] introduce three texture descriptors that are currently used in the MPEG-7 standard: homogeneous texture descriptor (HTD), texture browsing descriptor (TBD), and edge histogram descriptor (EHD). The HTD characterizes homogeneous texture regions and offers a quantitative description of texture regions through the mean energy and energy deviation of their frequency channel sets. The TBD provides a visual characterization of texture regions and is inspired by the human perceptual ability in differentiating the regularity, coarseness, and directionality of these areas. The EHD captures the spatial distribution of edges in an image, represented more specifically, as an ordered set of Local-edge distributions. Because of EHD's tendency to characterize Local image regions, this method is particularly useful in matching regions with partially nonuniform and nonhomogeneous texture.

Research on using wavelets to capture image textural information has widely increased after the introduction of wavelet transform in the early 1980s [137–139]. The wavelet transformation is a method of representing images at various resolution levels (i.e., sub-images), providing a spatial-frequency view at each level. It can therefore aid in evaluating distinct characteristics of an image. Wavelets possess a spatial Localization property that preserves the logical spatial relationship among image textural regions [140]. In the current work, a 20D feature vector is computed, based on the mean, μ and standard deviation σ, of a three-level wavelet decomposed version of each image [141].

In his paper, Ma et al. [142] proposed another method for texture representation of images based on the Gabor wavelet transform technique. These texture features can be found by calculating the mean μ and standard deviation σ of the Gabor-filtered image. Gabor filters are basically composed of a group of wavelets, in which each wavelet captures energy at a specific frequency and direction. Texture features are extracted from these energy distributions [143].

The 2D Gabor transform function $g(x, y)$ and its Fourier transform $G(u, v)$, for a given image $I(x, y)$ with size of $P \times Q$, can be calculated using Equations 6.1 and 6.2:

$$g(x, y) = \left(\frac{1}{2\pi\sigma_x\sigma_y} \right) \exp\left[-\frac{1}{2}\left(\frac{x^2}{\sigma_x^2} + \frac{y^2}{\sigma_y^2} \right) + 2\pi jWx \right], \tag{6.1}$$

$$G(u, v) = \exp\left\{ -\frac{1}{2}\left[\frac{(u - W)^2}{\sigma_u^2} + \frac{v^2}{\sigma_v^2} \right] \right\}, \tag{6.2}$$

where $\sigma_u = 1/2\pi\sigma_x$ and $\sigma_v = 1/2\pi\sigma_y$ are scaling parameters. In particular, the impulse response of Gabor filters in the spatial domain $g(x, y)$ is a 2D Gaussian-shape kernel modulated by a complex sinusoidal plane wave. The sinusoidal modulator is known as a carrier and the Gaussian-shape kernel is called an envelope. W in the above equations defines the spatial frequency of the sinusoidal carrier.

Gabor functions form a complete, but not orthogonal, basis set and provide a localized frequency description of a signal. The non-orthogonality of the Gabor wavelet implies that there is redundant information in filtered images, which must be reduced. Gabor wavelet is a collection of self-similar functions defined through Equation 6.3:

$$g_{mn}(x, y) = a^{-m} G(x', y'),$$ (6.3)

where m and n are integers that specify the *scale* and *orientation* of the wavelets, respectively. The scaling factor a^{-m} ensures that the energy is independent of m. x' and y' can be calculated as follows.

$$x' = a^{-m}(x \cos \theta + y \sin \theta),$$ (6.4)

$$y' = a^{-m}(-x \sin \theta + y \cos \theta),$$ (6.5)

where $\theta = n\pi/K$ and K is the total number of orientations. Variables in the above equations are defined as

$$a = \left(\frac{U_h}{U_l} \right)^{-\frac{1}{S-1}}, a > 1,$$ (6.6)

$$\sigma_u = \frac{(a-1)U_h}{(a+1)\sqrt{2\ln 2}},$$ (6.7)

$$\sigma_v = \tan \left(\frac{\pi}{2k} \right) \left[U_h - 2\ln \left(\frac{\sigma_u^2}{U_h} \right) \right] \left[2\ln 2 - \frac{(2\ln 2)^2 \sigma_u^2}{U_h^2} \right]^{-\frac{1}{2}},$$ (6.8)

where U_l and U_h are the lower and upper center frequencies of interest and S is the number of scales in the multi-resolution decomposition. The following filter parameters were employed in the current work: $U_l = 0.05$, $U_h = W = 0.4$, $K = 6$, and $S = 4$ [142].

As discussed earlier, the non-orthogonality of Gabor wavelets implies redundancy in the response of the filter. This redundancy can be reduced by designing a filter in such a way that the half-peak magnitude of the filter responses, in the frequency spectrum, touch each other. Consequently, for a given image $I(x, y)$, its Gabor Wavelet Transform can be extracted as

$$W_{mn}(x, y) = \int I(x_1, y_1) g_{mn}^*(x - x_1, y - y_1) dx_1 dy_1,$$ (6.9)

where $*$ indicates the complex conjugate of the Gabor wavelet itself. The mean μ_{mn} and the standard deviation σ_{mn} of the magnitude of the transformed coefficients can be calculated by Equations 6.10 and 6.11.

$$\mu_{mn} = \int \int |W_{mn}(xy)| dxdy. \tag{6.10}$$

$$\sigma_{mn} = \left[\int \int (|W_{mn}(x,y)| - \mu_{mn})^2 dxdy \right]^{1/2}. \tag{6.11}$$

For Gabor feature extraction purposes, a matrix of statistical descriptive features can be created where its columns and rows are constructed from 48D feature vectors using μ_{mn} and σ_{mn} for different images in the database.

6.2.3 Fourier and Moment-based Shape Descriptors

Shape provides powerful visual cues about the notion of similarity within objects and can be instantly detected by a human observer. These visual cues are identified by the topological closeness of lines and edges in space. Objects can be solely recognized by their shape information. This characteristic of shape features makes them essentially distinct from other types of descriptors including color and texture. Moreover, representation of shape requires some kind of regional information about an image, while both color and texture capture more Global attributes of an image.

Shape features can be classified into two distinct categories: *boundary-based* or *region-based*. Boundary-based shape descriptors represent an object based on the explicit representation of its outer boundaries. Region-based descriptors represent the shape in more detail by taking both the object's boundary and internal regions into consideration. Region-based descriptors are usually able to capture and describe complex attributes of objects with multiple disconnected or overlapping regions [136].

Fourier descriptors (FD) [144, 145] and Hu's seven moment invariants (HSMI) [146, 147] are among the most popular shape-based image descriptors and have been used in various applications, such as recognition, indexing, and retrieval. Although FDs are boundary-based shape descriptors, they are not directly invariant to image transformations. On the other hand, Hu's seven moment invariants are region-based image descriptors and have these invariance properties by their very nature [141].

Consider an image boundary region with K samples reside on the coordinate (x_k, y_k) where $k = 1, \ldots, K - 1$. For each pair of (x_k, y_k), a set of complex variables can be defined:

$$u_k = x_k + jy_k. \tag{6.12}$$

The FD for these K u_k points on the boundary are defined by Equation 6.13. Usually, a small number of FD descriptors provide sufficient discriminatory information about the boundaries of an object.

$$FD_l = \sum u_k \exp\left(-j\frac{2\pi}{K}lk\right); \quad l = 0, \ldots, K - 1. \tag{6.13}$$

In the current work, Fourier shape parameters are extracted using Sobel filters for the purpose of edge detection due to their low computational cost. The resulting edge parameters are then converted from the cartesian to the polar coordinate system. The Fast Fourier Transform (FFT) is then applied and the low frequency components are extracted to form a 10D feature vector. This truncated representation spectrum is indicative of the low frequency or smoothened aspects of the original boundary. The benefits of the coordinate conversion in this representation has the added advantage of inheriting the scale invariance property of the polar coordinate system.

The popular HSMI shape features, by contrast, are defined indirectly through 2D *geometric moments* described in terms of Riemann integrals:

$$m_{ij} = \int_{-\infty}^{\infty} \int_{-\infty}^{\infty} x^i y^j I(x,y) dx dy, \quad i,j = 1,2,\ldots \tag{6.14}$$

where m_{ij} is the $(i+j)$th order regular moment of the continuous image function $I(x,y)$.

Geometric moments are popular features for pattern recognition since they offer an equivalent representation of an image and provide rich information about its shape, size, and orientation [148]. An image can be reconstructed from its moments [149]. The zero-order moment m_{00} represents the total image power and can be used in conjunction with the first-order moments m_{10} and m_{01} to locate the centroid of the image $I(x,y)$, while the second-order moments m_{20}, m_{02}, and m_{11} characterize the size and orientation of an image.

Regular moments must be normalized in such a way that invariance properties can be established, since they cannot be directly used for characterizing the shape of objects. Invariance to position of an object can be achieved by using central moments of an image. Central moments, m_{ij} are defined as

$$m_{ij} = \int_{-\infty}^{\infty} \int_{-\infty}^{\infty} (x - \bar{x})^i (y - \bar{y})^j I(x,y) dx dy, \tag{6.15}$$

where $\bar{x}$ and $\bar{y}$ are centroid of the image and are defined as

$$\bar{x} = m_{10}/m_{00},$$
$$\bar{y} = m_{01}/m_{00}. \tag{6.16}$$

Scale and contrast invariance can be achieved through normalized central moments. The normalized central moments η_{ij} are defined as

$$\eta_{ij} = \frac{\mu_{ij}}{\mu_{00}^{(i+j+2)/2}}, \quad i,j = 2,3,\ldots. \tag{6.17}$$

Using different combinations of the normalized central moments based on the theory of algebraic invariants, Hu introduced seven moments:

$$
\begin{aligned}
\vartheta_1 &= \eta_{20} + \eta_{02}, \\
\vartheta_2 &= (\eta_{20} - \eta_{02})^2 + 4\eta_{11}^2, \\
\vartheta_3 &= (\eta_{30} - 3\eta_{12})^2 + (3\eta_{21} - \eta_{03})^2, \\
\vartheta_4 &= (\eta_{30} + \eta_{12})^2 + (\eta_{21} + \eta_{03})^2, \\
\vartheta_5 &= (\eta_{30} - 3\eta_{12})(\eta_{30} + \eta_{12})[(\eta_{30} + \eta_{12})^2 - 3(\eta_{21} + \eta_{03})^2] \\
&\quad + (3\eta_{21} - \eta_{03})(\eta_{21} + \eta_{03})[3(\eta_{30} + \eta_{12})^2 - (\eta_{21} + \eta_{03})^2], \\
\vartheta_6 &= (\eta_{20} - \eta_{02})[(\eta_{30} + \eta_{12})^2 - (\eta_{21} + \eta_{03})^2] \\
&\quad + 4\eta_{11}(\eta_{30} + \eta_{12})(\eta_{21} + \eta_{03}), \\
\vartheta_7 &= (3\eta_{21} - \eta_{03})(\eta_{30} + \eta_{12})[(\eta_{30} + \eta_{12})^2 - 3(\eta_{21} + \eta_{03})^2] \\
&\quad + (3\eta_{21} - \eta_{30})(\eta_{21} + \eta_{03})[3(\eta_{30} + \eta_{12})^2 - (\eta_{21} + \eta_{03})^2].
\end{aligned}
\tag{6.18}
$$

Calculating the moments of any order is possible using the algebraic invariants method; however, computing higher order Hu's moments is much more complex. Likewise, the extraction of image shapes from higher order moments will be complex [147, 148].

HSMI shape descriptors are extracted by converting color images into binary segmented images and then extracting shape parameters from resulting images using Equation 6.18. Binary image segmentations are performed through the processes described in Figure 6.3.

6.2.4 Feature Normalization and Selection

After extracting the individual image content descriptors, the calculated feature vectors are fused together to produce a more comprehensive and complete set. The resulting feature set is not suitable for similarity matching purposes directly because of two problems: (1) the features have distinct components, which might have various magnitudes and dynamic ranges, and (2) there are only some effective features from the initial set. These problems can be solved by feature normalization and feature selection.

The first problem deals with feature normalization, which is the process of readjusting feature components to a range that ensures their equal contribution and significance to the process of similarity matching. This range is normally defined in [0, 1] or [−1, 1] by proper data scaling.

Consider an $M \times P$ feature set $\mathbf{F}$ consisting of M images with the vector length of P:

$$
\begin{aligned}
\mathbf{F} &= [\mathbf{x}_1, \ldots, \mathbf{x}_m, \ldots, \mathbf{x}_M]^T \\
&= [x_{m,i}] \quad m = 1, \ldots, M, \quad i = 1, \ldots, P,
\end{aligned}
\tag{6.19}
$$

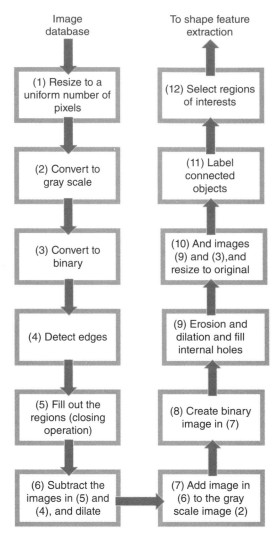

FIGURE 6.3   A flowchart for binary image segmentation process.

where $\mathbf{x}_m = [x_{m,1}, \ldots, x_{m,i}, \ldots, x_{m,P}]^T$ represents feature vector of image m in the database.

One method for normalization is to linearly readjust the entries in each column $\{x_{m,i}\}_{m=1}^{M}$ to the same dynamic range of $[0, 1]$ under the influence of the maximum and minimum feature values of the sequence as illustrated by Equation 6.20:

$$\mathbf{F}_{m,i} = \frac{x_{m,i} - \min_i}{\max_i - \min_i}. \tag{6.20}$$

where $\max_i$ and $\min_i$ refer to largest and smallest feature value of the ith column of matrix $\mathbf{F}$, respectively.

TABLE 6.1   Linear Normalization: (*a*) **Input Data** (*b*) **The Normalized Sequence to the Range of [0, 1]**

(a)			(b)		
0.1000	0.0800	0.2000	0.0010	0.0006	0.0030
0.4000	50.000	0.3300	0.0070	1.0000	0.0056
0.0500	0.3000	0.1500	0.0000	0.0050	0.0020

The drawback of this method is its dependency on two extreme feature values. This dependency will not ensure an equal dynamic range for all the members in the feature space due to the fact that any outliers may dominate scaling. For example, consider the following 3×3 input data and its normalized counterpart shown in Table 6.1. Clearly, this normalization puts more emphasis on outliers (i.e., 50) by devoting most of the [0, 1] range to them and compressing the rest onto a very slight range.

This problem can be addressed by applying a Gaussian-based normalization scheme. By making the assumption that sequence $\{x_{m,i}\}_{m=1}^{M}$ is a Gaussian sequence and is distributed evenly around the mean, the following process normalizes features linearly to zero mean and unit standard deviation as is illustrated by Equation 6.21:

$$\mathbf{F}_{m,i} = \frac{x_{m,i} - \mu_i}{\sigma_i}, \tag{6.21}$$

where μ_i and σ_i are the mean and standard deviation of the *i*th feature vector in the database, respectively. Table 6.2 illustrates the matrix of our example after performing the Gaussian normalization.

In the case that data are not evenly distributed around the mean, nonlinear normalization methods (e.g., exponential) can be employed to map data within specified intervals. Equation 6.22 illustrates one of the popular candidates of this type that compresses data in the range of [0, 1].

$$h_{m,i} = \frac{x_{m,i} - \mu_i}{k\sigma_i}, \quad \mathbf{F}_{m,i} = \frac{1}{1 + \exp(-h_{m,i})}. \tag{6.22}$$

This equation consists of two parts. The first part is a linear Gaussian normalization function that follows the $3 - \sigma$ rule for $k = 3$. According to the $3 - \sigma$ rule, approximately 99% (distance of 3 times the standard deviation for normal random variables) of the entries fall in the range of $[-1, 1]$. The second part is an exponential function that exponentially warps data onto the range of [0, 1]. For small values of $h_{m,i}$, $\mathbf{F}_{m,i}$ is a linear approximation of $x_{m,i}$, whereas large values of $h_{m,i}$ (values away

TABLE 6.2   Gaussian Normalization: (*a*) **Input Data** (*b*) **The Normalized Sequence to the Range of [−1, 1]**

(a)			(b)		
0.1000	0.0800	0.2000	−0.4402	−0.5812	−0.2870
0.4000	50.000	0.3300	1.1446	1.1547	1.1121
0.0500	0.3000	0.1500	−0.7044	−0.5735	−0.8251

TABLE 6.3 Nonlinear Gaussian Normalization: (*a*) Input Data (*b*) The Normalized Sequence to the Range of [0, 1]

(a)			(b)			
0.1000	0.0800	0.2000		0.4636	0.4517	0.4761
0.4000	50.000	0.3300		0.5942	0.5951	0.5916
0.0500	0.3000	0.1500		0.4416	0.4524	0.4317

from the mean) are exponentially condensed toward the mean [149]. Table 6.3 illustrates the same matrix after normalization. It is evident that the presence of outliers will no longer influence other feature elements [150].

The second problem deals with feature selection, which provides a hard decision on the trade-off between computational complexity and feature selection efficiency. The purpose is to eliminate as many features as possible to achieve maximum classification accuracy without concern for direct or indirect interactions among features. Feature weight detection provides an estimate on the importance of features through a soft-decision mechanism. In this regard, the soft decisions de-emphasize certain features rather than eliminating them completely, such that they no longer contribute significantly to the similarity calculation.

In Section 6.6, a GA-based approach is proposed to further guide the importance of individual features and the degree to which they contribute toward improving the retrieval process and overall performance of the system. The advantage of GA-based feature selection techniques lie in their ability to deal with multiple criteria including classification accuracy and feature cost measurement. This makes them particularly attractive in the design of pattern classifiers in many practical domains.

6.3 USER-ASSISTED RETRIEVAL

As illustrated earlier (Fig. 6.2), image retrieval based on the statistical representation of images and the linear approximation of similarity is limited in its ability to articulate the user's requirements on semantic levels. Past efforts to bridge this semantic gap attempted to capture perceptually relevant visual content by allowing the human to provide high level feedback through some interaction schemes. In such schemes, a learning mechanism allows the retrieval system to adapt to the user's requirements by tuning the similarity matching process to better reflect the semantic associations explicitly made by the user.

The tuning in the system's behavior is achieved by adapting an RF scheme accompanied by a weighted distance metric during the matching stage. In this process, different weights are assigned to individual components in a feature vector and are modified according to the user's preferences (i.e., the user directly teaches the system about her/his interpretations of an image).

The idea behind weighted distance is to re-weight the feature space in favor of relevant features (features that appear to correlate well with relevant selections made by the users). The weight parameters can be estimated from the standard deviation of the features in the relevant set selected by the user at each RF iteration process

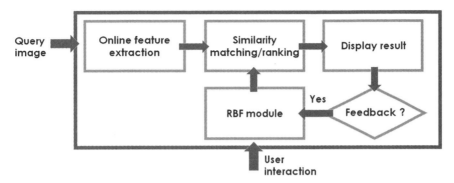

FIGURE 6.4   An adaptive human-controlled relevance feedback system.

[150–152], or through optimization techniques (i.e., GA) in the automatic RF CBIR system [130].

The RF approach is an extended application of the modern information retrieval, proposed by Salton and McGill [153]. In these systems, each document is represented by a set of key words and terms. These terms are then concatenated in a set of vectors and are then made available for search and retrieval. Some of the well-known implementations of this approach are [129, 154, 155], and [156]. In all the above systems, some kind of query refinement strategy (i.e., feature weighting) has been adapted to interactively create a new query with the goal of optimizing the search process.

Although above implementations have offered some improvement in the process of image retrieval, they still suffer from a limited degree of adaptivity due to inadequacy of distance metrics for modeling perceptual differences as seen by the human user. To overcome this problem, Muneesawang et al. [151] proposed a new architecture for the RF-based CBIR systems as is depicted in Figure 6.4. This system takes advantage of an adaptive technique based on a nonlinear RBF model [157] for learning the user's notion of similarity between images. In this process, the user is provided with a set of retrieved images and is asked to select those with the highest (semantic) similarity with respect to the query image. Feature vectors extracted from selected images are then used as training examples to determine centers and widths of different RBF units in the network. Using the RBF-based learning model offers further adaptability to the retrieval system for refining the search to different users and various types of images rather than enforcing a fixed metric for comparisons.

Since its invention, the RBF method has received much attention for application in multimedia search and retrieval. Ejaz et al. [158], for instance, has employed the RBF method to model user perception for selecting key frames for video browsing. In a training phase, K-Means clustering is performed on the feature space, where RBF is used as a similarity function. In the online phase, the system does not require user input, and thus, it is well suited for real-time web video browsing. This system has proven to outperform other techniques such as open video (OV) [159], Delaunay clustering technique (DT) [160], still and moving video story board method (STIMO) [161], and video summary and novel evaluation method (VSUMM) [162]. Since the music sequence may be subjectively classified in different ways by different users, RF can be applied to facilitate user need in retrieval procedures. RBF methods are applied for music retrieval using various features, such as the wavelet descriptor in [163] and temporal, spectral, tonal, and rhythm features in [164]. In the video domain, the audio content can be modeled by applying the Laplacian Mixture Model to wavelet coefficients of audio signal. The RBF method is then applied for measuring similarity for video retrieval [165]. For handwritten digital image databases, the studies in References 166 and 167 conduct context-sensitive ranking algorithm based on RBF nonlinear model. In Reference 168, Self-Organizing Map (SOM) was studied to minimize user interaction in the RBF method in order to retrieve content from algae image databases.

6.3.1 Radial Basis Function Method

Linear association between distance and similarity, according to traditional distance metrics, is not an optimal way of modeling human perceptual similarity. Instead, nonlinear models can be used to reflect this resemblance since pattern recognition and classification of visual content in the human visual system is performed on a nonlinear basis [169].

RBF is an attractive technique for simulating the human perception. RBF is a kernel function that has an outstanding approximation capability for nonlinear proximity evaluation. One of the major properties of RBF is its localization capability—a trait that is determined through its exponentially decaying (or growing) behavior with respect to the distance from a mean point [157]. Figure 6.5 a illustrates an example of a Gaussian-shape RBF located at zero with the width of one (i.e., $\mu = 0$ and $\sigma = 1$).

The Gaussian-shaped RBF in Figure 6.5a is generated using Equation 6.23. In this equation, μ is center of RBF and σ denotes its width:

$$G(x) = \exp\left[\frac{(x - \mu)^2}{2\sigma^2}\right].$$ (6.23)

This shows the nonlinear transformation of distance calculation $(x - \mu)$ into nonlinear space for similarity measurement. This technique has been employed for transformation of the Earthmover's distance to a nonlinear space for constructing a variable-length RBF classifier [170] and obtaining the likelihood function for conducting a posterior probability in Baye's theorem [171, 172].

In the current work, a 1D Gaussian RBF is associated with each component of the image feature vector and is used for the purpose of proximity evaluation between query $\mathbf{z}$ and input image $\mathbf{x}$ feature vectors. On the other hand, each RBF unit provides a nonlinear mapping of distance versus similarity, where the highest similarity is achieved when $\mathbf{z} = \mathbf{x}$. This process is illustrated by Equation 6.24 and subsequently in Figure 6.5b:

$$S(\mathbf{z}, \mathbf{x}) = \sum_{i=1}^{P} G_i(x_i - z_i) = \sum_{i=1}^{P} \exp\left[-\frac{(x_i - z_i)^2}{2\sigma_i^2}\right],$$ (6.24)

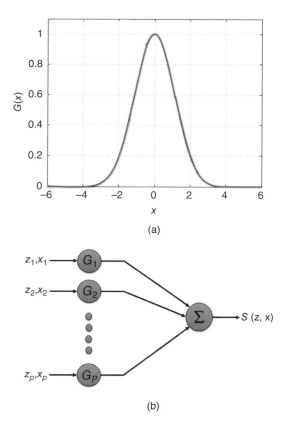

FIGURE 6.5 (a) Nonlinear Gaussian radial basis function (RBF) centered at zero with the width of one. (b) Nonlinear similarity measures using RBF network.

where σ_i, $i = 1, \ldots, P$ are tuning parameters in the form of RBF width centered at the query position. Each tuning parameter linearly approximates the relevance of individual features through Equation 6.27. The small value of σ_i reflects high relevance, whereas a larger value of σ_i declares low resemblance of the ith feature component.

In an RF cycle, the training vectors associated with selected images are used to form an $M \times P$ feature matrix $\mathbf{R}$ consisting of M images marked as relevant with the vector length of P. Similarly, the training feature vectors of irrelevant images are also used to construct an $N \times P$ feature matrix $\mathbf{N}$ where $N + M = Q$ as are illustrated by Equations 6.25 and 6.26, respectively:

$$\mathbf{R} = [\mathbf{x}_1', \ldots, \mathbf{x}_m', \ldots, \mathbf{x}_M']^T$$
$$= [x_{m,i}'] \quad m = 1, \ldots, M, \quad i = 1, \ldots, P, \tag{6.25}$$

$$\mathbf{N} = [\mathbf{x}_1'', \ldots, \mathbf{x}_n'', \ldots, \mathbf{x}_N'']^T$$
$$= [x_{n,i}''] \quad n = 1, \ldots, N, \quad i = 1, \ldots, P, \tag{6.26}$$

where $\mathbf{x}'_m = [x'_{m,1}, \ldots, x'_{m,i}, \ldots, x'_{m,P}]^T$ and $\mathbf{x}''_n = [x''_{n,1}, \ldots, x''_{n,i}, \ldots, x''_{n,P}]^T$ represent feature vectors of the mth relevant and nth irrelevant images in the database, respectively.

Given the matrix $\mathbf{R}$, the tuning parameters are obtained by

$$\sigma_i = \eta \max_{m \in \{1,\ldots,M\}} |x'_{m,i} - z_i|. \tag{6.27}$$

In this equation, η is an additional factor to ensure a large output for each exponential RBF unit G_i. In particular, highly relevant features allow a higher sensitivity to the similarity matching process in Equation 6.24, whereas poorly relevant features have a minimal affect in this process. Alternatively, η can be obtained by computing Local feature relevance [173–175]. This is assumed as the probability that feature vectors of images are labeled as relevant with respect to the query vector.

The training samples in Equations 6.25 and 6.26 are also used for obtaining a new query associated with the RBF center. Based on the selected images, the new query is subsequently created to adapt the search to the class that the query is embedded in. In the process of image retrieval there are situations where the selected query cannot entirely reflect users' preferences because of the uncertainty in image interpretations resulting from ambiguous image content (i.e., the presence of several objects of inter-est). Under such circumstances, the system often generates trivial or even irrelevant retrieval results due to its incapability in extracting all information required to lead it to converge toward the query (relevant) class. Moreover, query modification enables the system to readjust query location more toward a best representative class, with the objective of retrieving more relevant images at subsequent RF iterations. These modifications are carried out based on information (or preferences) provided by the user from earlier iterations of RF.

Several schemes have been studied for the purpose of query modification in the literature. In general, the query position is tuned to the center of mass of relevant samples by calculating the mean value of each column (i.e., feature elements) of the relevant matrix $\mathbf{R}$ in Equation 6.25 as is described by Equation 6.28. Since the relevant group indicates the user's preference, the modified query will also reasonably satisfy this preference [176].

$$\hat{\mathbf{z}} = \frac{1}{M} \sum_{m=1}^{M} \mathbf{x}'_m. \tag{6.28}$$

A better method for the query modification is realizable in situations where the matrix $\mathbf{R}$ contains a small subset of the actual relevant class. In this situation, the previous query modification scheme will not perform adequately, since sparse data resolution can extensively impact the modified query by diverging it from the true position of the relevant cluster center. To overcome this problem, the new scheme modifies the query based on the information extracted from both relevant and irrel-evant sub-samples (i.e., both $\mathbf{R}$ and $\mathbf{N}$ matrices). As a result, the query is adjusted to a new position by shifting it away from the irrelevant group and more toward the relevant image cluster. This process is illustrated by Equation 6.29.

$$\hat{\mathbf{z}}_k = \hat{\mathbf{z}}_{k-1} + \alpha_R \left(\frac{1}{M} \sum_{m=1}^{M} \mathbf{x}'_m - \hat{\mathbf{z}}_{k-1} \right) - \alpha_N \left(\frac{1}{N} \sum_{n=1}^{N} \mathbf{x}''_n - \hat{\mathbf{z}}_{k-1} \right), \quad (6.29)$$

where α_R and α_N are small positive constants, $\hat{\mathbf{z}}_{k-1}$ is the modified query at the previous iteration, and $\hat{\mathbf{z}}_k$ is the query under modification. The second term in the above equation represents the relevant image cluster, whereas, the third term indicates the irrelevant group. In practice, the constants in Equation 6.29 are chosen such that $\alpha_R \gg \alpha_N$; thus, a larger relocation is allowed toward the relevant samples while a slighter realignment is permitted away from the irrelevant group.

The second part of Equation 6.29, that is, $\frac{1}{M} \sum_{m=1}^{M} \mathbf{x}'_m$ assumes an equal importance (or weight) among all positive samples. Within the relevant sample cluster, however, some samples tend to carry more information about the query than others and, therefore, must contribute more toward the query refinement calculations. To overcome this issue, a weight algorithm can be adapted to characterize the contribution of each positive sample to obtain a new query on the positive term [177].

Based on the principles discussed above, researchers have been able to further improve the performance of RBF method. It has been observed that incorporating some information about the history of user feedbacks can enable the retrieval system to further narrow down semantic gaps by allowing more constraints on positive and negative cluster generations [178]. The RBF method can converge in a few iterations by applying the semantic learning space (SLS) [179]. This is done by training the system with SLS-based learning algorithm to obtain and store semantic features from every image in the database. Subsequently, in the online search stage, the system computes the similarity score by a weighted combination of similarity scores obtained from both RBF and SLS learning. In Reference 180, an online learning algorithm implements Fisher Information Matrix with previous results saved from other user retrieval sessions, permitting the RBF method to converge in just a single round of RF. Furthermore, the study in Reference 181 applies the adaptive clustering technique on previous search data to improve the convergence of RBF method. This technique performs clustering on relevant samples from the last step of the retrieval session, then memorizes and obtains the representative members of the resulting clusters for use in further searching procedure instead of all images from the database. The representative members enable faster and more subjective retrieval according to previous search results.

Dealing with the retrieval of data during online learning, clustering techniques can help to improve ranking performance [182]. A cluster-based ranking algorithm engages the consistency assumption [183] that the points on the same cluster structure are more similar to each other than to points outside the structure, which allow the exploitation of the inherent cluster structure revealed by an image dataset. The system implementing an RBF method with the cluster-based ranking algorithm has demonstrated its effectiveness outperforming the active leaning support vector machine (SVM) [184] and Falcon [185].

An approach similar to clustering techniques is to utilize Graphcut theory [186] for manipulation of data structure in a dataset. Zhang and Guan [187] introduced a technique for reformulating the database by applying Graphcut theory before RF. This can be done by calculating the minimum cut and dividing the total pool of the target image database into two groups. One of these groups represent a source group, which has a better real relevant image percentage rate than the original database, and thus, the RBF method can perform well, with a high probability of relevant images becoming available for selection. With regard to relevance judgment discussed in Equations 6.25 and 6.26, there is a different way to allow the user to judge the relevancy of retrieved images. In Reference 188, a fuzzy RBF network is implemented to consider fuzzy judgment of user feedback. In addition to relevant and nonrelevant, users are asked to label images as fuzzy if there is ambiguity in the retrieved images. A fuzzy membership function is applied to evaluate the relevancy of images; then, the network parameters undergo a gradient descent–based learning procedure. This enhances multi-class information in image matching and results in improved accuracy. In Reference 189, a study has been conducted to implement RBF network with regional search algorithms. The RF is performed on image regions to minimize the effect of background scene on image retrieval. It was shown that when an image contains some specific object or region over relatively large background, region-based search performs better than Global search, which uses the whole image data. It is also worth while mentioning that the RBF method implemented by Equation 6.24 considers a single-class learning algorithm. However, the multidimensional Gaussian function can be implemented to capture multi-class visual information within a semantic class. This enhances the retrieval capability of the RBF network [190].

6.4 SELF-ORGANIZATION FOR PSEUDO RELEVANCE FEEDBACK

This section discusses the application of self-organizing methods for adaptive retrieval in comparison with the user-controlled RF presented in the previous section. Figure 6.6 shows different configurations of retrieval systems. Figure 6.6c shows a diagram of an adaptive retrieval system that improves its performance without user interaction. This process can be done effectively by automatic RF [191] or pseudo-RF methods [192]. The philosophy behind these methods is that the system is able to make use of unlabeled data to improve the retrieval performance from the initial search results. The essential task is to obtain a set of pseudo labels (i.e., the label of samples that have been evaluated by a machine not the users) for training the RF learning module or supervised classifiers such as SVM [192]. Obtaining meaningful and effective sets of pseudo labels is challenging and has been researched extensively for text and multimedia database applications.

Pseudo-RF is also known as *blind* relevance feedback. Conventionally, an initial retrieval result is obtained and the system assumes that a small number of top-ranked objects in the initial set are relevant, and the lowest-ranked objects are irrelevant [192, 193]. These pseudo-relevant and irrelevant objects provide extra information that can be used to modify the query to improve the retrieval results; subsequently, this information is used as training data is a learning process for query adjustment.

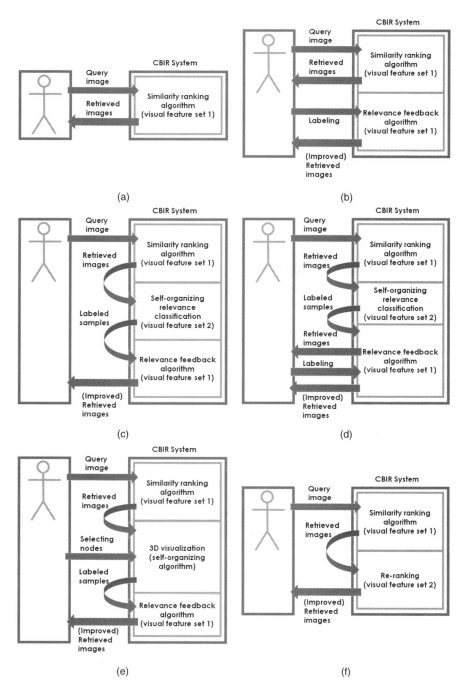

FIGURE 6.6 Different configuration of retrieval system: (a) nonadaptive system; (b) user-controlled relevance feedback (RF) system; (c) automatic-RF system; (d) semiautomatic RF system; (e) semiautomatic RF system with 3D model for user interface; and (f) re-ranking system.

In this process, the pseudo-RF applies a rule for labeling data in a given dataset, then uses this labeled data (query samples) to explore unlabeled data in order to increase the size of training set. This can be viewed as the transductive learning problem that has been studied to handle small numbers of labeled data in image retrieval [194, 195]. Transductive learning outputs a vector of labels instead of constructing an input–output mapping function. In the pseudo-RF, those labels are inferred using the nearest-neighbor rule applied to the unlabeled samples in the dataset.

Transductive learning assumes that the unlabeled examples are exactly the test examples [196], and the goal of learning is to minimize misclassification of just those particular examples. By contrast, inductive approaches instead consider the whole distribution of examples. The transductive learning plays an important role in the classifier for working with very small training sets [195]. For example, the transductive SVM [197] reduces the required amount of labeled training data dramatically. In Reference 195, the image retrieval is formulated as a transductive problem, in which the unlabeled data in the given database combined with labeled data are *both* used in training. The discriminant-expectation maximization (D-EM) approach is applied to select the most relevant features for classification.

The application of pseudo-RF to improve effectiveness of the SVM has been studied in [192, 198–200], particularly, when used to enlarge training sample sets for classification. In active leaning SVM [198], an initial set of retrieval images, together with unlabeled images, are incorporated into the bootstrapping of the learning process. In Reference 199, the SVM is enhanced by the pseudo-RF for spoken term detection in the construction of successful retrieval of spoken content. In general, the pseudo-labeled samples have a problem of imprecise embedding in their class information since they are not labeled by users. A possible solution to this problem is to assign fuzzy membership to pseudo-labeled samples and apply fuzzy SVM active leaning for retrieval [200]. There is also a case where the imprecision of class information occurs if most of the top-ranked images are assumed to be relevant. In order to remedy the possible errors incurred by such an assumption, the sigmoid weighting function can be applied to the output of one-class SVM to produce probabilities of image relevancy for re-ranking retrieved samples [201]. In order to reduce the performance degradation caused by irrelevant noise from pseudo labeling, the work in Reference 202 conducts a post-verified process when applying pseudo-RF to improve the bag-of-visual-word models for image retrieval.

There is a difficulty in making assumptions about the class labels assigned to unlabeled data, which can cause the imprecision of class information. Some works [203] have proven that sufficient positive and unlabeled data without any negative data can be used to build accurate classifiers. For a standard pseudo-RF applied to text retrieval, the top-ranked documents are viewed as positive samples used to update the query term [204]. However, in image and video, top-ranked samples are not always the relevant, correct answers that meet the user's information need, due to the limited accuracy of current multimedia retrieval systems [205]. Instead of assigning pseudo labels by using the ranking scores, the work in Reference 191 employs self-organizing methods for judgment of image relevancy. The K-top rankings are passed through SOTM clustering in order to perform the labeling task. The system labels the unlabeled points according to the clusters to which they naturally belong. The pseudo-positive samples are labeled relevant because they are packed very close to the query cluster. An advantage of the self-organizing method is that it may be able to make better predictions with fewer labeled point than standard pseudo-RF, because it uses the natural breaks found in the unlabeled points.

It should be mentioned that the automatic-RF method shown in Figure 6.6c employs two sets of features for retrieval: feature set 1—a standard feature used for retrieving image database; and feature set 2—a high quality feature used for relevance judgment by the self-organizing method. The application of feature set 2 provides more accuracy for pseudo labeling. The work in Reference 206 applies a region-based feature to the initial retrieval set for improving accuracy in classification. This feature is more accurate as compared with Global features extracted from the whole image. Thus, more information is provided to a 2-level SOFM for effective classification. In fact, the application of two feature sets (extracted from two modalities) for image retrieval appears to have become very popular for re-ranking image databases recently. The works in References 196, 207–209 are examples of pseudo-RF that use similarity from one modality (i.e., feature set 1 from visual space) to decide pseudo-positive samples for implementation of query expansion in another modality (i.e., feature set 2 from the text space). This is called intermedia pseudo-RF [209]. In Reference 207, the visual search engine FIRM [210] is used to process image query and associate the top-ranked images as pseudo-positive feedback. The XML associated with these images is used to modify the textual query for the text search engine (XFIRM system [211]). The final similarity scores are the linear combination of scores from the original query and the modified query. The use of metadata embedded in the top-ranked images for query expansion in the text domain is also presented in Reference 208. In some cases, text terms from the metadata can be enhanced by wordNet for obtaining noun synonyms as a thesaurus for term expansion. The intermedia pseudo-RF is applicable with web image retrieval [203, 212] because of the availability of metadata from web images. The pseudo-positive feedback in visual space may introduce some noise by the candidate terms extracted from those pseudo-labeled samples [203]. However, this noise can be reduced by a method for semantic selection restrictions [212].

Pseudo-RF is a very effective method for video retrieval since the video content can be indexed by multi-modalities. The early work in Reference 213 implemented pseudo-RF for adaptive cosine network for video retrieval. The network organizes the feature database and video database into a 3-layer network structure, and the retrieval is performed by pseudo-RF using positive and negative feedback through signal propagation. This increases retrieval accuracy within a few iterations. The work in Reference 199 implements visual ranking to select pseudo-relevant samples for query expansion in the text domain for video retrieval. In References 192 and 193, video files are indexed by visual and text features such as transcripts and movie titles. A set of queries are regarded as positive samples, while the negative samples are obtained by sampling the least-ranked samples from the search result. These are used for training on the SVM system that fuses the decision of multiple retrieval agents to compute and output overall similarity scores.

Active learning or selective sampling refers to methods that assume that the given learning algorithm has control on the selection of the input training data such that it can select the most important examples from a pool of unlabeled examples [196]. A human user is then asked to label those examples, with the aim of minimizing data utilization [214, 215]. This idea is illustrated by a semiautomatic retrieval system in Reference 216, where a self-organizing method is applied to select the clusters (the most important examples) from a pool of unlabeled data (i.e., the retrieved data set). The user can then label the relevant centroid nodes instead of labeling each of the retrieved samples. Figures 6.6e and 6.7b show the flow process diagram and the 3D clustering of the semiautomatic retrieval system, respectively. Once a centroid is selected, its associations (the membership of the selected clusters) are labeled as positive samples. Then, these pseudo-labeled data are used for training the standard RF algorithm for retrieval. The 3D visualization of data clustering is similar to Visual Thesaurus [217], where similar words are structured in a 3D space using networking of nodes as shown in Figure 6.7a. The user can click on a particular node and view its synonyms. The 3D visualization obtained by the self-organizing method in Figure 6.7b shows how similar nodes are to one another using the representative centroids of clusters. The main purpose of such 3D visualization of data clustering is to help the user to find the image or images that best fit his or her needs.

Finally, pseudo-RF can be applied for image and video re-ranking as shown in Figure 6.6f. The system takes a ranked list of results or concept models as an approximation of the idea semantics of the target. The initial list can then be mined to discover and leverage related concepts. In Reference 194, an initial video rank is obtained by text search, concept-based search, or image search. The high scoring shots are labeled as positive and lower scoring shots are labeled as negative. The pseudo labels can then be applied to discover and leverage related concepts to refine the initial results. The re-ranking for video files is also presented in Reference 218, where the re-ranking task is related to transductive learning by considering the strategy of using numerous unlabeled samples to boost a learning algorithm's performance. The work in Reference 206 outlines an optimum selection algorithm, applied to the initial visual ranking to select pseudo preference pairs for training the SVM in learning re-ranking models.

6.5 DIRECTED SELF-ORGANIZATION

One major advantage of the SOTM over classical Unsupervised Learning methods, such as SOM and K-mean algorithms, is its ability to work well with sparsely distributed data [219]. SOTM is chosen in the current application, as problems in image retrieval have different characteristics than those in other data classification tasks. Firstly, the training dataset retrieved for RF is very small, for example, a few to tens of samples. In addition, the feature space is of a very high dimension (combination of color, shape, and texture features). These tend to form sparsely distributed data. Secondly, a problem is caused by an unbalanced data distribution between relevant and irrelevant samples in the training set. It is expected that, after the first iteration of

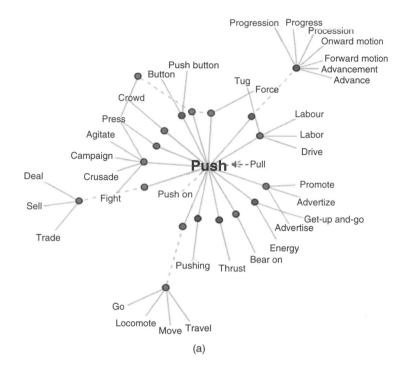

(a)

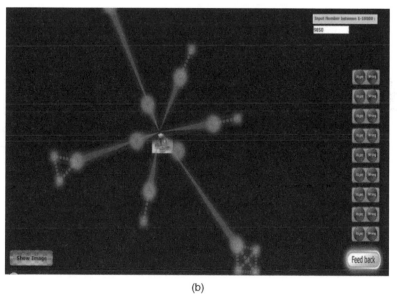

(b)

FIGURE 6.7 (a) 3D user interface of Thinkmap for visual thesaurus; (b) 3D user interference *via* self-organizing tree map for semiautomatic relevance feedback system.

RF, relevant items are retrieved more than irrelevant ones, and thus, the majority of relevant items will introduce an unbalanced space to the resulting clusters. To solve this problem the SOTM, by its nature, will attempt to maximize discrimination within subregions of the (unbalanced) training data. This efficient allocation and breakdown of class relationships minimize classification errors compared with that achieved through the SOM, which may distort when unfolding across low density feature space.

Despite advantages in the use of SOTM-based classifiers, there are two major drawbacks associated with the algorithm: it inappropriately decides on the relevant number of classes; and it often loses track of the original query position. The decision about which clusters are relevant in the SOTM is postponed until after the algorithm has converged. This is largely due to the absence of an innate controlling process in the algorithm to influence cluster generation around the query center. The loss of a sense of query location within the input space can have undesired effects on the true structure of the relevant class and can force the SOTM algorithm to spawn new clusters, form unnecessary boundaries within the query class, and make erroneous decisions about resemblance of the samples as illustrated in Figure 6.8. Therefore, partial supervision for the prevention of unnecessary boundary formation around the query class appears to be vital.

Due to the above limitations, a new member of the SOTM family, the DSOTM is introduced. The DSOTM algorithm not only provides partial supervision on cluster generation by forcing divisions away from the query class but also makes a gradual decision about resemblance of input patterns by constantly modifying each sample's membership during the learning phase of the algorithm. As a result, a more robust topology with respect to the query, as well as a better sense of likeness, can be achieved [130].

In addition, DSOTM relies on the query position as the a priori center of the relevant class and updates memberships according to this knowledge. The synaptic weight adjustments in the DSOTM are not simply limited to the winning node. The algorithm also constantly modifies all the centers according to the query position. If the winning center is not the query center, vector adjustments will affect both the winning node and the relevant center's position by moving the winning node (the center of the irrelevant class) toward the irrelevant samples and moving the relevant center toward the query center. Thus, as more samples are exposed to the network, the DSOTM algorithm will learn less from irrelevant samples and more from relevant ones, thus maintaining the integrity of a relevant center near the original query position. This action helps to foster a sense of preservation in the vicinity of the query class, effectively desensitizing partitioning in the region of the query.

6.5.1 Algorithm

The algorithm for generating the DSOTM map is given in the following steps [130, 220].

Step 1: *Initialization.* A root node $\{\mathbf{w}_j\}_{j=1}^{J}$ is chosen from the available set of input vectors $\{\mathbf{x}_k\}_{k=1}^{K}$ in a random manner. J is the total number of centroids (initially set to 1) and K is the total number of input vectors.

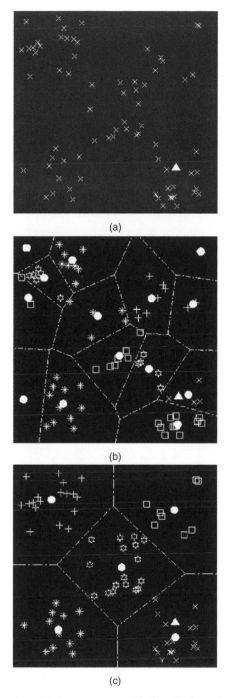

FIGURE 6.8 2D mapping: (a) input pattern with five distinct clusters; (b) 14 generated centers using Self-Organizing Tree Map (SOTM); and (c) five generated centers using Directed Self-Organizing Tree Map (DSOTM). The SOTM forms a boundary near the query (triangle) contaminating relevant samples, whereas some supervision is maintained in the DSOTM case, preventing unnecessary boundaries from forming.

Step 2: *Similarity Matching.* A new data point $\mathbf{x}$ is randomly selected and the best matching (winning) centroid j^* is found through the minimization of the predefined Euclidean distance criterion:

$$\mathbf{w}_{j^*}(t) = \arg \min_j \|\mathbf{x}(t) - \mathbf{w}_j(t)\|, \quad j = 1, 2, \dots, J. \tag{6.30}$$

Step 3: *Weight Update and Creation.*
If $\|\mathbf{x}(t) - \mathbf{w}_{j^*}(t)\| \leq H(t)$,
Then, $\mathbf{x}(t)$ is assigned to the winning node, and the synaptic vector is adjusted according to the reinforced learning rule:

$$\mathbf{w}_{j^*}(t+1) = \mathcal{W}(\mathbf{w}_{j^*}(t), \mathbf{x}(t)) \tag{6.31}$$

where

$$\mathcal{W}(\mathbf{w}_{j^*}(t), \mathbf{x}(t)) = \mathbf{w}_{j^*}(t) + \alpha(t)\beta(\mathbf{z}, \mathbf{x}(t))[\mathbf{x}(t) - \mathbf{w}_{j^*}(t)], \tag{6.32}$$

and $\alpha(t)$ is the learning rate, which decays exponentially over time as more neurons are allocated, $\alpha(t) = \alpha(t_0)\exp(-t/\max(t))$, $0.01 \leq \alpha(t) \leq \alpha(t_0)$, and $\alpha(t_0) = 0.1$.

Else, a new centroid node is formed starting with $\mathbf{x}$. The learning rate is changed to its initial value (i.e., $\alpha(t_0) = 0.1$), and j is increased by 1. The exponential ranking function $\beta(\mathbf{z}, \mathbf{x}(t))$ measures the similarity between query feature vector $\mathbf{z}$ and input feature vector $\mathbf{x}$:

$$\beta(\mathbf{z}, \mathbf{x}(t)) = \sum_{i=1}^{P} \exp\left[-\frac{(x_i - z_i)^2}{2\sigma_i^2}\right], \tag{6.33}$$

where P is the total number of features, σ_i is the tuning parameter in Equation 6.27, and η is an additional factor to ensure a large output for $\beta(\mathbf{z}, \mathbf{x}(t))$. A large value of $\beta(\mathbf{z}, \mathbf{x}(t))$ indicates a high relevance of the feature vector compared with the respective query feature at time t. As a result, the synaptic vectors are adjusted so that they learn more from statistically similar inputs and less from statistically irrelevant ones.

Step 4: *Identification of Relevance and Center Modification.* The index of the closest center to the query node $\mathbf{z}$ is identified by

$$\mathbf{w}_{j'}(t) = \arg \min_j \|\mathbf{z} - \mathbf{w}_j(t)\|, \quad j = 1, 2, \dots, J. \tag{6.34}$$

If $j^* = j'$ that is the closest center to the current input data is also the closest center to the query,
Then, the input vector $x(t)$ is marked as a relevant sample and the winning neuron is also moved toward the query position:

$$\mathbf{w}_{j^*}(t+1) = \mathcal{W}(\mathbf{w}_{j^*}(t), \mathbf{z}(t)) \tag{6.35}$$

Else If $j^* \neq j'$, the input vector $x(t)$ is marked as an irrelevant sample and this center is moved away from query center, for example,

$$\mathbf{w}_{j^*}(t+1) = \mathcal{W}(\mathbf{w}_{j^*}(t), \mathbf{x}(t)). \qquad (6.36)$$

Subsequently, the center $w_{j'}$ is moved toward the query position,

$$\mathbf{w}_{j'}(t+1) = \mathcal{W}(\mathbf{w}_{j'}(t), \mathbf{z}(t)) \qquad (6.37)$$

where the function $\mathcal{W}(.,.)$ is defined as in Equation 6.32.

Step 5: *Continuation*. Step 1 is repeated until the maximum number of iterations is reached, the maximum number of clusters is generated, and/or no noticeable changes in the feature map are observed.

In Step 3, $H(t)$ is the hierarchy function used to control the levels of the tree and decays exponentially over time from its initial value, $H(t_0) > \sigma_x$, according to $H(t+1) = \lambda H(t) \exp(-t/\rho)$, where λ is the threshold constant, $0 < \lambda < 1$, and $\rho = \max(t)/\log_{10}(H(t))$. The proposed threshold function is empirically established to decay faster than the one employed in the SOTM architecture. As a result, the network is given a better opportunity to generate the required centers at its initial training phase and learn from them at the later phase. In other words, the preliminary training phase in the DSOTM algorithm prioritizes node generation, while the later stages are dominated by learning about and adapting to existing information.

Step 4 of the DSOTM algorithm imposes some constraints on cluster generation near the query position and, thus, avoids the formation of unnecessary boundaries around it. As a result, a better sense of relevance measurements can be achieved as the tree structure develops. The growth of the DSOTM is biased *via* the ranking function to learn more from input vectors deemed to be similar to the query itself and less from images far from the query [191]. This promotes the generation of multiple irrelevant classes, while maintaining necessary plasticity in the relevant class [221].

As discussed in Reference 222, $H(t)$ provides a mechanism for the hierarchical exploration of an input space with different resolutions over time. It appears to be crucial to have a frontier on decaying $H(t)$ below a smallest meaningful resolution across feature space to avoid an indefinite growth of both SOTM and DSOTM networks. Beyond a maximally imposed limit on the number of neurons, the network can grow unnecessary centers, which can be generated until the number of classes equals (or even exceeds) the number of samples in the feature database. The threshold function used in the DSOTM architecture can be automatically adapted to a reasonable resolution before its existing topology reaches a stable condition as illustrated in Figure 6.8c. This is due to restrictions imposed by the query position as previously discussed. The threshold function of the SOTM algorithm, however, is unable to adequately decide on an appropriate number of centers and, thus, overclassifies the input space in Figure 6.8b. The smallest resolution was defined to be the Euclidean sum of the smallest resolution of all feature sets included in the feature space [222].

Figure 6.9 represents the timing diagram of the waveforms governing the evolution of DSOTM for the clustering result in Figure 6.8.

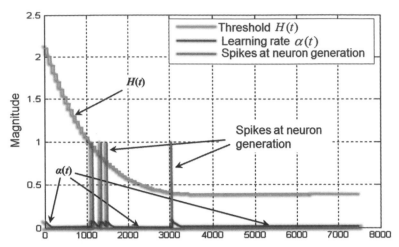

FIGURE 6.9   Timing diagram of the Directed Self-Organizing Tree Map based classification of Figure 6.8.

6.6   OPTIMIZING SELF-ORGANIZATION FOR RETRIEVAL

Although the use of the DSOTM method can be an effective solution for enhancing performance of image retrieval (results shown in Section 6.7), multiple criteria can still influence the optimality of this approach.

First, direction in the growth of the maps topology is entirely dependent on the location of the query in the space. If the query is located on the boundaries of a relevant group, some of the irrelevant samples might be mistakenly classified as part of the relevant class. In addition, the actual shape of the relevant class might also be jeopardized by generating unnecessary centers within this region. The GA shows capability of biasing the search process toward what is believed to be the best representative and distinctive traits among different image classes. This characteristic of the GA enables CBIR systems to tailor the retrieval process to the user's subjectivity by encoding the semantic information from image categories and using them for both classification and query modification.

Second, the choice on *number* and *variety* of features used to represent images and the degree of their *contribution* to successfully differentiate and distribute samples within their particular clusters can directly affect the DSOTM classification. The high dimensionality of low level features resulting from image indexing might impose an unfavorable influence on the classification process. It is usually thought that a better classifier can be achieved by applying more features to describe individual images. It has been observed that beyond a certain point, the inclusion of additional features leads to a worse rather than better classification result [223]. This is due to the deconstructive effect of redundant or even irrelevant features on the classification process. De-emphasis of the features that do not necessarily contribute significant information to the retrieval process can thus promote the discovery of common *conceptual* traits among image groups. This can improve the retrieval process as illustrated in Figure 6.12. In this figure, the contribution of individual features is accurately determined through the principle of feature weight detection. Figure 6.12b, represents the retrieval of a similar query after the process of GA feature weight detection. The GA operation appears to identify features important in capturing the information aspects of the query class, which in turn contributes to the DSOTM classification.

The main focus is therefore to further reduce the gap between low level descriptors and high level semantics, such that a CBIR system can achieve improved performance while in automatic retrieval mode. This combined framework is referred to as GA-based CBIR (GA-CBIR). GA-CBIR mimics the human feedback mechanism proposed in References 134 and 224, by automatically adapting the search process to what the system evolves to believe is significant content within the query. In this engine, DSOTM is a major component of GA analysis as it works closely with traditional GA operators to achieve a more robust perceptual classification—one that is more in tune with the apparent discriminative characteristics observed in an image by a human user [225].

6.6.1 Genetic Principles

The method for optimizing relevance identification in CBIR systems through GA-based feature weight detection is discussed here. The novelty of this scheme lies in the use of a base-10 GA method to measure the importance of individual features and their degree of contribution toward improving the retrieval process. The GA offers a particularly attractive approach, since it offers rapid Global search of large and nonlinear spaces.

The GA [226, 227] is one of the most commonly used optimization techniques among a set of evolutionary computational algorithms and was inspired by Darwin's theory of evolution [228]: *Individuals having advantageous variations are more likely to survive and reproduce than those without the advantageous variations.*

Together, Evolution Strategies, Evolutionary Programming, and Genetic Algorithms, form the backbone of the field of Evolutionary Computation [227]. The Evolution Strategies, an optimization technique based on principles of adaptation and evolution, was initially introduced by Rechenberg [229] and further developed by Schwefel [230] in the 1960s and early 1970s. Fogel, Owens, and Walsh [231] developed Evolutionary Programming, a technique in which finite state–machines are evolved by randomly mutating their state transitions and selecting the fittest. Several other pioneers working in the 1950s and the 1960s developed evolution-inspired algorithms for optimization and machine learning [227]: Fraser [232,233], Friedman [234], Bledsoe [235], Bremermann [236], and Reed, Toombs, and Baricelli [237]. The GA became especially popular through the work of John Holland in the late 1960s and early 1970s and was further extended by Goldberg in the late 1980s [226].

The basic concept of the algorithm is to model Darwin's evolutionary process, where members of a population of *potential solutions* compete with each other for survival based on their inherent behavior. These potential solutions are usually encoded as strings called chromosomes, and each chromosome is associated with

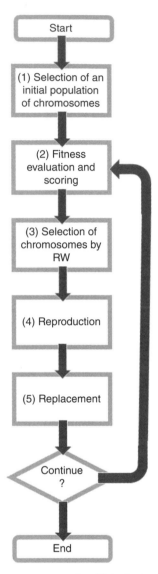

FIGURE 6.10 Single-point crossover operation. Note: in step 3, the selection of chromosome is performed by Roulette Wheel (RW) method.

a fitness value that indicates its optimality with respect to the current optimization criterion. The *fitness* of a solution will affect its probability of being selected for further evolution.

Figure 6.10 shows the flowchart of GA. The algorithm starts with the random selection of an initial population of chromosomes of size M. Typically, chromosomes are binary strings of a fixed length, but other forms of strings are also used to

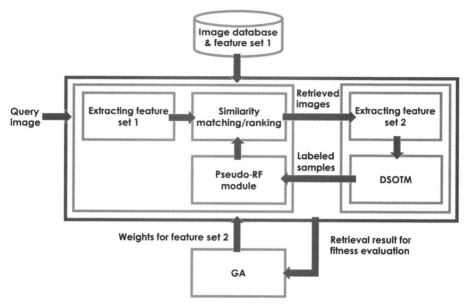

FIGURE 6.11 Block diagram of machine-controlled Genetic Algorithm (GA) based CBIR system.

encode the chromosomes. The goal of the evolutionary process is to select candidates associated with high fitness scores, while displacing the less optimal candidates from the population. The selected candidates are then used to generate new candidates by the reproductive operations of crossover and mutation, which introduce random variation into the solution [223, 238, 239]. We adopt GA to search for the suitable weight parameters.

6.6.2 System Architecture

The block diagram of the GA-CBIR system is illustrated in Figure 6.11. In this system, the GA is applied to measure the importance of individual features and the degree to which they contribute toward improving the retrieval process. To avoid the need for the encoding and decoding of chromosomes, a base-10 GA is employed, which operates similar to the binary GA described previously, except that genes vary between 0 and 9, and there is an extra digit for the sign representation [240]. Each chromosome carries information about a given number of traits: the feature weights, in our case, which are the actual parameters to be modified to improve fitness. These genes are combined with each other to create an initial population of M chromosomes in the range of $[m, 1]$, where m is a user-defined negative value specifying a boundary for the navigation of the GA algorithm. The empirical range for m is found to be $[-1, 0]$. This range will allow the GA to emphasize or de-emphasize features to a greater extent, as input feature vectors are initially normalized to the range of $[0, 1]$.

The first module of the system shown in Figure 6.11 deals with calculating features from a high volume image database. Consequently, a standard set of content descriptors (e.g., MPEG-7), is extracted to provide a more generic and rapid interface to existing databases. Extracted features are used to retrieve the most similar images based on a predefined distance metric. The top Q retrieved images are then redirected to the automatic relevance stage. This module extracts another set of features (usually of higher perceptual quality) from the top Q retrieved images from the initial search. Although computation of such features could be intensive, they become feasible at this stage since they are only computed for a few retrieved images from the previous rank-based process. This module allows for the use of more proprietary or specialty features, which may enhance perceptual discrimination beyond that which might otherwise be possible through standard features alone. These features are then used as seeds to train the unsupervised classifier. The normal procedure for the pseudo-RF is conducted and the retrieved results are obtained.

Color histograms, color moments, wavelet moments, and FDs were used in the feature set 1, while HSMI and Gabor descriptors accompanied with color histograms and color moments were used in feature set 2.

In order to calculate optimum weights for the retrieval system, the GA-based learning procedure is developed. The system first identifies the top Q similar images and then proceeds with unsupervised classification. The system's response to different weights is then quantified by measuring the ability of the DSOTM to correctly classify selected images. A new query, based on selected images from the previous iterations, is then adapted to represent the relevant class through the pseudo-RF module. The system's response to identified weights, in terms of retrieval accuracy, is detected by the system based on the pre-classified database in the fitness evaluation step of GA. A new population is then generated in the replacement step to identify and prepare the most fit chromosomes for replication through selection and reproduction operations. The detected feature weights and final retrieval results are then displayed back to the user upon the convergence of the algorithm.

The DSOTM seeks to provide a better conclusion regarding the resemblance of input samples to one another, and while the GA aims at selecting and reproducing a more fit population of candidate solutions, a combination of DSOTM and GA can replace the RF learning process to achieve a fully automated retrieval engine. Feature weight detection seeks to emphasize certain characteristics in an image (i.e., its color, texture, and/or shape) that might provide significant information to the DSOTM for a more robust classification. In Figure 6.12, this is illustrated by selecting/manipulating feature weights manually. As seen in Figure 6.12b, there exists a more appropriate weighting that leads to a higher retrieval rate.

6.6.3   Genetic Algorithm for Feature Weight Detection

In this section, we elaborate on the proposed GA-based feature weight detection algorithm (in Fig. 6.11). A chromosome in the base-10 GA is defined as $\mathbf{c} = \{c_c, c_t, c_s\}$, where c are the weight parameters of color, texture, and shape, respectively. Each $c \in \Re$ is defined in the range of $m \leq c \leq 1$, where m is a user defined negative value.

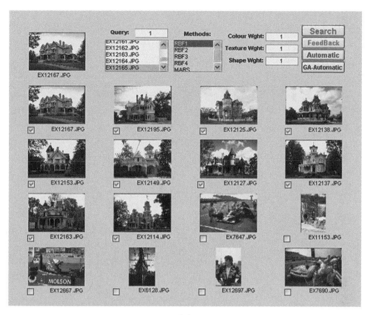

(a)

(b)

FIGURE 6.12   The degree of contribution of individual feature descriptors can affect both the Directed Self-Organizing Tree Map (DSOTM) classifier and the CBIR system: (*a*) 62.5% retrieval rate for the query image (on top-left corner) using the DSOTM classifier without feature weighting (with the same degree of feature weights); and (*b*) 100% retrieval rate for the same query using manually adjusted feature weights. Color feature offers the least contribution, while texture and shape features provide maximum amount of information for the DSOTM classifier.

Length of the chromosome depends on desired precision of the weights, in terms of digit decimal fraction. These chromosomes are used as feature weights for the current query and are the main variables to be manipulated by GA operators with the aim of enhancing retrieval results. The process of the GA weight detection is summarized as follows.

Step 1: *Initial Search.* Let $z = [z_c; z_t; z_s]$ represent the selected query image described by its color, texture, and shape feature vectors. Top Q statistically relevant images are selected by minimizing a predefined distance criterion.

Step 2: *Feature Weight Detection.* Dominant query features and their weights are identified with the aid of GA. This process is summarized in the following steps.

1. *Query Redefinition:* A new query feature vector, z', is created where $z' = [c_c \times z_c; c_t \times z_t; c_s \times z_s]$. Query feature weights, c_c, c_t, and c_s, are initially set to 1 in order to give them an equal opportunity to compete against each other in the weight detection process.

2. *Classification:* The DSOTM algorithm is applied to identified relevant class of the retrieved samples.

3. *Similarity Matching:* Query position is modified to the center of mass of the relevant class using the method described in Equation 6.29, and similarity measurement is performed by RBF method.

4. *Fitness Evaluation:* A new set of feature weights, c_c, c_t, and c_s are calculated to maximize DSOTM classification and retrieval precision using GA operators. The precision of the retrieval, $P_r(N_c)$, is calculated by $P_r(N_c) = \frac{N_R}{N_c} \in [0, 1]$, where N_R denotes the number of relevant images retrieved, and N_c denotes the number of retrieved images. The fitness function $F(w)$ is calculated by

$$F(w) = e^{-P_r(N_c)}. \tag{6.38}$$

The above equation measures the system's performance against various feature weights. Throughout the process of feature weight detection, GA aims at maximizing the above function by minimizing the inverse of retrieval precision $P_r(N_c)$. Since function maximization is essentially the minimization of the inverse of the same function, retrieval precision is increased by maximizing the above equation. Also, the use of an exponential operator can discriminate the system's performance nonlinearly and greater than a linear function.

5. *Termination:* The current system state is evaluated against termination conditions (see Table 6.5). If termination criteria is met, the optimization process will stop and the system's control will move to Step 3. Otherwise, new set of feature weights are detected and control of the system goes back to Step 2 for further optimization.

Step 3: *Display Results.* The evaluated feature weights are applied to the query image and top Q relevant images are displayed back to the user.

6.7   RETRIEVAL PERFORMANCE

The experiments were conducted in two parts. First, the performance of DSOTM was compared with SOM and SOTM. This was done by measuring the performance of an automatic image retrieval system using pseudo-RF. Second, the GA-CBIR system was evaluated for identifying dominant features of randomly selected images through the process of feature weight detection. The experiments were carried out using a subset of the Corel image database [241] consisting of nearly 12,000 JPEG color images, covering a wide range of real-life photos, from 120 different categories, each relating to a particular semantic class containing 100 images. Three sets of query images were constructed for testing and evaluation (A, B, C). In each set, one random sample was selected from each class; thus, one set of test queries included an example for every class (120 in total). Retrieval results were calculated for each set, with the average retrieval rate reported over all queries in the set. In these simulations, a total of the 16 most relevant images were retrieved to evaluate the performance of retrieval. This was measured in terms of Retrieval Rate (RR).

6.7.1   Directed Self-Organization

The system architecture of pseudo-RF discussed in Figure 6.6c was implemented. This is similar to the system in Figure 6.11 with the exception of not having the GA to optimize unsupervised data classification. The experimental results are illustrated in Table 6.4. In the SOM and SOTM algorithms, maximum number of allowed clusters was set to eight. A 4×2 grid topology was used in the SOM structure to locate the eight possible cluster centers (fixed topology). A *hard decision* on the resemblance of the input samples was made—if the sample was closer to one center than any other centers, in terms of a predefined distance metric, it was considered to be part of the cluster represented by that center.

Figures 6.13, 6.14, and 6.15 illustrate screenshots of the system's behavior using the same query sample as Figure 6.2. SOTM has shown effective behavior in minimizing human interactions and automating the search process by efficiently classifying an unknown and nonuniform data space into more meaningful clusters. Moreover, the flexible tree-like topologies of the SOTM allowing top-down data exploration make it less prone to classification errors and more attractive for retrieval applications.

TABLE 6.4   **Experimental Results in terms of Retrieval Rate (RR)—The Automatic Content-Based Image Retrieval (CBIR)**

Classifier	Set A	Set B	Set C	Average
Rank-based	37.8%	39.2%	39.8%	*38.9%*
SOM	51.2%	49.1%	52.3%	*50.9%*
SOTM	52.1%	50.6%	54.4%	*52.4%*
DSOTM	54.8%	56.4%	58.6%	*56.6%*

FIGURE 6.13 Machine-controlled CBIR system using Self-Organizing Map.

FIGURE 6.14 Machine-controlled CBIR system using Self-Organizing Tree Map.

FIGURE 6.15   Machine-controlled CBIR system using Directed Self-Organizing Tree Map.

Despite the advantages of using SOTM-based classifiers, the retention of some degree of supervision to prevent unnecessary boundaries from forming around the query class appears to be crucial. In the DSOTM algorithm, decisions about the association of input patterns to the query image are gradually made as each sample is presented to the system. The DSOTM keeps track of the query center forcing the center of the relevant class to remain in the vicinity of query position. Therefore, it biases the generation of new centers and can determine the relevance of input samples, with respect to the query, as its structure grows.

6.7.2   Genetic Algorithm Weight Detection

A number of experiments were conducted to compare behaviors of the GA-based CBIR system, presented in Figure 6.11, using the SOM, SOTM, and DSOTM clustering algorithms. Table 6.5 illustrates the adapted GA parameter settings in our

TABLE 6.5   Parameter Setting for the Genetic Algorithm

Parameter	Setting
Population size	50
Crossover type	Two-point
Crossover probability - P_C	80%
Mutation probability - P_M	5%
Selection mechanism	Roulette Wheel
Termination criterion	Best score does not change over 20 s

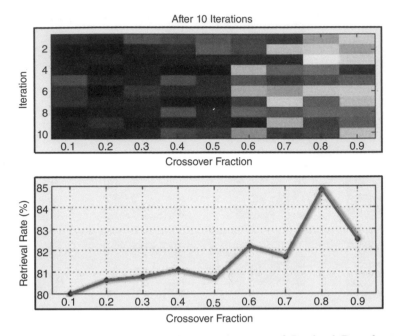

FIGURE 6.16   Comparing CBIR performance in terms of Retrieval Rate for various crossover rates.

experiments. A base-10 GA algorithm with an initial population of 50 chromosomes, defined within the range of $[-1, 1]$, with a maximum of 100 iterations, was employed. The size of the initial population was kept constant throughout the entire process of feature weight detection. Figure 6.16 shows the effect of various crossover probabilities on the automatic CBIR performance. The crossover probability was defined as the probability of exchanging segments between any two selected chromosomes. In this figure, the highest RR was achieved at the 0.8 level. Therefore, a two-point crossover operation with a probability of 80% was utilized. Mutation, the probability of randomly flipping a gene to another value, was set to 5%. The RW method was used to select chromosomes in proportion to their score as indicated by the fitness function. Consequently, a chromosome with higher fitness score would have a better chance of being selected for reproduction.

The experimental results are illustrated in Table 6.6. DSOTM outperforms both SOM and SOTM in the GA-CBIR framework. The effectiveness of the genetic-based algorithm in the structure of CBIR systems is also evident from these results.

TABLE 6.6   Experimental Results in terms of Retrieval Rate

Classifier	Set A	Set B	Set C	Average
SOM	61.2%	59.9%	63.6%	*61.6%*
SOTM	66.8%	65.7%	67.5%	*66.7%*
DSOTM	71.2%	68.8%	72.3%	*70.8%*

As discussed in Reference 242, GA performance is usually measured by the number of fitness function evaluations done during the course of a run. For a fixed population size, the number of fitness function evaluations is given by the product of population size by the number of generations. Number of generations in the GA-CBIR algorithm depends on the quality of features describing an image; therefore, retrieval speed can fluctuate from one image to another. With the presence of good quality features, DSTOM can produce more distinct clusters and retrieval might converge toward the information need more rapidly. On the other hand, in the presence of poor quality feature descriptors, the DSOTM might have difficulties generating meaningful clusters so the GA can face difficulties to find important weights. In our experiments, GA weight detection can take anything from a seconds to a few minutes on an average speed computer processor.

6.8 SUMMARY

In this chapter a methodology for guiding adaptations of an RBF-based RF for automatic CBIR systems, using dynamic Self-Organization was explored. The main focus of this chapter was twofold—introducing a new member of SOTM family, the DSOTM, that not only provides a partial supervision on cluster generation by forcing divisions away from the query class, but also presents an objective verdict on resemblance of the input pattern as its tree structure grows. A base-10 GA approach was also proposed to accurately determine the contribution of individual feature vectors for a successful retrieval in a Feature Weight Detection process. The DSOTM is quite attractive in CBIR since it aims to reduce both user workload and subjectivity. Repetitive user interaction steps are replaced by a DSOTM module, which adaptively guides RF, to bridge the gap between low level image descriptors and high level semantics. To further reduce this gap and achieve enhanced performance for the automatic CBIR system under study, a GA-based approach was proposed in conjunction with the DSOTM. The resulting framework is referred to as GA-CBIR and aims to maintain human subjectivity by automatically adjusting the search process to what the system evolves *to believe* is significant content within the query. Throughout this architecture, traditional GA operators work closely with the DSOTM, adapting to the more discriminative characteristics observed in an image by a human user.

CHAPTER 7

The Self-Organizing Hierarchical Variance Map

In this chapter, a new model for clustering data is introduced and developed, offering a number of enhancements and features over the self-organizing tree map (SOTM). The model is known as the Self-Organizing Hierarchical Variance Map (SOHVM). In the spirit of the SOTM, the SOHVM is a dynamic, growing self-organizing network of nodes that evolve toward a representation of an input data/feature space. This evolution takes place through the process of competitive learning, wherein network nodes compete and associate with one another in order to represent information presented as each new input pattern (stimulus) is exposed to the network.

Among the highlights of this particular model, is a built-in mechanism for estimating an appropriate number of prototypes for any given clustering result. In addition, the network works to establish and refine topological relationships between discovered clusters, thereby revealing a more faithful representation of the underlying structure of feature space. Such topologies are deemed to be useful for the discovery and evaluation of higher level associations existing within the data. The model is thus more suitable for extracting dominant sets of patterns existing in a dataset, with potential to simplify applications that require automated, unbiased assessment and description of previously unlabeled data. In the following chapter, backbone descriptions extracted with the SOHVM model will be utilized in the segmentation and labeling of complex biological image data.

The remainder of this chapter is broken down as follows. In Section 7.1, the SOTM is revisited, and we highlight some of its limitations. In so doing, a motivation is provided for a more advanced clustering algorithm, one that retains some of the desirable properties of the SOTM. In Section 7.2, the key components and principles of operation for the new model are outlined and justified. In Section 7.3, implementation details are discussed. Finally, in Section 7.4, a series of visual simulations on synthetic two-dimensional (2D) data are presented, with the goal of providing a

Unsupervised Learning: A Dynamic Approach, First Edition.
Matthew Kyan, Paisarn Muneesawang, Kambiz Jarrah, and Ling Guan.

simple and clear demonstration of the new model in operation, highlighting some of its key features and strengths over popular existing architectures from the literature.

7.1 AN INTUITIVE BASIS

The driving force behind the proposed SOHVM model revolves around how the decision is made as to whether or not the network (map) should be grown (extended through the addition of new prototypes) or adapted (the refinement of already existing prototypes) toward an improved representation of feature space.

In the SOTM, an unseen pattern presented to the network as a feature vector will automatically trigger the growth of the map (i.e., by spawning a new prototype as a child of the closest one in the current map). This is achieved when some distance metric (evaluated between the input pattern and the closest prototype pattern in the existing map) exceeds a globally decaying threshold $H(t)$, as previously depicted in Figures 4.3 and 4.4—the condition whereby an input pattern is *not* proximal to, and is thus deemed *significantly dissimilar* to the current representation of feature space, warranting insertion of an input pattern directly into the map's memory as a new prototype. Input patterns within the proximity of existing prototypes stimulate a refinement that imparts a small portion of information from the input into the map's existing memory.

This process, by design, is somewhat blind. This is particularly evident in the early stages of learning. During this time, new prototypes may easily be formed in outlying or noisy regions, wherein the prototype may become trapped and unable to sufficiently *track back* to more suitable regions of density (particularly as competition becomes increasingly fierce). Thus, it would seem that a proximity threshold alone may not be indicative of the most likely regions of input space warranting further exploration or modeling. Instead of blind insertion based on a Global threshold, the proposed model attempts to make a more *informed* decision for node insertion by considering the interplay between both Global (top-down) proximity information and localized (bottom-up) variance information.

The principal idea for the proposed SOHVM model is as follows—if at any point in the evolution of the map, its prototypes are each able to *probe* the region of data within their local proximity and somehow form an idea of the nature of such local variations in the underlying data, then it follows that this knowledge might be utilized in making a more *informed* decision when it comes to extending the set of representing prototypes. The challenge, of course, is that generally such a network only has access to a single input pattern at any given instance in time. To store and remember every input seen thus far is generally not desired in applications with excessively large datasets (e.g., content retrieval or microbiological image analysis), as memory requirements would be prohibitive. As will be discussed, such an online *probe* is achievable, through the use of Hebbian Maximal Eigenfilters (HME), which model maximal variance in the data *local* to a cluster's prototype.

Assuming such a probe (q_i in Fig. 7.1 b) is incorporated into each memory element (node) of the map (previously a centroid $\mathbf{w}_k$ in an SOTM), each cluster prototype

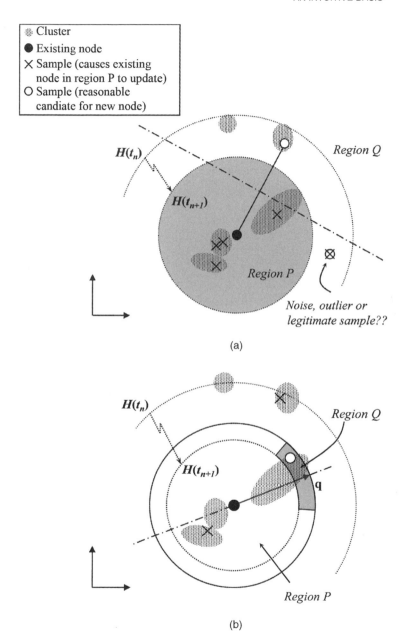

Cluster
● Existing node
✕ Sample (causes existing node in region P to update)
○ Sample (reasonable candiate for new node)

H(t$_n$)

Region Q

H(t$_{n+1}$)

Region P

Noise, outlier or legitimate sample??

(a)

H(t$_n$)

Region Q

H(t$_{n+1}$)

q

Region P

(b)

FIGURE 7.1 SOTM vs. SOHVM growth strategies—blind vs. informed insertion. (a) SOTM *blind* insertion, showing nodes inserted and tracking back, plus nodes getting trapped in the outskirts/noisy areas of feature space (b) SOHVM *informed* insertion, showing an alternative region Q for node insertion, one that considers local variance information extracted from within the *local* scope of a discovered cluster group, using a variance probe *q*.

would then become more *aware* of how data is distributed within its cluster. It would thus be desirable for new prototypes to be added near the extremities of *known* density, rather than simply at the location of an arbitrary input sample. Intuitively, if a large region of density contains multiple clustered subregions, it would then be more likely to warrant subdivision.

Insertion of a new prototype in the outskirts of the overall distribution should cause both the original and newly spawned prototypes to each begin to compete over a subset of the original data—causing each individual variance probe to adjust and become more localized. Thus, with every new input stimulus, each probe progressively indicates more local, natural sites for further insertion, and so on, cascading down such that the underlying data distribution is gradually partitioned. In this sense, the network partitions hierarchically according to cascading local variances; thus the new model is termed the Self-Organizing Hierarchical Variance Map.

Due to the inconsistent tree structures and the fact that connections exist between nodes quite removed from one another in the early phases of the mapping, very little *associative* learning can take place in an SOTM, since neighboring nodes are not guaranteed to remain so over the entire course of learning. The new model integrates a *Competitive Hebbian Learning* (CHL) mechanism into the framework such that dynamic connections may be generated throughout learning to reflect the underlying density connecting prototypes. In this way, associative learning may be included. The goal is to allow neighboring nodes to alleviate those trapped in suboptimal regions, acting as attractors to draw them back toward regions of the space that have previously discovered density.

With an ability to generate relatively consistent topological maps, the information encoded by the new model is expected to serve the additional purpose of conveying information about higher level associations in the data, which may then serve to guide post-processing and interpretation tasks—a feature that is explored through the automated segmentation and visualization of microbiological image data presented in Chapter 8.

7.2 MODEL FORMULATION AND BREAKDOWN

The SOHVM process is formulated as follows. Let $\mathbf{X}$ represent an input data/feature space of dimension N_f and sample size N_s to be clustered:

$$\mathbf{X} = \left[\mathbf{x}_1, \mathbf{x}_2, \mathbf{x}_3, \dots, \mathbf{x}_N \right] ; \mathbf{x}_j \in \mathfrak{R}^{N_f} \tag{7.1}$$

Let $\mathbf{x}_{i*}$ represent an individual input pattern vector drawn at random from $\mathbf{X}$ and presented to the network at iteration i. The SOHVM process then works to generate a topologically aware representation in the form of a map, $M = \{V, E\}$, of the dominant clusters existing in the data space $\mathbf{X}$. The map is formed as a network consisting of a set of prototype memory elements (nodes) V, each connected by a set of edges E:

$$V = \left[v_1, v_2, v_3, \ldots, v_{N_c} \right] \tag{7.2}$$

$$E = \left[e_1, e_2, e_3, \ldots, e_{N_e} \right]; e_j = \{ v_p, v_q \} \equiv \{ v_q, v_p \} : v_q, v_p \in V; p \neq q \tag{7.3}$$

where N_c and N_e represent the number of discovered classes/clusters and the number of edges, respectively.

Each node v_k in M contains a dual memory element:

$$v_k = \{ \mathbf{w}_k, \Lambda_k \} : k \in \left[1, 2, \ldots, N_c \right] \tag{7.4}$$

$$\Lambda_k = \left(\lambda_k, \mathbf{q}_k \right) \tag{7.5}$$

where $\mathbf{w}_k$ represents the kth prototype's position (cluster center), whilst Λ_k forms a maximal eigenvalue (λ_k) /eigenvector ($\mathbf{q}_k$) pair describing the maximum variance of data in the vicinity of $\mathbf{w}_k$. This second memory element acts as a local variance *probe*, as discussed in the previous section. These probes are then used as an aid in controlling the growth of the network.

As indicated, the goal of the clustering process is twofold. The first goal is for the nodes of the map (memory elements V) to capture a representation of the dominant clusters existing in the underlying data space. The second goal is for the edges E to form a representation of the topology of the underlying data space. Specifically, this topology defines the way in which discovered clusters are related to one another—formed so as to indicate the way in which underlying density is distributed between discovered clusters.

To achieve these goals, the SOHVM process implements three key mechanisms over and above that considered in a typical SOTM.

- Topology extraction through CHL;
- Local Variance Mapping through HME;
- Global and local variance interplay for intelligent map growth and termination.

The second feature, in particular, is exploited at both the Global and local levels toward an intelligent map growth strategy. In the next section, the theory behind the first two mechanisms (CHL and HME) will be outlined, before moving on to a detailed description of the third mechanism, and the SOHVM algorithm itself.

7.2.1 Topology Extraction via Competitive Hebbian Learning

Inspired by Hebb's postulate of learning [6], the principal of CHL [243] was first introduced to more accurately estimate the topology of an input space.

Rather than imposing a fixed topological structure a priori, CHL allows for topological connections to be adjusted as the network adapts, by *dynamically* forming

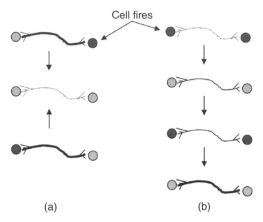

FIGURE 7.2   Illustration of Hebb's postulate of learning: nerve cells that fire in (a) an uncorrelated fashion that weakens synaptic connectivity; (b) correlated fashion, strengthening the synaptic connectivity. The connection serves to enhance a firing cell's efficiency in triggering its related neighbors.

connections between nodes that tend to span more dense regions of the underlying data. This topological inference is especially important for generative maps, as the topology between the limited nodes discovered in the early phases of learning is unlikely to be suitable for relating larger numbers of nodes discovered in later phases.

Hebb's postulate of associative learning essentially states that (on the cellular level) when two neuron cells are within significant proximity enabling one to *persistently* excite another, some form of physiological/metabolic growth process results. This process works to *enhance* the firing cell's efficiency in triggering the other, that is, a synaptic path evolves and strengthens between the two neurons, so that future associations occur much more readily. Thus, the action of strengthening the association between two nodes in a network functions as a *correlation* between their two states, as illustrated in Figure 7.2. CHL offers a means of strengthening and weakening associations between discovered prototypes by forming connections between pairs of nodes found to be *most* representative of any given input, akin to triggering or refreshing a correlation between the two nodes.

Typically, each neuron, as a memory element, signifies a cluster prototype in the input space. Upon clustering, each neuron partitions the input space relative to nearby neurons resulting in a *Delaunay* triangulation of the neuron prototypes (or cluster centers). The triangulation defines intersecting boundaries (Voronoi cells) that would occur given a specific distance metric describing the similarity of data points. Simulating Hebbian association by establishing a connection between the two closest nodes to an input data sample produces what is known as an Induced Delaunay Triangulation (Fig. 7.3). This triangulation has been shown to preserve topology in a general sense [244]. Connection of nodes, with or without a measure of strength, offers a path through which information may be distributed among neurons in a network.

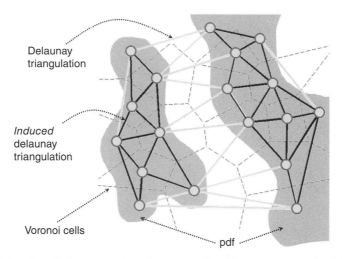

Delaunay
triangulation

Induced
delaunay
triangulation

Voronoi cells

pdf

FIGURE 7.3 Associative connections between nodes (cluster prototypes) within a given network defining an *Induced Delaunay triangulation* of the underlying data distribution. The links (bold) are emphasized in regions of the data space where the probability density function is nonzero.

Formation of connections is only half the story. To account for the likely scenario of associations being formed in earlier states, amounting to false assertions at a later stage of learning, a complementary scheme for *disassociation* of prototypes is necessary. An *edge aging* scheme [243], proposed for combining Neural Gas (NG) and CHL is used in this current treatment. In such a scheme, stimulation of the two closest nodes to an input gives birth to an edge, which is progressively aged (weakened) unless restimulated by other inputs from the underlying data. Edges restimulated are reset to a zero age (strengthened), while old edges are eventually removed, thereby disassociating prototypes.

7.2.2 Local Variance via Hebbian Maximal Eigenfilters

In attending to the question of how the variance of data represented by a given node might be estimated, one might consider the following. The network could be stopped at given intervals (preferably as current nodes settle in terms of their location) to examine the data currently associated with each cluster. To do so, however, would require that the entire dataset be labeled with their representing nodes, before performing some kind of general variance measure or principal component analysis (PCA), on each individual subspace.

With the new information, we could proceed with evolving the network. This is undesired, as it requires labeling steps that might be prohibitive if the number of samples is large. This type of approach also could not be used in online learning processes, where all that is known is the current input (e.g., data mining temporal datasets where inputs are transient and cannot be recovered). Alternatively, an error

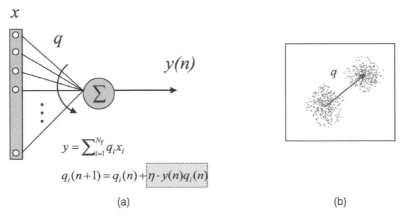

$$y = \sum_{i=1}^{N_f} q_i x_i$$

$$q_i(n+1) = q_i(n) + \boxed{\eta \cdot y(n) q_i(n)}$$

(a)   (b)

FIGURE 7.4   A simple Hebbian perceptron: (a) utilizing a Hebbian learning rule; (b) weights from the simple perceptron evolve toward the maximal eigenvector (first principal component vector through the data, axis through which variance is maximized).

statistic could be accumulated for each node (as is performed in Growing Neural Gas (GNG)); however, an additional scheme to stop/relax the accumulation of such errors becomes necessary and often becomes the dominant influence on the clustering result.

The Hebbian-Based Maximum Eigenfilter (HME) [245] offers an attractive mechanism that fits well into the framework of our proposed Self-Organizing Map strategy. It turns out, that the correlation sensitivity of the Hebbian learning rule leads to more than just the CHL principle outlined earlier. Oja showed that a single Hebbian-type adaptation rule for its synaptic weights can evolve into a filter for the first principal component of the input distribution.

To demonstrate, consider the simple neuronal model shown in Figure 7.4 a. Let $q_i, i = 1, \cdots, N_f$ represent a synapse that maps an input x_i onto an output y, such that

$$y = \sum_{i=1}^{N_f} \mathbf{q}_i \mathbf{x}_i \qquad (7.6)$$

where $x_i, i = 1, ..., N_f$ is an input sample from the space $\mathbf{X}$ and N_f is the dimension of input space or, alternatively, the number of features if x_i is a sample from a feature space.

The model is linear in the sense that its postsynaptic output is a linear combination of its presynaptic input signals [2]. According to Hebb's postulate, unlike the Kohonen learning rule, the synapse (memory element) should grow a strong output response when the input signal x_i is similar to $\mathbf{q}_i$. This learning rule can be instantiated as

$$\mathbf{q}_i(n+1) = \mathbf{q}_i(n) + y(n)\mathbf{x}_i(n) \qquad (7.7)$$

where η is the learning rate, and n represents the current iteration (unit time or presentation cycle).

One can see that, over a period of time, $\mathbf{q}_i$ will continue to grow indefinitely should it continue to detect correlations between the respective jth components of $\mathbf{x}_i$ and $\mathbf{w}_i$. As such, Oja suggested a convenient form of normalization to force the synapse into stability [245]:

$$\mathbf{q}_i(n+1) = \frac{\mathbf{q}_i(n) + y(n)\mathbf{x}_i(n)}{\sqrt{\sum_{i=1}^{N_f}\left[\mathbf{q}_i(n) + y(n)\mathbf{x}_i(n)\right]^2}} \tag{7.8}$$

Normalization amounts to a necessary condition for Self-Organization, namely, the competition among the synapses of a neuron over limited resources (as indicated in Chapter 3). If η is small, Equation 7.8 reduces to the power series expansion (ignoring second and higher order harmonics in η):

$$\mathbf{q}_i(n+1) = \mathbf{q}_i(n) + y(n)\left[\mathbf{x}_i(n) - y(n)\mathbf{q}_i(n)\right]. \tag{7.9}$$

The negative term here offers stabilization due to normalization and amounts to a *forgetting* or *leakage* factor that becomes more pronounced with a stronger response $y(n)$. There is neurobiological support for this type of control [246].

By projecting samples from X onto this neuron, it has been shown [245] that $\mathbf{q}_i(n)$ will converge to the maximal eigenvector of X [245], namely, the first principal component $\mathbf{q}_1$ of X (the vector describing the axis through the data X, along which variance is maximized). This is depicted in Figure 7.4 b. In addition, $y(n)$ will simultaneously converge to the largest eigenvalue λ_1 of X (i.e., the expected value of the variance along the axis defined by $\mathbf{q}_i$).

In the context of the current SOHVM map model, a single Hebbian unit embedded within the construct of each self-organizing node within the network then acts as a *Maximal Variance Probe* that dynamically captures the distribution of the local data that it represents.

The dual nature of each node V_k allows one set of synapses to capture centroid information ($\mathbf{w}_k$) and one to capture the maximal eigenvector and its eigenvalue ($\Lambda_k = \lambda_k, \mathbf{q}_k$). Each memory element is driven by a synchronous learning rate and acts simultaneously on any given input as it is presented to the network (given that it belongs to the winning node). Learning rates decay, then reset with the introduction of each new node and act to force convergence of local variance properties, as the node itself converges upon a position in the input space.

In order to cast the Hebbian unit into the Self-Organizing Map framework, manipulations within Equation 7.9 must be made with respect to a nonstationary origin. To ensure that the eigenvector is localized to the current self-organizing node, we need a translation to the frame of reference defined by the current location of that node. This amounts to constructing a virtual input vector $\mathbf{x}_i'$ that describes the

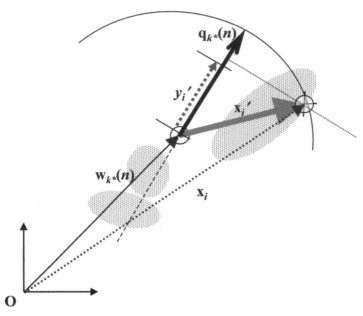

FIGURE 7.5 Recasting the calculation of maximal variance such that it relates to the scope of an individual node in the network. The graphic is a geometric representation of Equations 7.10–7.13.

relative position of the current input to that of its closest node (depicted in Fig. 7.5), calculated as

$$\mathbf{x}'_i = \mathbf{x}_i - \mathbf{w}_{k^*}(n) \tag{7.10}$$

$$y'_i = \sum_{j=1}^{N_f} \mathbf{q}_{k^*j}(n) \cdot \mathbf{x}'_{ij} \tag{7.11}$$

$$\mathbf{q}_{k^*}(n+1) = \mathbf{q}_{k^*}(n) + \alpha_k(n) \cdot y'_i \cdot \left[\mathbf{x}'_i - y'_i \cdot \mathbf{q}_{k^*}(n)\right] \tag{7.12}$$

$$\lambda_k^*(n+1) = \lambda_k^*(n) + \alpha_k^*(n) \cdot \left[y'_i - \lambda_k^*(n)\right] \tag{7.13}$$

where $\mathbf{w}_{j^*}$ is the winning node's centroid, $\mathbf{x}_i$ is the current input, $\mathbf{x}'_i$ is the *effective* input, and α_{j^*} is the learning rate of the current winning node; y'_i represents the projection of $\mathbf{x}'_i$ onto $\mathbf{q}_{k^*}$, which is a transient projection of the current input onto the maximal eigenvector of the winning node. To store y'_i, as it too converges, we can use a Kohonen update equation in the same way as we do to capture the centroid, as shown in Equation 7.12. Note that y'_i is a scalar, so too is $\lambda_{k^*}(n)$, which stores a running estimate of the maximal eigenvalue at the winning node k^*.

Figure 7.6 demonstrates the HME in action, under the condition of a *nonstationary* reference point (a lone winning centroid $\mathbf{w}_{k^*}$). The convergence properties of multiple trials are demonstrated for various 2D input spaces. The central and rightmost figure

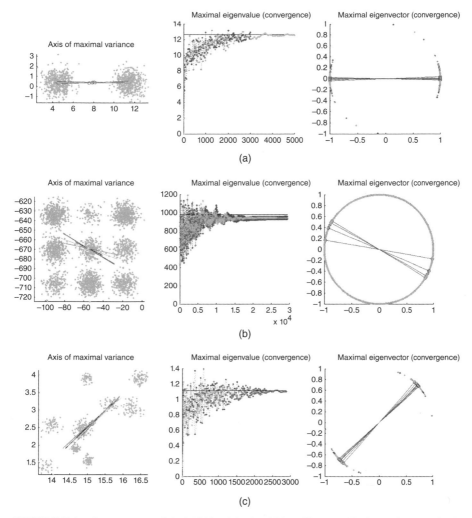

FIGURE 7.6 Convergence of the Hebbian Maximal Eigenfilter (HME) for various synthetic 2D data spaces—the HME is a perceptron whose synaptic weights adapt toward the maximal eigenvector of the underlying space of patterns it is presented with. This amounts to the first principal component (or axis through the data along which variance is maximized). In this figure, convergence properties of the HME are demonstrated under a nonstationary environment. Eigenvectors $\mathbf{q}_k$ may be initialized either at a random position within or on the unit circle and examples shown include: (a) two clusters of equal density; (b) symmetrically spaced grid of nine closely packed clusters of similar size, differing densities; (c) nine clusters of differing size and densities.

for each test set shows a graph of the converging eigenvalue and eigenvector pairs for a single node in motion while it settles to the centroid of the data, over a number of trial runs. The horizontal line at the maximal eigenvalue, as determined by PCA, is depicted by the central figures as a ground truth.

Ultimately, the HME calculations described in this section, as adapted to the self-organizing framework, estimate local variance properties that can then be utilized in a new scheme for the control of map growth and even have some implications for map termination, as outlined in the next section.

7.2.3   Global and Local Variance Interplay for Map Growth and Termination

7.2.3.1 Map Growth   Essentially, the goal of node insertion in the SOHVM should be to bias the possible choices of inserting new nodes, in favor of locations at maximal points of variance with respect to the given winning node. In this sense, the chance of a node being generated on a noise point or outlier, and staying there, is reduced. Essentially, we then want to recreate the conditions (at later stages of evolution) allowing for a similar resilience to noise as experienced in the early stages of a typical SOTM process. As mentioned previously, during this phase, $H(t)$ is large enough that a noise point is able to track back toward regions of density (should it in fact belong to those regions), under the assumption that there must be *some* dense structure(s) existing *within* bounds dictated by the maximal variance probe.

The decision to grow in the SOHVM is thus delayed until such time as the Global vigilance $H(t)$ drops to within the local scope of any given winning node—indicated by the winning node's variance probe. $H(t)$ is thus initialized to a value that exceeds the maximal range in the data, as per the SOTM (see Chapter 4. The map stabilizes while $H(t)$ cascades down in SOTM stepped fashion, to meet with the local variance of the root node (i.e., the maximal variance of X).

After this period, the node with the highest degree of variance is identified, providing a lower bound for the region P. At the same time, the winning node's local variance λ_{k*} provides an upper bound on the region P. The region P (see Fig. 7.7) is then defined as

$$\max_{j\in\{1,...,N_c\}} \left(\sqrt{\lambda_j}\right) \leq P \leq 3 \cdot \sqrt{\lambda_{k*}} \qquad (7.14)$$

where $k*$ is the index of the winning node. The justification here is that P sits between the first and third standard deviations of the most variant and winning nodes, respectively. In the initial case, when there is only a root node, this will reduce to a region within the outer *radius* of the local data (under the Gaussian assumption). If the subspace under the winning node does contain multiple clusters, then insertion here should lead to their discovery, that is, there should be sufficient freedom for an inserted node to freely migrate to regions of density within the scope previously described by the winning node.

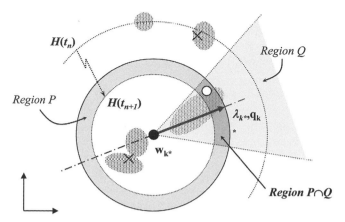

FIGURE 7.7   Global and local variance interplay for node insertion (map growth). The intersection of region P and Q defines a *hot spot* for node insertion. Nodes encountered outside $H(t)$ will be treated as noise/outliers under the assumption that clusters have already been dispatched to those regions at a previous level of $H(t)$. Nodes within $H(t)$ will cause the winning node to adapt.

As $H(t)$ decays, new nodes are only inserted if they fall within region P and are also at a distance of at least $H(t)$ from the winning node. As a result, stimulation of map growth is governed by the interplay between Global vigilance $H(t)$ (*top-down*), and local variance (*bottom-up*) information—prioritizes the subdivision of more dispersed regions of density.

Under mixtures of different clusters prior to any given partition, orientation in the local variance is more likely; thus, inserting anywhere within the region defined by P may not be entirely appropriate. The information encapsulated in the eigenvector of the maximal variance probe may be used to further constrain insertion by imposing the region Q.

$$Q : \hat{x}'_i \cdot q_{k*} \geq \zeta \tag{7.15}$$

where ζ is some projection factor defining an angle of incidence from w_{k*}. The intersection $P \cap Q$ identifies a hot spot that is more confined to the outer regions of known density, within the local context of each winning node. In keeping with the SOTM strategy of insertion through a cascading threshold, the SOHVM thus utilizes a stricter, more informed search strategy that attempts to achieve insertion through the consideration of cascading local variances, which are each unique to the individual regions in which they reside. $H(t)$ then acts as a guide, overseeing this process hierarchically from the Global down to the local context.

The proposed decision region of the SOHVM (Fig. 7.7) can be thought of as a localized *annulus of significant dissimilarity*. If any samples are encountered that trigger a given node as their winner *and* they fall into this decision region, they are considered likely candidates for the generation of a new node.

7.2.3.2 Map Termination   Two primary ways of stopping the SOHVM are considered. The first method proceeds as with the SOTM, by imposing a minimum limit on $H(t)$. The second utilizes both topological and local variance information extracted by the SOHVM, to assess cluster validity *on-the-fly*, and thereby infer an appropriate number of clusters at runtime (as opposed to running an entire algorithm multiple times with different numbers of classes).

Specifically, there are two cluster validity indices introduced in Chapter 2, that are directly compatible with the information supplied by the HME's and the SOHVM's dynamic topology: the Calinski–Harabasz index (CH) and the recent Geometric index (GI).

To recap, CH considers the traces of both the between and within cluster scatter matrices (Equation 2.22). Initially, one might consider that the $|C_k|$ term in Equations 2.23 and 2.24 might be reflected by some kind of hit rate, that is, if a particular neuron/node is fired more than another, then this might serve as an indication of the density of underlying data belonging to it. Counting the number of hits alone, however, does not accurately portray the relative density of a cluster under the condition of dynamic growth, as some nodes have been in existence longer than others. In addition, over the duration of learning, different nodes may be representative of different densities due to the hierarchical nature of the partitioning process.

It turns out, that by incorporating a conscience learning (CL) mechanism [247] into each node, we can obtain an accurate density estimate that adapts with the evolving network. This mechanism works by evolving a scalar density ρ on the interval $[0, 1]$ either toward 1 or toward 0, depending on whether or not a *hit* is registered. If a winner registers a hit (or rather a match), for example, its density ρ is evolved toward 1 by a constant factor η, while at the same time all other nodes' ρ values are evolved toward 0:

$$\Delta\rho_{k*} = \eta\left(1 - \rho_{k*}\right) \tag{7.16}$$

$$\Delta\rho_j = -\eta\rho_j; j = 1, \cdots, N_c : j \neq k^*. \tag{7.17}$$

When a new node is spawned, its density is halved and distributed across both nodes; from there it will continue to adapt to the underlying data. The ρ_j term can be related to $|C_k|$ via

$$\rho_k = \frac{|C_k|}{N_s} \tag{7.18}$$

Thus, based on HME and CL information, $\text{Tr}(B)$ (Equation 2.18) can be reformulated by substituting Equation 2.23 in for $|C_k|$. Likewise, $\text{Tr}(W)$ (Equation 2.24) is related to the sum of local variances as estimated by the HMEs for each node in the network:

$$\text{Tr}(B) = \sum_{k=1}^{N_c} \rho_k N_s \cdot \|\mathbf{w}_k - \bar{w}\| \tag{7.19}$$

ALGORITHM   **173**

$$\operatorname{Tr}(W) = \sum_{k=1}^{N_c} \lambda_k. \tag{7.20}$$

Thus, a CH-type index based on HME information, CH_{SOHVM}, might be considered as

$$\text{CH}_{\text{SOHVM}} = \frac{\sum_{k=1}^{N_c} \rho_k N_s \cdot \|\mathbf{w}_k - \bar{w}\| / (N_c - 1)}{\sum_{k=1}^{N_c} \lambda_k / (N_s - N_c)} \tag{7.21}$$

In addition to CH, the GI is also well set up to work with the SOHVM model. In this case, rather than use the sum of all possible eigenvectors, as in the standard GI, a rough estimate is made using just the maximal eigenvector, which is assumed to represent the bulk of that sum. Thus a GI-type index GI_{SOHVM} might also be considered:

$$\text{GI}_{\text{SOHVM}} = \max_{1 \le k \le N_c} \frac{\left(2\sqrt{\lambda_k}\right)^2}{\min_{1 \le q \le N_c} \|\mathbf{w}_k - w_q\|_2} \tag{7.22}$$

As the network is evolved and $H(t)$ cascades down in values, the indices can be tracked for each state of the map immediately prior to each new node insertion. At some minimal $H(t)$ value, or after several consecutive insertions result in no improvement in quality according to one of these indices, map growth may be ceased. Generally, it would be advantageous to revert back to the best state seen thus far, and allow the network to re-converge (with the desired number of classes fixed) from this position.

7.3   ALGORITHM

The algorithm for generating the map is summarized in a simplified flowchart depicted in Figure 7.8. Details associated with each component are then given below.

7.3.1   Initialization, Continuation, and Presentation

The process of *initialization* begins by forming a map (M) with a single node only. The initial (root) node v_0 comprises a variance probe component and a randomly selected centroid $\mathbf{x}_0$, from X. That is to say, $\mathbf{w}_0 = \mathbf{x}_0$. The variance probe for the root node is then initialized to a unit eigenvector of random orientation and zero eigenvalue.

Presentation of each individual input involves first identifying the best matching unit (BMU) or winning prototype from within the current map. This is achieved as with the SOTM and self-organizing feature map (SOFM), by selecting the closest prototype according to some distance/similarity metric: $v_{k^*} : k^* = argmin_j \left(\mathbf{x}_i, \mathbf{w}_j\right)$;

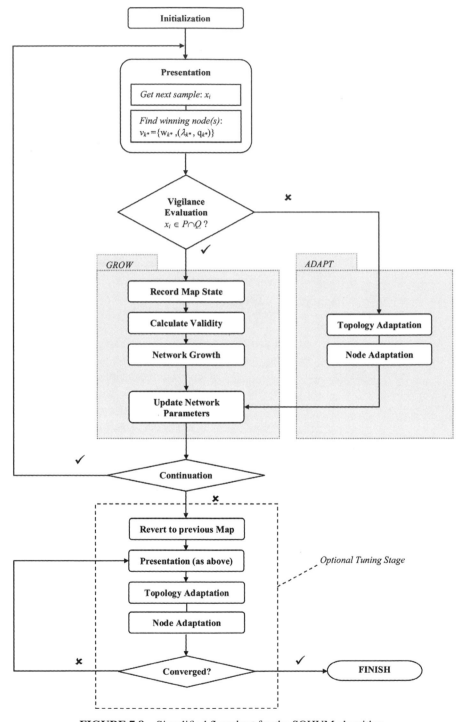

FIGURE 7.8   Simplified flowchart for the SOHVM algorithm.

ALGORITHM   **175**

(e.g., $d_j(\cdot)$ might be Euclidean). As such, all existing prototypes essentially compete for the opportunity to learn something from the input pattern, and the closest prototype (indexed by k^*) is regarded as the winning node. The current input is either used to trigger map *growth* or *adapt* the current map prototypes until some stop criterion is met. As discussed earlier, this might be due to one of either of the following.

1. A limit on the number of nodes has been reached and the map has converged.
2. A limit on the number of epochs has been reached.
3. A minimum limit on $H(t)$ has been reached and the map has converged.
4. Optional extension: A validity index has shown no improvement in the solution over a number of consecutive node insertions.

7.3.2   Updating Network Parameters

After performing any necessary growth or adaptation steps (see following sections), the network parameters are *updated* before iterating back through the continuation test to consider the next sample, where the process repeats. Network parameter updates include

1. Increment counters: iterations (per input); epochs (once every N_s iterations).
2. Decrement learning rate(s): $\alpha(t)$, (as with SOTM). We note that empirically, the HMEs tend to learn slightly more slowly than the centroids; thus, we use two different learning rates that follow the same decay schedule but are initialized differently: $\alpha_w(t)$, $\alpha_q(t)$; where $\alpha_w(0) = 0.1$, $\alpha_q(0) = 0.5$.
3. Decrement $H(t)$ (as with SOTM).
4. Calculate any changes in the map (note $|\cdot|$ denotes cardinality): ($\Delta M_i = |M_i - M_{i-1}|^2$; if $|M_i| = |M_{i-1}|$, otherwise $\Delta M_i = \infty$).

7.3.3   Vigilance Evaluation and Map Growth

The test for vigilance (i.e., that an input sample occurs within the region $P \cap Q$) is an implementation of Equations 7.10, 7.14, and (7.15) and requires that all three of the following conditions hold.

$$d\left(\mathbf{x}_i, \mathbf{w}_{k^*}\right) > H(t) \tag{7.23}$$

$$\max_{j \in \{1,\dots,N_c\}} \left(\sqrt{\lambda_j}\right) \leq d\left(\mathbf{x}_i, \mathbf{w}_{k^*}\right) \leq 3 \cdot \sqrt{\lambda_{k^*}} \tag{7.24}$$

$$\hat{x}_i' \cdot \mathbf{q}_{k^*} \geq \zeta \tag{7.25}$$

Typically, ζ is chosen such that $0 \leq \zeta \leq 1$. A value of $\zeta > 0.707$, for instance, will bias insertion toward the direction specified by $\mathbf{q}_{k^*}$. Ignoring the projection term all together will remove this constraint, causing the SOHVM to act more like an SOTM while still maintaining the property of local variance modulated vigilance.

Actual insertion follows that of the SOTM, in that a new node is formed ($k_{new} = N_c + 1$) at the location of the input sample. Additional variables used by the SOHVM as a part of its node include

1. HME element: initialized by choosing $\mathbf{q}_{k_{new}}$ as a random value on the unit circle and $\lambda_{k_{new}} = 0$.
2. The density parameter $\rho_{k_{new}} = 0$. An alternative is to halve or distribute the density of the winning node across both the winner and the new node. However, on the odd chance that the new node is a noise point (at lower levels of $H(t)$), then its density may not recover sufficiently, influencing validity indicators.
3. Insert an edge $e\left(k^*, k_{new}\right)$ of zero age, between the winner and the new node

7.3.4   Topology Adaptation

Adaptation is broken into two parts—one part for updating edges to reflect the topological status of the map and one part for refining node prototype information.

An essential step in adapting prototypes is the estimation of underlying topology. In the SOHVM, this is achieved through a combination of SOTM tree links, and an adaptive CHL mechanism. The SOTM process of inserting a new node and attaching it to the winning node tends to form a tree structure as depicted earlier. Over time, however, such a tree may lose significance in lower branches—clusters may have been disassociated before enough information was known.

The SOHVM attempts to maintain the tree hierarchy early but gradually allows this condition to be relaxed as new associations take shape later in the evolution of the network. The hierarchical structure is important during evolution as it helps the SOHVM to efficiently span the data across all phases of network resolution. CHL is used in combination with the SOTM linkage, in order to force some rigidity of structure initially, that over time is gradually relaxed and modified by the underlying distribution.

Specifically, we employ an edge aging scheme similar to that used in the GNG algorithm, where the edges e_k are either inserted during growth, or formed in M once we have more than one node in the map: $|V| > 1$. With each $\mathbf{x}_i$ presented to the system,

1. Select the two closest nodes to $\mathbf{x}_i : k^*, k_2^*$ such that

$$d\left(\mathbf{x}_i, \mathbf{w}_{k^*}\right) \le d\left(\mathbf{x}_i, \mathbf{w}_{k_2^*}\right) \le d\left(\mathbf{x}_i, \mathbf{w}_j\right) : \forall_j, j \ne k^*, j \ne k_2^*. \quad (7.26)$$

2. If $\sim \exists$ an edge $e\left(k^*, k_2^*\right) \in E$ (i.e., no edge between nodes), then add a new edge $e\left(k^*, k_2^*\right)$ to E.
3. Reset the age of the existing (or newly formed) edge e to zero: $Age\left(e\right) = 0$.
4. Age all edges emanating from k^* (increment ages by 1).

5. After each adaptation phase, edges in the network above a certain limit Age_{max} are removed, leaving a skeleton of only the most relevant associations currently in the network.

7.3.5   Node Adaptation

Once the winner has been chosen as the best representative for $\mathbf{x}_i$, and node generation is deemed unnecessary by the vigilance test, information is then imparted to the network by updating both the winning node $v_{k^*} = \{\mathbf{w}_{k^*}, (\lambda_{k^*}, \mathbf{q}_{k^*})\}$ and selected neighbors, as indicated by the adapting topology. This involves two major steps: updating the node's position $\mathbf{w}_{k^*}$; and second, the node's variance probe $(\lambda_{k^*}, \mathbf{q}_{k^*})$. The winner's center $\mathbf{w}_{k^*}$ and its topological neighbors $\mathbf{w}_{nbr(k^*)}$ are updated using

$$\mathbf{w}_{k^*}(n+1) = \mathbf{w}_{k^*}(n) + \alpha_w(t)\left[\mathbf{x}_i \mathbf{w}_{k^*}(n)\right] \tag{7.27}$$

$$\mathbf{w}_{nbr(k^*)}(n+1) = \mathbf{w}_{nbr(k^*)}(n) + \alpha_{nbr}\left[\mathbf{x}_i \mathbf{w}_{nbr(k^*)}(n)\right] \tag{7.28}$$

where k^* is the index of the winning prototype, and $0 \leq \alpha_{nbr} \ll \alpha_w(t) \leq 1$ are neighborhood and winning node learning rates respectively. $\alpha_w(t)$ decays exponentially with each iteration from an initial value (~ 0.1) and is reset as new nodes are spawned to foster local plasticity in the map. Associative learning (α_{nbr}) is fixed at a relatively low rate (~ 0.0005).

To adapt the winning node's HME, the coordinate system is then translated to the frame of reference centered on $\mathbf{w}_{k^*}$, as described in Section 7.2.2. The relevant update calculations are thus given in Equations 7.10–7.13.

7.3.6   Optional Tuning Stage

In the optional tuning stage, no node growth is permitted, and the above adaptation rules are implemented until convergence or an epoch limit is reached, after first reverting back to the previous state of the network (i.e., the hierarchy of previous states) deemed *most valid* by the validity indicators: CH_{SOVHM} and GI_{SOVHM}.

7.4   SIMULATIONS AND EVALUATION

In the remainder of this chapter, the results of a number of simulations were conducted on synthetic 2D datasets, each consisting of a series of Gaussian-based clusters in 2D input space, of varying density, size, and separation. Visual comparisons are made between both dynamic and static unsupervised architectures; and between more closely related self-organizing-based models. Through such, the basic properties of the SOHVM are highlighted. The results in this section are by no means meant to be comprehensive, rather illustrative. A more detailed analysis on both synthetic and real world data is provided at the end of this chapter, where the cluster validity

TABLE 7.1   Table of Parameters and Initial Values for the SOHVM Algorithm

Category	Parameter	Initial	Description
Learning rates			
	$\alpha_w(0)$	**0.1**	Initial *winning* centroid learning rate
	α_{Nbr}	0.0005	Neighbouring centroids learning rate
	$\alpha_q(0)$	0.5	Initial *winning* HME learning rate
	η	0.001	Conscience learning factor
Time constants			
	τA	**floor(0.5N_s)**	Decay rate for learning: $\alpha_w(t)$, $\alpha q(t)$
	τH	2N_s	Decay rate for $H(t)$
	$\tau Hstep$	**floor(0.25N_s)**	Period for stepped $H(t)$ decay
Hierarchical control			
	$H(0)$	**8,σ_{Xt}**	Initial $H(t)$
	H_∞	$Hf\sigma_{Xt}$	Minimum limit for $H(t)$
	H_f	**0.1**	Minimum limit factor for $H(t)$
Edge ageing			
	eAgeMax	floor(0.1 N_s)	Age above which edges are removed
General			
	epochsMax	**20**	Upper limit on presentations of X_T
	NcMax	**100**	Upper limit on nodes allowed
	$\Delta mapTol$	**0.001**	Tolerance for map convergence
	ζ	0.9	Projection factor used in HMEs

indices introduced in Chapter 2 are used to assess the relative performance of different algorithms.

For most of the simulations, unless otherwise specified, the SOHVM was run using the network parameters shown in Table 7.1, many of which are built-in and based on the size and general properties of the training set and would not typically be required as input by the user. These parameters were thus found to work across a variety of different datasets. If more control is desired, this is typically exercised through the user's selection of H_∞. Unlike imposing the number of clusters, choosing H_∞ provides a more objective and natural parameter to adjust, one that will produce an appropriate number of clusters based on the data itself. Of course, the SOHVM does incorporate a self-stopping mechanism, however, is not limited to use in that mode of operation alone. Note also, that some parameters, such as this, are shared in common with the SOTM. Where this occurs, both algorithms are run using the same values.

7.4.1   Observations of Evolution and Partitioning

In the first simulation, we observe the partitioning process of the SOHVM, which is demonstrated for two synthetic 2D datasets: *synth2D-A* and *synth2D-D*, in Figures 7.9 and 7.10, respectively. Both sets of data contain clusters of differing densities, with *synth2D-A* containing different-sized clusters also.

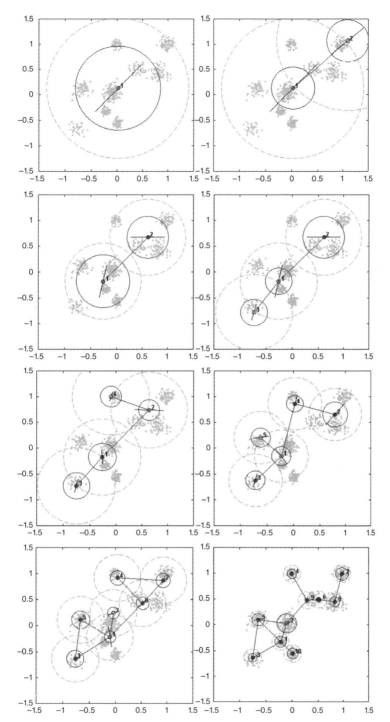

FIGURE 7.9 An example of SOHVM evolution on the dataset *synth2D-A*. Progression follows from right to left, top to bottom. Broken circles represent H(t) w.r.t. each centroid. The axis through each centroid represents the adaptive Hebbian Maximal Eigenfilter (or principal eigenvector/eigenvalue), and the closed circles represent cluster density.

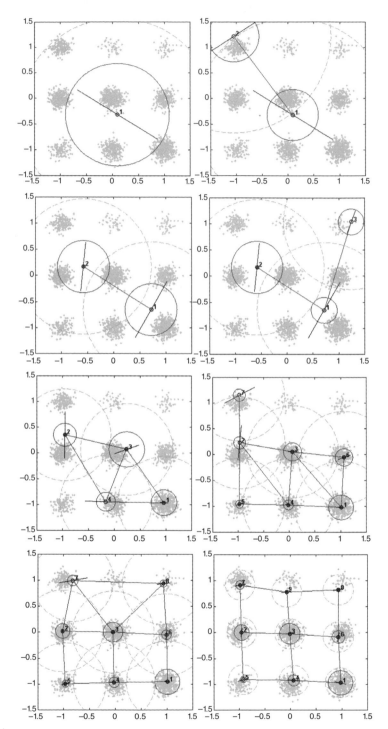

FIGURE 7.10 An example of SOHVM evolution on the dataset *synth2D-D*. Progression follows from right to left, top to bottom. As with Figure 7.9, the SOHVM focuses on revealing primary regions of inferred density. Hebbian Maximal Eigenfilters axes can be seen to extend as *feelers*, probing into unknown regions before considering insertion.

There are two key properties to observe from these samples. The first is that the local variances (HME properties) are represented by the axes plotted through each node (cluster centroid). The SOHVM is shown just prior to node insertion, where the nodes are numbered in increasing order as new nodes are generated. From the figures, it is clear that the HMEs adapt to the local regions of the input space, as it is gradually partitioned across newly inserted nodes.

The orientations and size of the local variances impact node insertion such that priority is given to the discovery of the more dominant parts of the underlying distribution. In Figure 7.10 this is especially evident, as the spread of density along the diagonal is revealed early. The process also biases the maximal separation of this density before considering smaller or more local separations. This is indicative of the hierarchical nature of the partitioning process. In addition, it is interesting to note that once a new node is dispatched to a local region, the HME component is able to reach out much like a *feeler* or *tentacle* to probe the local region of which it has now been made aware. In doing so, it is soon able to trigger any necessary insertions. Insertions also may lead an existing node to reassess its local region (as impacted by growth in another part of the map). Such interactions also work to allow the map to explore and adapt to new sites of possible density.

7.4.2 Visual Comparisons with Popular Mean-Squared Error Architectures

In this test, preliminary comparisons are conducted between SOHVM and some popular static methods: *K-Means* (KM) [28, 29], *Fuzzy C-Means* (FCM) [32], and advanced FCM variants *Gustafson–Kessel* (GK) [33] and *Gath–Geva* (GG) [35] (discussed in Chapter 2). Such methods find extreme popularity in the clustering literature. On a number of test runs, limiting the number of clusters in the search to nine, we find clues as to the possible inconsistencies in such models, as have been indicated in Chapter 3. This is also explored further in Section 7.6.

In Figure 7.11, the goal was to gain some level of insight into the efficiency of allocation (cluster representation) offered through the SOHVM against methods even when the user supplies such *a priori* information regarding the desired number of clusters in the data.

Density contours were projected over the cluster results using tools from Reference 248. As shown, SOHVM appears to locate a more reasonable set of cluster positions. Fuzzy methods such as GK and GG do demonstrate some propensity toward capturing elongated and different-shaped regions, and show sensitivity to a possible (perceived) overlapping cluster in the mid top right. This is, however, at the expense of intuitively obvious clusters in the mid lower region. Furthermore, GK and GG operate following an FCM initialization, yet still do not resolve two clusters in the lower central region. FCM and KM on the other hand remain quite sensitive to initialization of cluster centers, and it is often left to the user to decide when an appropriate solution is found.

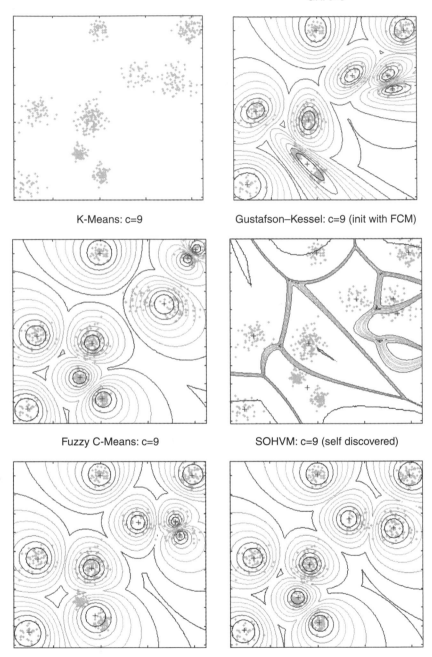

FIGURE 7.11 Comparison of SOHVM with popular static clustering methods. This figure overlays a Fuzzy Sammon mapping (contours are through data points that share a common fuzzy membership to a given cluster). The SOHVM demonstrates good efficiency in allocating nodes to perceived clusters and does so without knowledge of an appropriate total number of classes into which it should cluster. The top left shows the original synthetic dataset *synth2D-A*, consisting of nine clusters of unequal density and size. A predefined total of nine target clusters was supplied as an input for the other methods.

7.4.3 Visual Comparison Against Growing Neural Gas

In Figure 7.12, performance of the SOHVM against GNG is demonstrated for the datasets *synth2D-A* and *synth2D-D*. In this figure, additional blue lines represent major Voronoi class boundaries. It is apparent that GNG operates from the inside out—a skeletal backbone grows from an initial state of two nodes, in an error-driven manner, gradually attempting to fill out the data space. Regular insertion of nodes and their insertion between two existing nodes (along an existing edge) tend to lead to proliferation of prototypes, even with a possible error limit as a stopping criterion. An appropriate error value for a given dataset must be known *a priori*, or must account for all the sized clusters in the data, otherwise some dense clusters will be forced to subdivide prior to all clusters being found. Later phases of the GNG show that by the time all clusters are finally discovered, previous clusters have been compromised.

By contrast, the SOHVM quickly spans the entire dataset by initially favoring insertion at the extremities of Global maximal variance, then in progressively more localized orientations. Clusters most distant from one another are thus discovered earlier. This gives a more hierarchical breakdown of clusters, and consequently, across all stages in its evolution, gives a more faithful representation of the underlying topology of the input space. In this experiment, both models were allowed to continue indefinitely and were manually stopped at the point where each had located all dense regions.

7.4.4 Comparing Hierarchical with Tree-Based Methods

In the following tests, the SOHVM is compared with the more similar SOTM, under the condition that for each test run, different limits be imposed on the minimum value of $H(t)$: controlled as a factor of the standard deviation of the training set $\sigma(X_T)$. Sample results from two datasets are considered in Figures 7.13 and 7.14.

In both figures, we notice that the early stages for both the SOTM and SOHVM are quite similar in terms of node positioning, with the exception that the SOHVM has a more adaptive sense of topology as expected—in fact, for the SOHVM, the order in which inputs are presented has less of an effect on topology than in the SOTM. At smaller values of $H(t)$, however, differences begin to surface.

The SOTM shows sensitivity to outliers at small $H(t)$, as can be seen for $H(\infty) = 0.5\sigma(X)$, $H(\infty) = 0.25\sigma(X)$ in both figures. SOTM tends to spawn new nodes in outlier positions too readily; thus, they quickly become trapped and impact the competition between other nodes. In Figure 7.14, in particular, clusters are quite noisy and dispersed; thus the impact is far more profound.

The SOTM therefore appears to maintain efficiency more so in lower coarse grain resolution, higher levels in the partitioning hierarchy. The SOHVM is far more conservative in this regard, maintaining cluster integrity down to much smaller values of $H(t)$. One might speculate from such, that the SOHVM demonstrates improved ability to generalize or smooth over noisy clusters compared with the SOTM, particularly at finer scales of resolution in the space being partitioned.

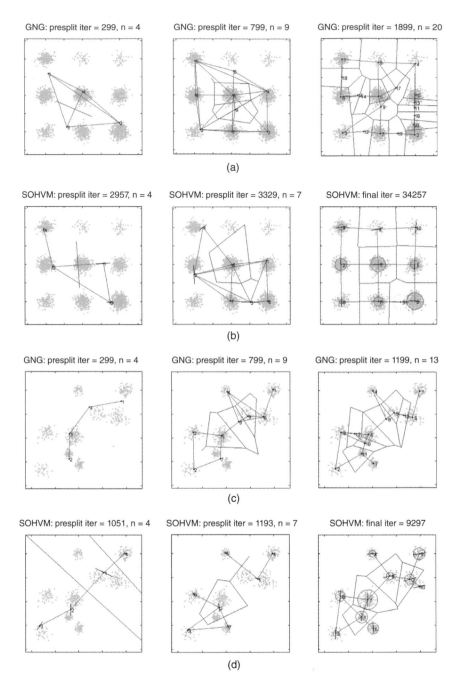

FIGURE 7.12 Visual comparison of Growing Neural Gas (GNG) vs. the SOHVM evolution. GNG (a, c) evolves from the inside out onto data space but splits prematurely, well before capturing all cluster positions. The rightmost image for (a, c) shows the point where GNG has discovered all dense regions; however, node insertion leads to premature subdivision. SOHVM (b, d) maximally spans the data space early through hierarchical partitioning also forming a more faithful or intuitive topological representation of the data across insertions. While GNG is effective for capturing topology, it does not place a priority on the location of valid clusters as does SOHVM.

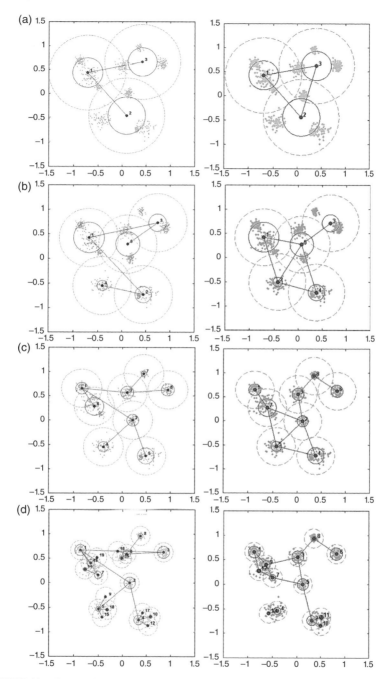

FIGURE 7.13 Comparison of SOHVM with SOTM, demonstrating reduction in node proliferation at low $H(t)$. SOTM (left) vs. SOHVM (right), for equivalent settings of $H(\infty)$ top to bottom: (a) $H(\infty) = \alpha(X)$; (b) $H(\infty) = 0.75\alpha(X)$; (c) $H(\infty) = 0.5\alpha(X)$; (d) $H(\infty) = 0.25\alpha(X)$. Both strategies act quite similar at earlier stages of evolution; however, the SOHVM maintains relevant topological connections throughout. At low resolutions of $H(t)$, the SOTM shows more sensitivity to noise and outliers. Broken circles represent $H(t)$, while closed circles represent densities ρ_k. Dataset = *synth2D-B*.

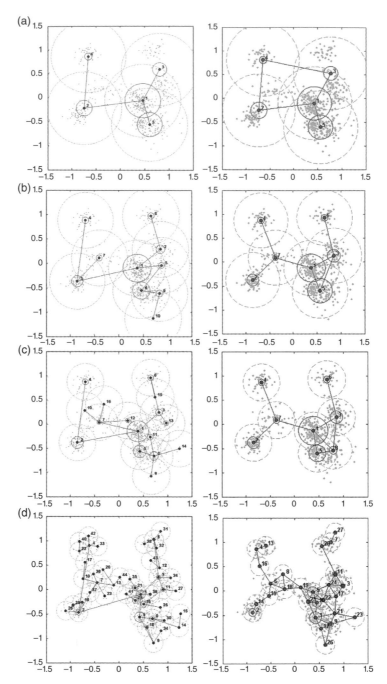

FIGURE 7.14 Comparison of SOHVM with SOTM—independent runs to completion, demonstrating reduction in node proliferation at low $H(t)$. SOTM (left) vs. SOHVM (right), for equivalent settings of $H(\infty)$ top to bottom: (a) $H(\infty) = \alpha(X)$; (b) $H(\infty) = 0.75\alpha(X)$; (c) $H(\infty) = 0.5\alpha(X)$; (d) $H(\infty) = 0.25\alpha(X)$. Both strategies act quite similar at earlier stages of evolution; however, the SOHVM maintains relevant topological connections throughout. At low resolutions of $H(t)$, the SOTM shows more sensitivity to noise and outliers. Broken circles represent $H(t)$, while closed circles represent densities ρ_k. Dataset = *synth2D-C*.

7.5   TESTS ON SELF-DETERMINATION AND THE OPTIONAL TUNING STAGE

In the final simulation, the optional stop condition is briefly considered, and a comparison drawn between the SOTM and the SOHVM (with and without the optional stop), under the scenario that all models are resolved down to a $H(t)$ of a very low limit of $0.1\sigma(X_t)$.

As can be seen from Figures 7.15 and 7.16, the CH_{SOHVM} mechanism for estimating the number of clusters works quite well. This is perhaps due to the fact that the CH measure fits in well with the information supplied by the HMEs. An alternative $CH2_{SOHVM}$ index was also considered. This version incorporated the density parameter into the calculation of the $Tr(W)$ term in Equation 7.20. This measure for the most part mimics CH_{SOHVM}, however, is degraded occasionally with increasing N_c. GI_{SOHVM} shows equal promise; however, it was not in exact agreement with CH_{SOHVM}. In this experiment, the condition to stop and switch to the refinement stage was made if the number of consecutive nodes inserted exceeds three without improving the quality measure. For all datasets, the clustering solution achieved appears to be both intuitive and a desirable improvement over both the SOHVM standard and SOTM models.

7.6   CLUSTER VALIDITY ANALYSIS ON SYNTHETIC AND UCI DATA

In this section, a comparison is conducted between the SOHVM, SOTM, SOFM under various configurations, KM, FCM, and the Gaussian Mixture Model (GMM). The reason for selecting this subset of models is that they are all related in terms of identifying similar types of clusters in the data, under the loose assumption of Euclidean style similarity metrics. Agglomerative or binary-tree forming hierarchical methods are not included due to heuristic-driven pruning needed to obtain comparable clustered groupings.

The goal here is to evaluate the regularity and quality with which the SOHVM model is able to provide useful partitions of the data space and how readily its solutions lead to accurate identification of an optimal number of clusters in the data.

In these simulations, four alternative cluster indices (Xie Beni (XB), I-index, CH, and GI) are considered in their pure forms (see chapter 2), which for some, require that the data itself be used in the calculation. As such the analysis is conducted a posteriori to cluster formation. As both the SOHVM and SOTM models are constructive in nature, we constrain experiments such that these models are operated in a relatable fixed mode (i.e., with imposed limits on either the vigilance threshold or the maximum number of clusters to seek). They still remain generative, however, in the sense that clusters are allocated dynamically throughout the course of learning. Each algorithm is run over a series of 20 trials, such that the variability in solutions and the impact of clustering method on cluster quality/optimality may be evaluated.

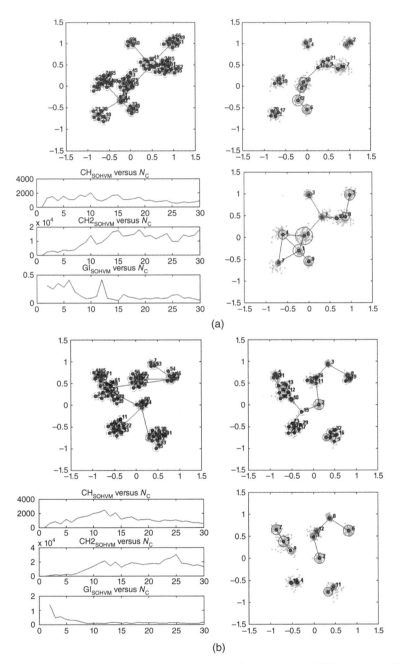

FIGURE 7.15 SOHVM automatic cluster selection for datasets *synth2D-A* and *synth2D-B*: (a) *synth2D-A*; (b) *synth2D-B*. SOHVM automatic cluster selection: SOTM (top left); SOHVM (top right); SOHVM with refinement (bottom right); SOHVM-based validity measures (bottom left): CH$_{\text{SOHVM}}$ used for N_c selection.

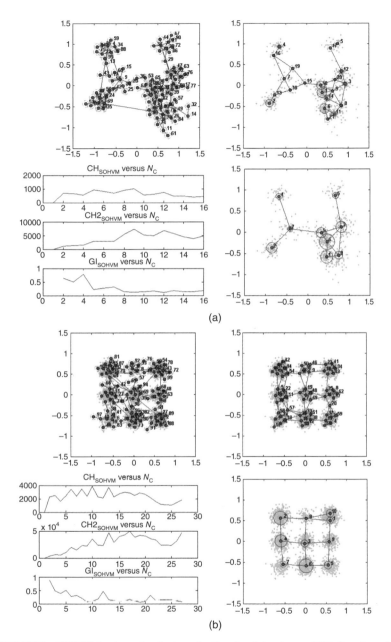

FIGURE 7.16 SOHVM automatic cluster selection for datasets *synth2D-C* and *synth2D-E*: (a) *synth2D-C*; (b) *synth2D-E*. SOTM (top left); SOHVM (top right); SOHVM with refinement (bottom right); SOHVM-based validity measures: CH$_{SOHVM}$ used for N_c selection.

Three datasets are considered in the following experiments: one synthetic test case (*synth2D-A*) and two popular multidimensional real-world datasets from the UCI repository of Machine Learning Databases [249]: *IRIS* and *WINE*. *IRIS* contains 3 classes of 50 instances each, where each class refers to a type of plant. One class is linearly separable from the other, two are not linearly separable from each other. Each sample is defined with four features: $x_1 =$ sepal length (cm); $x_2 =$ sepal width (cm); $x_3 =$ petal length (cm); and $x_4 =$ petal width (cm). The WINE dataset contains samples from the chemical analysis of 178 wine samples grown in the same region in Italy. Each sample has 13 continuous features derived from the chemical analysis.

7.6.1   Performance vs. Popular Clustering Methods

For a fixed number of clusters N_c, a series of 20 separate trials were run for each algorithm, each consisting of K individual runs of each algorithm, each time for a new value of $N_c = 1 \cdots K$. The mean of each index over the 20 trials was plotted against N_c, and is shown in Figure 7.17(a, c, and e). The objective of these graphs is to depict the average quality of the clustering result for each algorithm, given the imposed constraint of N_c. In all four indices (XB, I-index, CH, and GI), the SOHVM shows the best average quality and appears to favor $N_c = 9$ as an optimum.

Comparisons are made between the SOTM and the SOHVM for individual traces of test runs in Figure 7.18, where the arrows indicate the most common path taken by each algorithm. The SOHVM appears to have more consistency. This is mirrored also in cluster selection histograms of Figure 7.17(b, d, and f), where the frequency with which individual trial runs (considered in isolation) predict N_c is shown. The SOHVM selects $N_c = 9$ the most consistently of all models tested and shows minor indecision restricted to ± 1 cluster. The SOTM also performs better than the other models, however, not quite as consistently as the SOHVM. GMM, KM, and FCM give much lower quality readings at the optimal N_c than both SOTM and SOHVM. This is likely due to inconsistent placement of cluster centers between individual runs of these algorithms. Figure 7.17(b, d, and f) reflects this, depicting more radical predictions of an optimal N_c in both the GMM and FCM. This may corroborate the tendency for such algorithms to become more easily trapped in local minima. Interestingly, FCM appears to exhibit indecision, albeit over a smaller range about the optimum. It is conjectured that Self-Organization, through its inherent reliance on associative learning and sharing of information between prototypes, in fact, emulates to a certain extent, a form of nonlinear generalization that might be considered similar in many ways to the fuzzy boundaries inherent in FCM.

It is also noted (in Fig. 7.17), that two SOFM configurations were considered, $\text{SOFM}_{K \times 1}$ and $\text{SOFM}_{M \times N}$, due to the difficulty in forming a lattice when N_c is a prime number. The $\text{SOFM}_{M \times N}$ configuration attempts to make the lattice as square as possible, given the value of N_c, for example, $N_c = 9$ would use a 3×3 lattice, $N_c = 10$ would use a 2×5 lattice. For prime values of N_c, $\text{SOFM}_{M \times N}$ reverts to the same configuration as $\text{SOFM}_{K \times 1}$. This explains the occasionally erratic performance of $\text{SOFM}_{M \times N}$, which can be accounted for by the topological mismatch between the imposed lattice and the underlying data. In fact this is an indication of why the

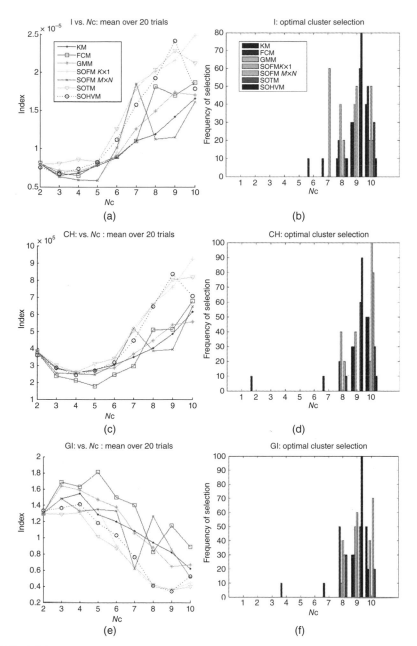

FIGURE 7.17 Average cluster validity index values for different choices of N_c, over 20 trials for the dataset *synth2D A*. From right to left, top to bottom. (a) I-index; (c) Calinski–Harabasz (CH) index; (e) Geometric index (GI). This set of indices appears to be more reliable, in that a number of algorithms exhibit a more obvious maximum/minimum. Quality at the optimum for SOHVM is shown to be superior over the course of the trials.

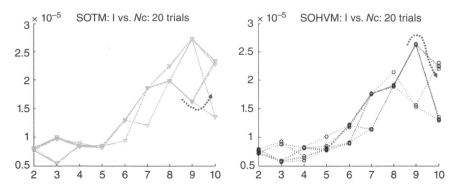

FIGURE 7.18   Explicit traces of the I-index for individual trials of the SOTM and SOHVM, for cluster validity calculations on *synth2D-A*. In terms of actual paths, SOHVM (right) has 80% passing through maximum at $N_c = 9$, while SOTM (left) shows roughly 40% traversing the alternate route (indicating by arrows), leading to $N_c = 10$.

dynamic topology in the SOHVM is an important feature. SOTM and $SOFM_{K \times 1}$ are quite flexible in terms of topology due to their configuration, and their solutions appear to follow SOHVM well in terms of quality; however, according to the CH index, for example (widely considered as giving most accurate performance), $SOFM_{K \times 1}$ consistently considers N_c to be 10, while the SOTM is more undecided: $9 < N_c < 10$.

To further evaluate the variability exhibited by each algorithm, we look to Figure 7.19, which depicts statistical box-plots of the variation in CH index for each algorithm over the course of the 20 trials depicted in Figure 7.17. In this figure, KM and FCM both show far greater variability in the quality of solutions for different N_c, particularly, around the true $N_c = 9$ and hence can be quite arbitrary when attempting to choose an optimal N_c. GMM shows more variability than self-organizing models, yet appears to settle more than KM and FCM around $N_c = 9$, although shows many outliers. SOFM models show some variability at or near the optimum. SOTM and SOHVM show low variability up to the optimum; SOHVM has reduced outliers. Along with quality levels, SOHVM shows strongest response to optimal cluster configurations for *synth2D-A*.

7.6.2   IRIS Dataset

Results of analysis with IRIS are depicted in Figure 7.20. The I-index appears to be the most accurate in terms of all models for predicting the optimal $N_c = 3$, while GI only predicts $N_c = 3$ for some SOTM and SOHVM solutions. The GI also shows that SOTM and SOHVM solutions are of better average quality. One possible reason for why the SOTM continues to improve in terms of the GI might be its heightened sensitivity to noise at low vigilance thresholds. The I-index appears to be more useful for situations of extreme overlap existing in data such as the IRIS set, where 2 classes are linearly inseparable—note that FCM demonstrates a high response along with

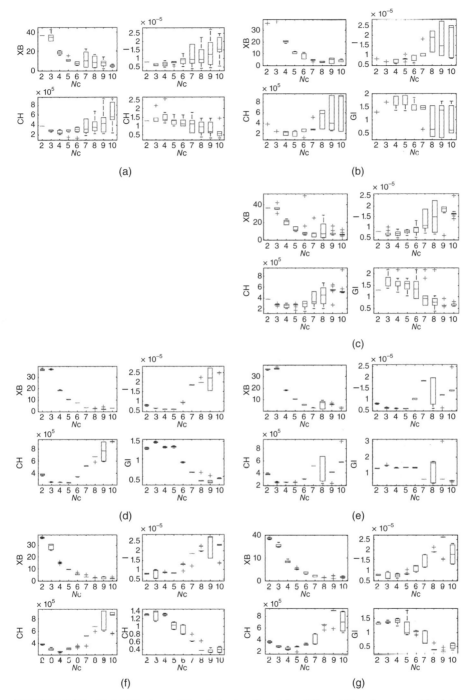

FIGURE 7.19 Variability in quality of clusters found for different N_c values over 20 trials, for dataset *synth2D-A*: (a) KM; (b) FCM; (c) GMM; (d) SOFM$_{K\times1}$; (e) SOFM$_{M\times N}$; (f) SOTM; (g) SOHVM.

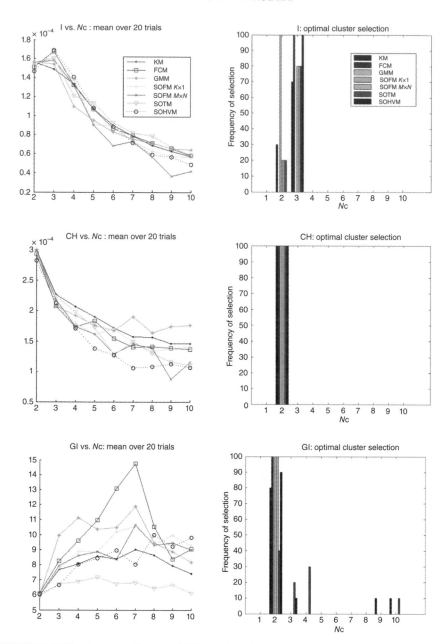

FIGURE 7.20 Average cluster validities and optimal cluster selection histograms for the IRIS dataset.

SOHVM at the optimum. Again, in general, SOTM and SOHVM exhibit higher average quality than the other algorithms tested.

7.6.3 WINE Dataset

With the WINE dataset, the SOHVM is considered in fully automatic mode. A simple comparison is made against KM, and evaluated on the basis of local (LCE) and Global (GCE) consistency errors in the solutions (see Appendix A). Such errors are generally used to assess the relative consistency between two alternative segmentation solutions (often used in image segmentation), under the condition where the number of separate clusters in each solution is not necessarily guaranteed to be the same, nor is there any viable method of matching clusters across both solutions. LCE and GCE are based upon defining a local refinement error (LRE), which expresses an error in terms of a weighting of how many samples (feature vectors) are not common between the two clusters it belongs to in each solution versus the size of a cluster. LCE then considers the average minimal refinement error between the two solutions, over all samples. Globally, GCE looks at the minimum cumulative refinement errors over all pixels in each pairing of clusters and averages this over all clusters.

The WINE dataset represents a high dimensional feature space, with 3 classes expected. Figure 7.21 shows the relative LCE and GCE errors of the SOHVM classification versus KM, where KM is run three times (KM1, KM2, and KM3) with the number of classes preselected, $K = 1, 2$, and 3, respectively. The bottom graph shows that the SOHVM automatically selects the optimal cluster number $N_c = 3$ on 8/20 trials, and within ± 1 cluster 18/20 times. The graphs above show that the relative errors in classification performed on the original data (according to known labels), compares favorably with KM results for similar K values. KM also shows one outlier where it seems to have converged to a nonoptimal configuration of cluster centers (even though K was chosen as 3 before running the algorithm). SOHVM shows favorable integrity in terms of classification in cases where N_c was overestimated.

7.7 SUMMARY

The framework and justification for a novel dynamic clustering technique: the Self-Organizing Hierarchical Variance Map was introduced. The new model retains some of the useful properties of the SOTM algorithm, in terms of conducting a hierarchical search and partitioning strategy over the input space. In the SOHVM, however, this is achieved through the consideration of cascading local variance maxima. The local variances are mapped along with the cluster centroid, by a dual-element, nonstationary perceptron. The component responsible for mapping local variance information is known as a Hebbian Maximal Eigenfilter, which, through a Hebbian-style learning rule, causes a simple perceptron to extract the maximal principal component from the space of patterns with which it is presented.

Incorporating the HME as the key feature in a self-organizing tree-based framework, a novel architecture and insertion strategy was proposed and justified. In

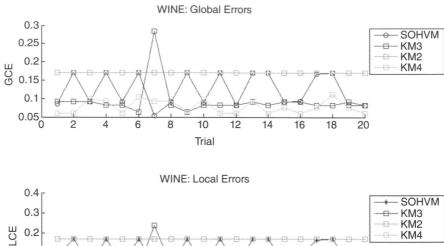

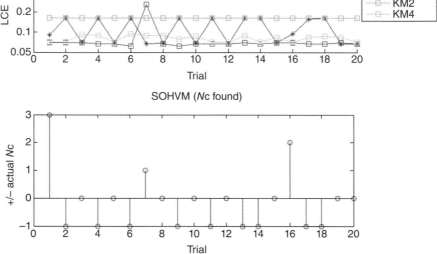

FIGURE 7.21   Global (GCE) and local (LCE) consistency errors during SOHVM classification of WINE data samples into similar clusters over 20 trials, according to a labeled ground truth set of clusters ($K=3$); (top) GCE; (middle) LCE; (bottom) error in number of clusters SOHVM selects as optimal over 20 trial runs.

essence, node insertion works to bias the location of inserted nodes into regions of known density; thus in comparison to the SOTM, map growth is more of an *informed* rather than *blind* process.

Visual experiments were conducted outlining the parsing process of the SOHVM, and a variety of other features and benefits as compared with the more popular clustering models from the literature. Specifically though, the SOHVM shows promise in achieving a more intuitive, efficient breakdown of feature space over the SOTM and other models and also demonstrates some propensity toward estimating an appropriate number of clusters at runtime.

CHAPTER 8

Microbiological Image Analysis Using Self-Organization

In this chapter, the potential and flexibility of self-organizing tree map (SOTM) based and Self-Organizing Hierarchical Variance Map (SOHVM) based learning are considered for tasks in microbiological image analysis. Approaches are first suggested for how the SOTM may be adapted to address issues such as how to fuse information effectively across both intensity and spatial domains to better extract image structure. The SOTM is then applied to the more specific problem of elucidating structures inherent within heterogeneous microbiological images. The SOHVM, introduced Chapter 7, is then explored as a more consistent mechanism for building a compact and functional description of the input space for microbiological image segmentation.

The argument presented is that knowledge of both clusters and their intercluster relationships (topological associations) extracted by the SOHVM, can further assist in analysis or post-processing tasks. Performance of the SOHVM is explored in the context of two problems: one of inferring a suitable multilevel thresholding to isolate the constituents of complex, heterogeneous biofilm images; and one for the extraction of chromosomes from phase-enhanced confocal images. As a demonstration of the SOHVM's ability to mine topological information from an input space, the chapter concludes with an example for how such information can be used to simplify the task of visualizing a large three-dimensional (3D) stack of phase-contrast acquired plant chromosomes imaged during an advanced state of mitosis (cell division).

8.1 IMAGE ANALYSIS IN THE BIOSCIENCES

Microscopy has long been considered an essential investigative tool in the biosciences, affording a unique visual avenue through which the biologist may probe more deeply into the vast, yet relatively untapped microbiological landscape. Although microscopy has been around in developing forms for over a century, its primary function has

Unsupervised Learning: A Dynamic Approach, First Edition.
Matthew Kyan, Paisarn Muneesawang, Kambiz Jarrah, and Ling Guan.
© 2014 by The Institute of Electrical and Electronics Engineers, Inc. Published by John Wiley & Sons, Inc.

remained as an observational, rather than rigorous analytical tool. In the last two decades, however, significant advances in the fields of computer hardware, digital image processing, physical optics, and genetic engineering have combined in dramatic fashion to revolutionize this notion and, along with it, the world of biological research [250]. As it stands today, microscopy is rapidly becoming the biologist's research tool of choice, with the growing realization that, over and above the improved abilities to see, comes newfound opportunity to extract more quantitative information regarding the physical and chemical structure of biospecimens and their environments.

Confocal Laser Scanning Microscopy (CLSM), in particular, is one of the many recent bioimaging technologies that have helped usher in this new era, through its ability to produce a highly resolved 3D description of biological specimens. Often used in conjunction with conventional (CM) and electron microscopy (EM), CLSM technologies have the added bonus of being able to collect multiple, high resolution channels of information corresponding to specific biochemical markers that assist in isolating and rendering specific properties of a specimen [251]. Confocal modalities enable this information to be captured in a simultaneous and noninvasive, *in situ* manner [252]. As such, living specimens may be observed in their natural states. This has profound implications for improving the understanding of true structure, dynamics, and function of living organisms embedded within their complex ecologies.

Microscopy data, in general, shares a number of characteristics in common with data from the fields of medical imaging (e.g., macroscopic imaging of tissues and structures: CT, Ultrasound, MRI) and geophysical imaging (e.g., satellite, remote sensing, seismic data):

- extremely high bandwidth, high resolution data, often volumetric in nature and may involve multiple channels;
- typically collected for exploratory research and analysis, thus lacks reference to a suitable ground truth description (emphasized more so in microscopy);
- requires intensive, meticulous, and tedious interpretation by the professional observer (biologist, physician, radiologist, or geologist) to assess, diagnose, and segment data before computerized analysis can proceed;
- the collection of large datasets is occurring at a high rate, and thus, prompts the need for faster and more computerized approaches to annotation and description for the purpose of computer-assisted visualization, characterization, archiving, and retrieval.

8.1.1 Segmentation: The Common Denominator

A crucial first stage to the *automation* of tasks such as visualization, characterization, analysis, and archiving is the ability to formulate suitable separation of imaged specimens into materials of interest (MOI). For instance, if an image is acquired from a sample of bacteria embedded in a conglomerate of other bio-materials, then it becomes useful to extract or separate the image information relating to bacteria of interest from the other materials present or, even further, to separate different materials deemed present from one another within the image. This process is termed *image segmentation.*

Armed with a segmented dataset, the process of isolating and measuring properties of the different materials becomes more tractable. Furthermore, by identifying different characteristic materials present, it becomes possible to measure and draw conclusions about how the different materials relate to one another both structurally and dynamically. For instance, we may notice that a set of small bacteria tend to form or conglomerate in regions of high concentration of some specific biochemical or certain other species may tend to form a degree of symbiosis under certain conditions. These are the types of questions that biologists can ask and then proceed to better *quantify* if armed with the 3D spatial representation of physicochemical information possible with today's microscope technologies.

8.1.2 Semi-supervised versus Unsupervised Analysis

In the absence of prior knowledge regarding a particular biological specimen under investigation, biologists are often forced to *manually* generate their own segmentation by labeling/marking individual pixels, voxels (volumetric pixel), or sets of voxels. As one might expect, when dealing with extremely heterogeneous, complex images, this process can become extremely tedious. Furthermore, it becomes very subjective, often leading to interoperator variance. One might imagine a situation in which a whole series of ensuing measurements are taken on the basis of a user-driven segmentation. Seemingly slight interoperator variances can very easily translate into quite marked differences in quantitative results. To alleviate tedium, *computer-assisted* segmentation is heavily relied upon [253].

The development of automated tools to assist in the segmentation process can be divided into two categories: *semi-supervised* and *unsupervised*. In semi-supervised approaches, the user has control over some key property of the tool and through its manipulation is able to make simple adjustments until satisfied that key features of interest have been labeled appropriately. The most common example of this used in bioimaging is simple foreground/background thresholding, where the user manipulates an intensity level (threshold) for the image data, and voxels above an intensity threshold are separated from those below.

Similarly, a user may define multiple threshold ranges (*multilevel thresholding*), over an intensity profile or histogram, in order to separate content. In other, more advanced tools, the user may select a number of voxels relating to material(s) of interest, wherein an algorithm seeks to identify a relationship between the chosen samples and uses this to partition all remaining voxels. This has been used, for instance, in color segmentation studies of bacterial species [253, 254], and extensive methods are available in the general image processing literature—some of the more popular approaches include deformable contours and meshes [255], region growing [256], and the more recently successful graphcut methods [257]. Of course, if a priori information is available (e.g., regarding the nature, size, shape of the specimen imaged), it may be embedded into such algorithms to improve their performance.

In unsupervised approaches, no user-centered labeling or a priori information is used. One reason may be that the samples of data are in a high dimension (as is the case in multichannel microscope data) and might escape intuition for how a reasonable segmentation should proceed. Another reason might be that the user may not wish to impose a perceived relationship on the data and would rather that any relationships be mined from the data automatically—this equates to the notion of *data mining*. The idea here is that some natural relationship discovered in the data might become useful for its subsequent classification and analysis. This presents an attractive option for the biologist, freeing them to focus on the *biology* of an experiment, while the computer is left to extract possible signal/spatial relationships that may be tested against corresponding experimental conditions at the time of imaging. Of course, in doing so, the experimenter must never lose sight of the minimum requirements of the analysis process in order that results retain biological significance. This being said, however, it is quite possible that inherent correlations automatically mined may lead to important features that help characterize, describe, or shed light on the specimens under investigation.

In cases where there are multiple channels of information, individual voxels assume a multidimensional description (i.e., multiple signal values or intensities) that, as stated, become difficult to divide into useful groups. In the case of microscope data having 2 or 3 channels, pseudo coloring is often applied such that a user can more easily distinguish between materials present. However, if there are excessive combinations of mixtures across these channels, it may become difficult to ascertain what an appropriate material, or number of materials, might be. In cases where the number of channels is even higher, it may not be feasible for a user to even make a sensible segmentation using a semi-supervised approach.

8.1.3   Confocal Microscopy and Its Modalities

Unlike traditional microscopy, recent modes of imaging (such as confocal microscopy) have the ability to collect spatially registered information through separate channels, each capturing a unique perspective of the biological specimen under examination. Such modalities have the ability to achieve lateral *sectioning* (ability to reject light/energy incident on the image sensor coming from outside the focal plane), thus allow for much higher resolutions in both the axial and lateral planes of a specimen volume.

The principle governing confocal microscopy (optical sectioning), for instance, stems from the combination of a point source and point detector (implemented by a laser illumination with a pinhole detector, as seen in Fig. 8.1). Traditionally, the pinhole detection is through an optical barrier (aperture); however, more recent advances achieve this through the physics of light absorption—Multi-photon Microscopy (MM) [252]. Since out-of-focus blur is essentially rejected, the confocal microscope is able to observe a very highly resolved location within the specimen. As only one point is observed at a time, the object must be scanned in x and y directions—achieved by controlling a scanning mirror that deflects the illumination beam accordingly.

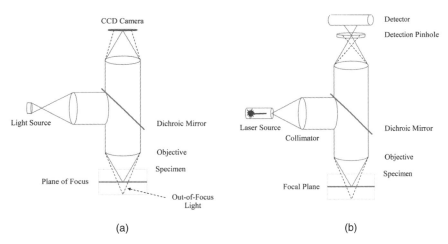

(a)   (b)

FIGURE 8.1 Schematic diagram of Conventional Microscopy (CM) vs. Confocal Laser Scanning Microscopy (CLSM). Unlike CM (a), CLSM (b) is characterized by an ability to reject out-of-focus blur at the detector using an optical barrier (pinhole detector) or, more recently, the physics of light absorption (via related, multiphoton microscopy modalities).

Scanning through a series of optical planes, on the other hand, is controlled by computerized movement of a mechanical stage on which the specimen resides [251]. The combination of stacks yield a 3D signal representation of the subject.

While the techniques presented in this chapter are applicable to other forms of microscopy, we focus our attention on the segmentation and visualization of confocal image stacks, for which there are three commonly used modalities.

8.1.3.1 *Transmission and Reflectance*
Such modes are more indicative of traditional approaches to image acquisition, where light is either passed through the specimen with the pinhole and photo multiplier tube (PMT) detector located on the other side or, as is more common, in reflectance mode, where the optics used to illuminate the specimen serve the dual purpose of deflecting returning light through to the PMT detector (Fig. 8.1).

8.1.3.2 *Phase-Based Modes*
In this unique mode, the interaction between two or more illumination beams (offset and adjacent in the xy plane) are recombined and allowed to form an interference pattern at the detector. The resulting signal reflects any change in the optical path between the sources and is due to a change in refractive index in the specimen. This represents an effective mode for detecting translucent structures.

8.1.3.3 *Epi-fluorescence*
Fluorescence microscopy, itself discovered almost a century ago, represents perhaps the most exciting new prospect for bioimaging, however, all on account of a major discovery in the field of genetic engineering, made

as recently as 1994, where Chalfie et al. [258] succeeded in expressing a naturally fluorescent protein (GFP) in living organisms. This discovery was so paramount, in fact, that it paved the way for a whole new class of tagging or labeling methods— ways for scientists to attach fluorescent probes to specific proteins of interest within the biological environments under study. In combining such technology with fluorescence microscopy, it becomes possible not only to extract spatial information of more than just the physical structure of specimens, but also, to a certain extent, have an idea of the spatial distribution of chemical or functional properties within these environments. Modern confocal microscopes have the capability of using multiple excitation filters on the illumination path in order to excite specific fluorescent probes that subsequently emit at different characteristic wavelengths. Corresponding emission filters act to direct the emitted wavelengths through to the detector. In modern confocal instruments, multiple channels can be captured simultaneously through a series of filters, thus reflecting spatially registered information from multiple labels, each targeting a different aspect of physical or chemical structure. An example of such is shown in Figure 8.2c.

8.2 IMAGE ANALYSIS TASKS CONSIDERED

Essentially, this chapter considers two types of microbiological image data in order to demonstrate the potential for the proposed algorithm to achieve unsupervised, fully automatic segmentations. In essence, we are concerned with two fundamental tasks: one of segmentation for the purpose of visualization, while the other involves segmentation suitable for characterization and quantitative analysis (as outlined in Fig. 1.2).

8.2.1 Visualising Chromosomes During Mitosis

In visualization, segmentation offers visual enhancement for the process of rendering volumes acquired in their natural 3D state. Essentially, by forming a description of the primary materials existing in the data, it becomes possible for regions or materials of interest to be selectively viewed or removed from the data or sets of associated regions/properties to be visualized automatically. This is extremely important when viewing in 3D, as the relative opacity levels of different materials govern whether or not they obstruct the viewer from seeing other internal structures embedded in the data volume. Strategies for how to automatically achieve opacity and color assignment remain an unsolved task, and it is principally left up to the observer to manipulate by trial and error an infinite combination of thresholds, opacity maps, and color maps (collectively, *transfer functions*) in order to enhance possible structure in the data. Such manipulations are found to be completely counterintuitive. Our goal, with respect to visualization then, is to make use of a natural or unsupervised segmentation that automatically attempts to mine and group related content from the volume, such that the task of visualization is simplified to the simple switching on/off of classes discovered. More so, we consider how the mining of relationships *between* the

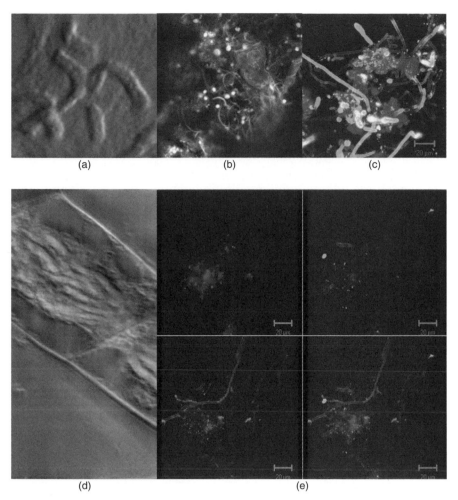

FIGURE 8.2   Sample confocal image datasets from various biological specimens: (a, d) chromosomes imaged using a phase-contrast Nomarski Differential Interference Contrast modality; (b) a single channel from a FITC-stained biofilm; (c, e) examples of 3 channel stained Biofloc samples from water-treatment studies.

homogeneous materials extracted can assist in forming fully automatic visualization strategies in the future.

The data considered for such investigations is from two samples of a set of orchid root-tip chromosomes.[1] This data is a representative example of studies in the field of *cytology* research (the study of cells and subcellular components). A slice from each dataset is shown in Figure 8.2a: *chromo18*, and Figure 8.2d: *chromo83*. Both

---

[1] Data courtesy of the Physical Optics Department, University of Sydney, Australia.

sets were acquired using a phase-contrast technique known as Nomarksi Differential Interference Contrast (DIC). Such phase-based modalities are quite useful as they allow scientists to visually probe the contents of cells, which would otherwise be translucent, often with the ability to achieve higher resolution than with fluorescent-based modalities. In combination with fluorescence-based modalities, such methods allow for the opportunity to combine functional information with highly resolved structural information.

The problem, as presented in this test case, is one of attaining a reasonable visualization of the important chromosomes, which, by virtue of the acquisition method, are embedded in a grey matrix of relatively *unchanging* background. Simple thresholding will not suffice in this instance, nor will direct volume rendering, as the chromosomes will remain hidden and embedded within their background. Extraction of important regions from such data volumes offers a means to record structural properties of otherwise translucent cell constituents essential to the understanding of the various signaling mechanisms at work in live cell division.

8.2.2   Segmenting Heterogeneous Biofilms

One area of investigation in the biosciences dramatically impacted by recent advances in microscopy, is that of Biofilm research. The term *Biofilm* is used to describe a collection of microorganisms anchored to some form of substrata [252], which may exist in a variety of different situations, from the dental plaque found on teeth to microbial *flocs* (highly complex aggregations of microbial cells or bacteria, bioorganic, and inorganic material) suspended in aqueous environments [259]. In such environments, physical structure plays a crucial role in the many key processes that occur.

Knowledge of the structural factors affecting such processes becomes important in formulating solutions to many pertinent environmental problems. In the performance of wastewater treatment, for instance, a process known as *activated sludge* is utilized to promote the stabilized formation of flocs. This process then aids in the separation of suspended microbial contaminants from treated effluent. A common problem occurs in such systems when flocs form with poor settling properties, thereby, degrading the overall treatment process [259]. To gain insight into the structural properties and microbial behavior in this and many other environmental applications, epi-fluorescent modalities remain a major tool through which noninvasive study may be conducted *in situ* at the cellular level. At this point, however, *biofilm* structure is understood more in a qualitative rather than a quantitative sense [252]. As such, the linking of parameters characterizing biofilm performance with structural features remains a hot topic of research.

The majority of available techniques attempt to quantify biofilm structure from microscope images by segmenting the image into foreground and background pixels. Most frequently reported techniques in use within microbiological applications are based on more traditional image processing approaches that utilize boundary and edge information. Such techniques, however, are typically tested only in situations where microbial constituents are clearly defined [260]. These approaches often become ineffective when applied to biofilm, in which objects are *not* clearly defined, often existing within a dense, spatially heterogeneous mixture of bacterial species, extracellular polymeric substances (EPS), and other organic material. This heterogeneity is further magnified in the case of floc studies, as is evidenced in the sample epi-fluorescent images of biofilm and biofloc seen in Figure 8.2(b, c, and e).

Automatic techniques for thresholding have been proposed for use with biofilm. A series of entropy- and histogram-based approaches are reviewed in the literature [261], for their applicability to biofilm. Some of the more well-known methods include iterative selection [262] and Otsu's method [263], as utilized by the popular biofilm characterization software ISA5 [264] (developed by the Center for Biofilm Engineering at Montana State University). There is some debate within the biofilm community, however, as to what constitutes a more appropriate and robust method of biofilm segmentation [265], arguing in favour of alternative methods such as the minimum-error algorithm [266] or the ICM: Iterated Conditional Mode [267] algorithm.

At this point, the majority of these approaches treat biofilm images as essentially bimodal in nature. While this might be a reasonable assumption for some experiments where the biofilm is relatively homogeneous, it is rarely the case in the study of floc (as seen in the samples of Fig. 8.2). In such instances, segmentation via crude thresholding of foreground from background will result in the loss of much, potentially, significant information. In Figure 8.3, for example, Otsu's method clearly overgeneralizes on the nature of underlying materials present. As a result, researchers often resort to the arduous task of manual or semiautomated segmentation—wherein operator discretion plays a key role impacting any subsequent characterization measurement taken.

In addition, popular quantitative approaches generally measure morphological and textural parameters [268, 269]. Morphological measures discussed in the literature are dependent almost exclusively on an initial thresholding. Any form of particle property measured (porosity, size, etc.) must then assume that the particles existing in the "foreground" are of the same type—when in fact they may be a conglomerate of overlapping types, with different intensity profiles or shapes. Presently, multimodal or multilevel considerations have received little attention in the field. It is from this then, that we draw motivation to develop new unsupervised methods for the automatic formulation of a multilevel segmentation by mining natural homogeneities from the data.

The general idea is that if more robust and repeatable segmentations can be made for the isolation of biomaterials present in a specimen, then parameters measured may more appropriately characterize the distribution and nature of materials present. Furthermore, relationships *between* the biomaterials present in any one specimen may be more representative of *functional* processes that are taking place in such environments.

8.3 MICROBIOLOGICAL IMAGE SEGMENTATION

In exploring the effectiveness of the SOTM for segmentation of biological image data, a set of features is fed into the network (as outlined in Fig. 1.2), each describing

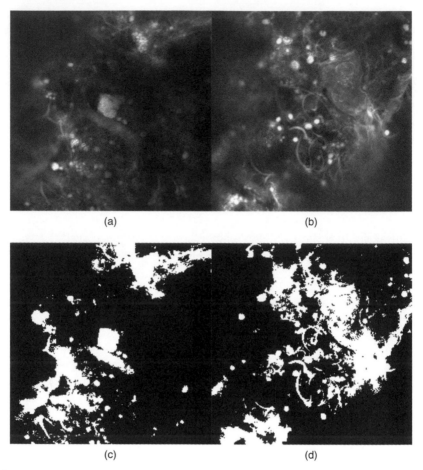

FIGURE 8.3 Two slices of FITC-stained biofilm image data and associated Otsu-thresholded binary representations. Low contrast *hazes* in raw image data (above) are indicative of trace distributions of fluorescent molecular markers—often not noise, yet are truncated through thresholding (below), while clusters of cells are blended together making subsequent particle analysis difficult.

a different aspect of the input data. In the following investigations we have chosen a small set of features fundamental to a basic description of objects in a gray-level scene, as segmented by the human visual system (HVS). These features include Gray-level (GL) of an individual pixel, which describes highly localized intensity variation within an object; Average gray-level of a disk-shaped region (GL_{dsk}) surrounding the current pixel, which describes more regional variation across an object; Phase Congruency (PhC) [270], which is more akin to describing the edge information present in an image, however, unlike traditional edge detectors, with the added advantage of incorporating scale information into its calculation, thus highlighting significant features that the HVS is thought to respond to; Position (XY), which simply relate to the positional coordinates (x,y) of pixels in the image plane, considered here such that partitioning across position will give formed clusters a sense of proximity within the spatial domain of the image. Of course, in reality it is highly likely that there are many additional features and factors that contribute to object discrimination as performed by the HVS.

We also note that, in this application, although we primarily need to segment 3D data obtained from the confocal microscope, we restrict our experiments at this stage to the 2D segmentation of an individual slice, so that the significance of these features with respect to one another (as fused through the SOTM) can be assessed along with the impact of the proposed refinements to the SOTM model.

Experiments were conducted on individual 2D confocal image slices from a sample of FITC-stained biofilm. Of the slices, one was chosen for this presentation (Fig. 8.4a), such that adequate comparison could be drawn as to the impact of feature adjustment on the resulting SOTM segmentation. A number of experiments were conducted, and in each, constraints were imposed both in the sets of features to be fused by the SOTM and by imposing a bias or weighting to the competitive search phase of SOTM learning (Step 3 in the SOTM algorithm, Section 4.4). Three main dynamics were explored.

8.3.1 Effects of Feature Space Definition

The first experiments explore the dynamic feature space definition. In this test, the goal was to consider how the SOTM responds when features are added to the feature space description, one by one. With each new definition, the impact on segmentation is evaluated. A 64 neuron (upper limit) SOTM was utilized in this process. The stop criterion based on limiting $H(t)$ was not enforced.

Feature spaces (FS_i), are defined as follows, with segmentation results presented in Figure 8.4(b) $FS_1 = (GL)$; (c) $FS_2 = (GL, GL_{dsk})$; (d) $FS_3 = (GL, GL_{dsk}, PhC)$; (e) $FS_4 = (GL, GL_{dsk}, PhC, XY)$. We consider both X and Y to be of equal significance, to be used in unison to represent position of a pixel. All features remained unbiased throughout learning and were normalized to eliminate any possibility of natural ranges in the data adversely affecting the outcome of the segmentation (X and Y normalized together). Two images were obtained for each case; however, we omit the segmented dataset labeled with the GL component of the classifying neuron. Since the analysis is subjective, we present an image of the segmentation with a randomly gray-level-labeled version, such that any assessment of region/object localization is not biased by our own tendency to segment the resulting GL images naturally using our own built-in HVS.

As can be seen from the labeled images in Figure 8.4, both (b) and (c) demonstrate little in the way of a contiguous region (connected set of labels), with the exception of regions of extreme uniformity in GL existing in the background. With PhC, in (d), we start to observe some mild regional associations. The overall segmentation, however, is still rather contaminated by the signal-based pixel statistics, each competing (in an equal fashion) for the right to represent the input space. As a side note, forcing the partition to create 64 groups may represent significant over-segmentation. If one

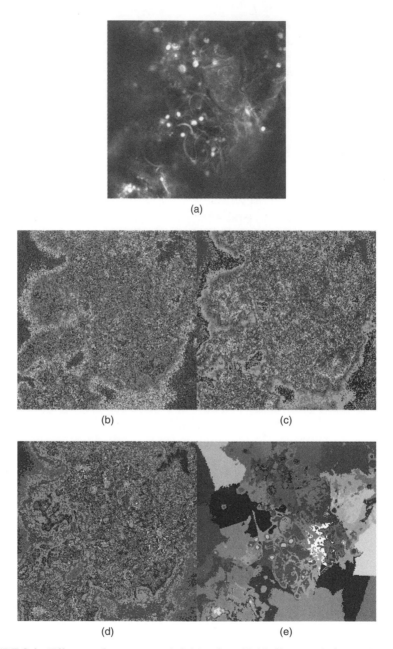

FIGURE 8.4 Effects on feature space definition for a 2D biofilm sample image: (a) original slice—for reference; (b) GL only; (c) GL, GL_{dsk}; (d) GL, GL_{dsk}, PhC; (e) GL, GL_{dsk}, PhC, XY.

considers the PhC feature, in being more representative of significant features and edge information, one might assume that a large dynamic range of PhC values might exist, but over a more limited expanse of the input dataset. As such, the network would tend to encounter large differences in PhC more often, thus partition in this dimension more readily. Even with this though, the majority of the labeled segmentation appears quite random and with little grouping across regions.

When adding position to the mix, the SOTM appears to immediately discover more regional-based associations. While not delineating all structures *per se* (limited by its restriction to 64 neurons maximum), a good number of neurons appear to favor a relatively uniform partitioning of XY space. One would assume that the same occurs in the other dimensions (based on the relative density of information in those dimensions). In the XY plane, the density is always uniform, as the X and Y vectors carry no information on their own. The partitioning in this plane, however, allows for neurons to separate and yet still learn from GL regional information. This could offer an insight into how separate notions of objects may be formed within the memory of the SOTM, due to their separation in proximity. At any rate, it seems clear that there is strong interplay between the knowledge of signal characteristics and proximity, and the SOTM demonstrates potential in differentiating this.

8.3.2 Fixed Weighting of Feature Space

In a second experiment, we consider applying bias to the signal and spatial components of feature space. In separate runs of a 16-node SOTM, we adjust the significance weighting of XY components, to investigate how the segmentation is impacted when the competitive learning process is biased toward different features. At this stage we also draw a comparison between the popular K-Means clustering method [271] and the SOTM.

The results of initial bias experiments are presented in Figure 8.5(b–d). In all cases, GL, GL_{dsk}, and PhC remain unbiased (weighting of 1), while XY is changed. In (b) the weighting for XY is 0.01; in (c) 0.02; and (d) 0.1. A high ratio of Signal versus XY weightings favor a relatively weaker partitioning in the XY plane. Thus the number of neurons split across (GL, GL_{dsk}, PhC) will tend to outnumber those split across XY. Sensitivity of the SOTM to proximity is then considered via a range of fixed XY weightings.

From the segmentation results in Figure 8.5, we notice that, as expected, significantly fewer neurons are dedicated to the representation of the background as compared with Figure 8.4e, thereby freeing up neurons to capture foreground regions, where microbial material exists (i.e., regions of high signal activity). The extent of these regions is reduced or tightened as we increase the significance of XY features across Figure 8.5(b–d), while the range of intensities captured by each neuron (region) is extended or relaxed. From this it becomes evident that there is an inherent trade-off between signal and proximal resolution as we bias the significance ratio between signal and position.

It is at this point that we compare the SOTM's performance with the popular clustering technique: K-Means. The features were weighted as for Figure 8.5d; however,

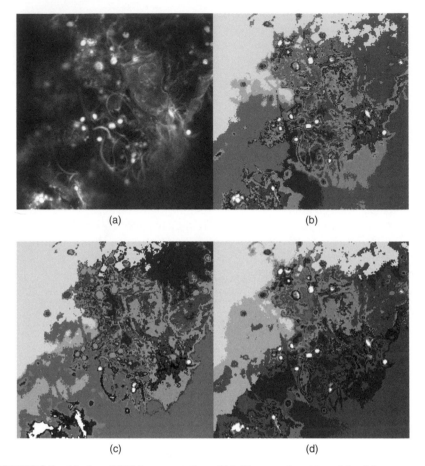

FIGURE 8.5 16-class SOTM segmentation of biofilm sample with weighted feature space: GL, GL_{dsk}, and PhC are all weighted by 1.0. (a) top left (original slice for reference); (b) top right: XY weight = 0.01; (c) bottom left: XY weight = 0.02; (d) bottom right: XY weight = 0.1.

the SOTM was allowed to decide on the appropriate number of clusters by itself, by restricting the minimum level to which $H(t)$ decays to $H(\infty) = 0.3$. A total of 31 clusters (or class centers) was discovered at this limiting resolution of $H(t)$.

The K-Means algorithm was then run with a limit of 31 clusters, in order to get a direct indication of performance. We also used a randomly generated, but ordered gray scale, so that the labels thus discovered by each algorithm (also ordered in terms of their gray scale property) might be compared. What we find from Figure 8.6 is that there is quite a marked clarity exhibited through the SOTM result. Clusters discovered tend to form well-packed groupings of similar signal characteristics. The large bacterial clumps, for instance, are quite pronounced and grouped into two localized regions, as opposed to the K-Means case. This is likely due to the systematic

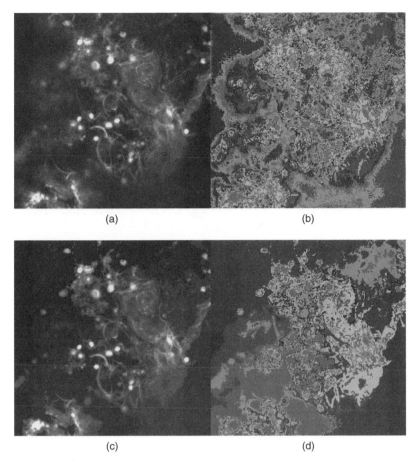

(a)   (b)

(c)   (d)

FIGURE 8.6   Comparison of K-Means vs. SOTM for biofilm segmentation: (a) (b) K-Means at 31 centers; (c)–(d) bottom: SOTM at 31 centers (self-discovered).

way in which the SOTM parses the feature space. Partitioning is biased toward the selective allocation of new classes (neurons) with the occurrence of either slight variations in signal or large variations in the proximity of similar signals.

The K-Means approach does not share this flexibility, as it essentially begins with a choice of random samples from across the entire feature space, attempting to then adjust the centers from what may in fact be ill-fated initial positions. In addition, it will tend to blur or average across boundaries, while the SOTM inserts so as to maximize separation. Perceptually, the SOTM gives a much clearer result and appears to offer a more efficient representation across feature space. The higher the feature-space dimension grows in any one application, the more important this property will become. A more automated allocation of class numbers is also a major advantage of the SOTM here, as the allocation is somewhat data driven.

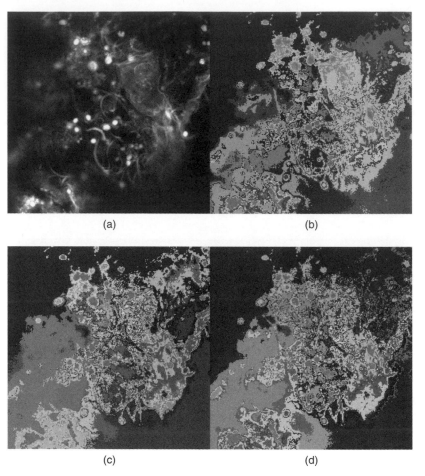

(a) (b)

(c) (d)

FIGURE 8.7 Exploring effects on biofilm segmentation due to dynamically switching weights during SOTM learning: (a) original slice (b) top right: 28 centers, β_{xy} decayed from 1 over duration $1*N_s$, $H(\infty) = 0.3$; (c) bottom left: 47 centers, β_{xy} decayed from 1 over $2*N_s$, $H(\infty) = 0.2$; (d) bottom right: 42 centers, β_{xy} grown from 0, $H(\infty) = 0.2$.

Biologically speaking, the segmentation achieved by the SOTM in Figures 8.5, 8.6, 8.7 offer a number of implications for the study of biofilms. In Figure 8.6, out-of-focus and void space (interstices) have been grouped into large background classes and may easily be removed (operator selection). Such regions may be considered background and represent avenues for the transport of nutrients to the biofilm—a factor that is often assessed by porosity measurements. In crude thresholding methods alluded to in Figure 8.3, out-of-focus blur can *bleed* into the image and contaminate thresholding (upon which porosity measures rely), similarly for the large cyan clumped regions (likely protozoa related and not considered significant to biofilm function). The smaller clumps of bacterial clusters and fine grain material (individual bacteria), however, is deemed important to biofilm function. As is evidenced in both Figures 8.5 and 8.6, reduced significance of the XY feature results in a push toward greater representation of these foreground bio-constituents. The gel-like EPS (exopolymeric substances) are often the byproduct excreted from the cellular biomass (bacteria)and are also thought to be important in biofilm architecture, as they act as an adhesive *glue* that binds the microbial aggregate. This material can be seen in the segmented regions encapsulating the bacterial clumps and the speckled bacteria elements, present as the hazy matrix in which they are embedded in the original image. In the following segmentations, dynamic weighting is incorporated into the SOTM in order to further enhance these foreground components.

The advantage of having these multilevel segmentations means that characterizing measurements may be conducted on the materials separately—for example: assessing the relative porosity or spatial concentration of bacteria within the EPS matrix; or considering the sites wherein larger bacterial clumps tend to form with respect to the distribution of EPS and interstitial nutrient channels. The two major groupings of bacterial clumps seen in Figure 8.6, for instance, appear to thrive where the EPS matrix is more prevalent.

8.3.3 Dynamic Feature Fusion During Learning

Based on the results of applying fixed Global weightings to each of the above features for SOTM clustering, we suggest that the network's ability to cluster across an input data space—while efficient and optimal in a vector quantization sense—may not necessarily converge to locate clusters that represent objects as perceived by the HVS. We propose that in the natural course of learning, certain features may become more (or less) significant. This would have the effect of a nonlinear biasing or warping of the final topology of the network away from the vector quantized topology. The resulting topology potentially offers a more object- or region-based partitioning of the input feature space and thus more of an object-based segmentation suitable for the delineation of constituent materials existent in biofilm/floc images.

Theoretically, there are quite a number of parameters one could vary in the competitive search, learning, hierarchical function decay, or clustering phases of SOTM segmentation. One might even apply weightings to selectively control all such parameters differently. In this section, however, we introduce a dynamic set of weights in the competitive search phase of learning only. We start by applying a set of initial feature weights (β) to the competitive Euclidean distance measure in the SOTM algorithm such that the test to decide on a winning node now becomes

$$d_j : d_j\left(\mathbf{x}_l, \mathbf{w}_k\right) = \min_j \left[\beta \cdot \gamma \cdot d_j\left(\mathbf{x}_i, \mathbf{w}_k\right)\right] \tag{8.1}$$

where $\gamma(t)$ denotes a set of exponential functions that force individual feature weights to grow or decay on the interval [0 1] or remain constant throughout learning.

More specifically, as a contrived test of this principle, we utilize a sigmoid function to control the gradual switching of individual weights from one state to another:

$$\gamma\left(t, c_s, g, T\right) = \frac{1}{1 + e^{-(q/T) \cdot g[T/2 - (t - c_s)]}} \tag{8.2}$$

where t is the current cycle number (each presentation of a new input vector to the SOTM represents one cycle/iteration); c_s is the delay in cycles before switching should commence; g takes on a value of either $(-1, 0, 1)$, controlling whether the function decays, remains constant, or grows (respectively) over time; T is the transition period (in cycles) over which the switching occurs; and finally, q controls the shape of the transition profile.

It follows that if individual weights are dynamically increased or decreased gradually (toward the weights of the other features) over the entire learning process, then partitioning would begin by favoring the highest weighted feature(s), shifting toward the other features as they, in turn, become (relatively) more significant.

If feature weights cross over in value, the ratio between them would also switch, thus promoting the shift of partitioning from one feature to another. During this progression, neurons are being allocated in a manner that would favor the highest weighted feature dimension at any one time during learning. This might be a significant dynamic in terms of object segmentation, where neurons to be allocated could favor one dimension until sufficient information is learned from that dimension, before shifting focus to another dimension.

In the third experiment, we investigate what would happen if there is such a compromise between features over the course of learning. Using the modifications discussed above, results are demonstrated for the dynamic weight adjustment of XY features, decreasing or increasing their role in the search phase of competitive learning, over time. Figure 8.7 shows the results and experimental conditions. We also reduce the minimum limit on $H(t)$ for cases (b) and (c) to see what happens if more neurons are allowed to generate.

In each case Figure 8.7(b) and (c), we begin with an initial XY weight of 1, which then decays to zero over two different periods (denoted by multiples of Ns, the number of samples in the image data). In (b), more vigorous partitioning occurs in XY while it is as significant as the GL features; thus tight regions are captured as in Figure 8.4e. This is somewhat offset though, by the large initial values of $H(t)$, which force partitioning in XY to only occur across well separated data. In essence, if two data points are encountered that have similar signal properties, then their separation must be large if they are to be considered as different. As the XY significance switches to zero, signal features now dominate and neurons generated tend to be pushed toward capturing signal variations. Unlike Figure 8.4e, background regions not having much variation in signal tend not to be further partitioned as the constraint on XY is relaxed, while biomass regions (foreground) are. The result is more detail in the foreground (which is what we prefer to delineate). In Figure 8.7c, we relax the XY weighting more slowly. The danger here is that as $H(t)$ decreases, more of the background partitions may in fact be split, while the same is true for foreground. Such is a trade-off that may need to be addressed through some mechanism to reduce the impact of background partitions. Some domain knowledge can be used here (background should have the lowest intensities). Figure 8.7d shows the opposite case—growth of the XY weighting. This pushes neurons to represent signal early, then split across XY later; the same danger thus exists if the weight grows too fast, before $H(t)$ is limited.

As indicated in the discussion of the previous section, the process of biasing the SOTM to allocate more resources to foreground material has increased the detail with which the important bacterial and EPS-related information has been captured in the segmentations (particularly of Fig. 8.7b). While the dynamic mechanism allows the SOTM to capture and focus on foreground information in the segmentation, the tendency for SOTM to spawn nodes prolifically at low $H(t)$ may result in over-segmentations, as may be the case for Figure 8.7(c and d).

8.4 IMAGE SEGMENTATION USING HIERARCHICAL SELF-ORGANIZATION

The flexibility and efficiency of the SOTM to adaptively build a representation of the input feature space reveals interesting properties via dynamic adjustment of feature significance in the competitive search phase of learning. An important interplay between positional and gray-level characteristics when building a representation of an object or region in an image with the SOTM was identified. Evidence further suggests that the SOTM can adaptively warp its topology from the traditional means-squared sense into forms that better reflect the types of segmentations typical of the human visual system.

In an effort to take advantage of these properties, yet better limit the prolific spawning of nodes at low $H(t)$, the SOHVM model introduced in Chapter 8 is applied to both single and multichannel image samples.

Initially, we consider the segmentation of chromosomes from an orchid root-tip specimen, *chromo18*. We restrict our attention to a single slice of the 18 slice 3D stack, for comparisons between K-Means (KM), self-organizing feature map (SOFM), SOTM and SOHVM. In a later section we revisit the result of segmenting such chromosomes in a 3D context on a larger, 83 slice set of chromosome data, taken from the same sample. In the second experiment, we compare the gray-level segmentation produced by the SOHVM in its fully automated mode, with that produced by KM (fixed to the same number of nodes). In this case a patch from a stack of FITC-stained biofilm, *FITC1* (investigated in the previous section) was used. The sample test cases are shown in Figure 8.8.

8.4.1 Gray-Level Segmentation of Chromosomes

In Figure 8.9, we present four equivalent runs of the SOHVM and SOTM for direct comparison. In the SOTM and SOHVM experiments, we apply limits to $H(t)$ at

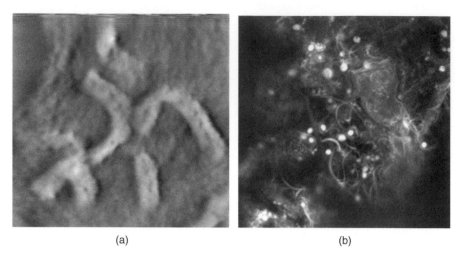

(a)   (b)

FIGURE 8.8 Sample test cases for gray-level image segmentation comparisons: (a) a slice from an orchid root-tip specimen, *chromo18*; (b) a patch from a single channel of FITC-stained biofilm, *FITC*1.

different resolutions in order to allow the number of classes mined to depend on the data. We then choose similar class numbers for comparison with fixed models as shown in Figure 8.11.

In general, both the SOTM and SOHVM are quite proficient in terms of mining dominant gray-level homogeneities from the image. In fact, over the course of different numbers of clusters, they maintain their description of the data quite well with respect to KM and SOFM. In Figure 8.9, from top to bottom, we vary the lower limit for $H(t) : H(\infty) = \sigma(X), 0.75\sigma(X), 0.25\sigma(X), 0.1\sigma(X)$. The left column shows the SOHVM results, with SOTM on the right. SOHVM selects corresponding N_c values of 16, 21, 33, and 39 nodes, while SOTM selects N_c values of 13, 18, 30, and 52. In the early stages, SOTM, it would seem, has prematurely allocated nodes to noisy outliers in the data, as its representation of foreground structure is not as complete as the SOHVM's (as evidenced in the zoomed chromosome in Fig. 8.10). The second difference we notice is that the SOHVM appears to maintain cluster integrity across all values of $H(t)$, experiencing far less degradation than the SOTM at the lowest $H(t)$ limit of $0.1\sigma(X)$. With the breakdown of the SOTM at this level, and its leap in node insertion, clusters formed previously are very rapidly subdivided. Since their subdivision is very Local at this level, the cluster centers previously describing classes are easily redistributed throughout the volume of the density they were describing. This causes increased blurring between cluster groups seen in the final case.

In Figure 8.11, the classes describing individual pixels can be seen to undergo more shifting to different states (gray-levels) in the compared models versus SOHVM when moving to finer resolutions (as corroborated by the close-up versions in Fig. 8.10). This is evidence of the SOHVM's efficiency in allocating nodes to, and keeping them

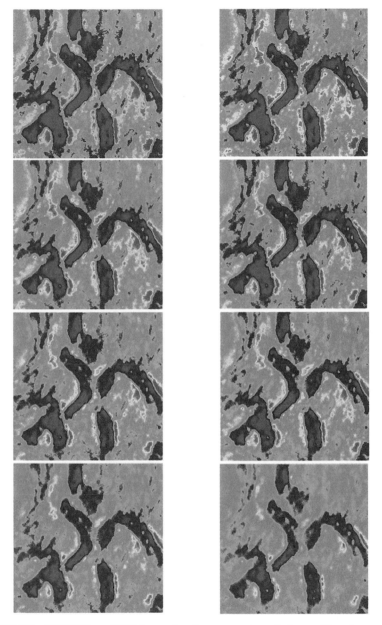

FIGURE 8.9 SOHVM vs. SOTM gray-level segmentation of *chromo18* under equivalent $H(t)$ limitation: (top to bottom) $H(\infty) = \sigma(X), 0.75\sigma(X), 0.25\sigma(X), 0.1\sigma(X)$; (left) SOHVM; (right) SOTM. Excessive node spawning at low $H(t)$ by the SOTM works to over-segment, thus degrade previously mined clusters (regions of homogeneity in gray-level).

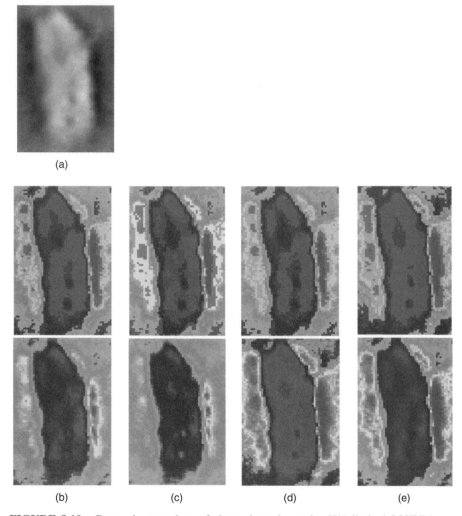

FIGURE 8.10 Cropped comparison of cluster integrity under $H(t)$ limited SOHVM segmentation of chromosome image data. Cropped sections show zoomed version of (a) lower central chromosome; (b) SOHVM results for $\sigma(X)$ (top) and $0.1\sigma(X)$; (c) SOTM results; (d) SOFM results for 4×4 (top) and 7×7; (e) KM result for $N_c = 16$ (top), $N_c = 49$. This figure highlights both the efficiency of the SOHVM and its increased robustness to degradation of its previously discovered groups.

in the more *important* regions of Local density at earlier stages (not simply most distant or most satisfying in a MSE sense). We note that the SOFM has quite similar performance to the SOTM and SOHVM with smaller maps; however, on using larger lattices, saturation begins to occur—most likely as a result of some nodes becoming trapped between regions of density, thus not allocated to useful chromosome structure. KM, on the other hand, appears to saturate early, as it averages across the few

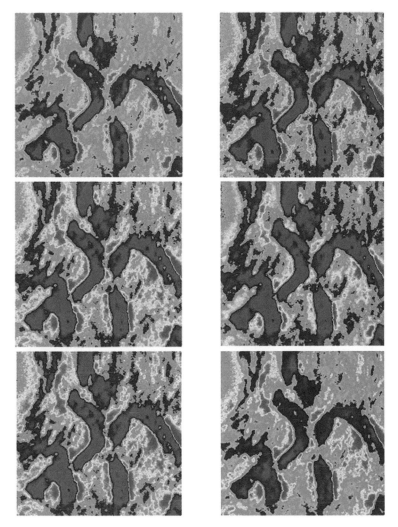

FIGURE 8.11   SOFM vs. KM gray-level segmentation of *chromo18* under node limited conditions equivalent to cases tested in Figure 8.9. (left) Top to bottom: SOFM 4×4, 6×6, 7×7 (matches $\sigma(X)$, $0.25\sigma(X)$, $0.1\sigma(X)$)—shows saturation in the chromosome regions, blending resolvable structure together; (right): KM with 16, 25, 49 nodes from top to bottom, respectively.

known classes, then degrades as does SOTM at higher N_c values (without topological structure to keep it in check). It would seem that the Hebbian Maximal Eigenfilters (HME) units embedded in each prototype act as a form of protection over the integrity of each cluster discovered. The ability of the SOHVM then, to generate and keep nodes in important regions, relatively intact under further allocation, makes it a powerful algorithm for resolving and extracting microstructure of the specimen.

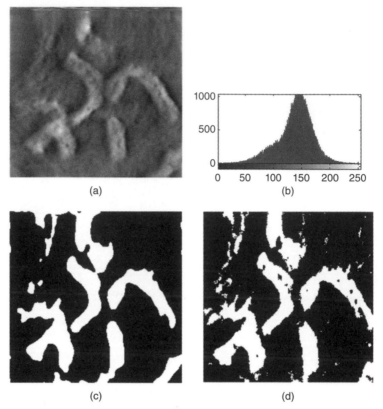

FIGURE 8.12 Automatic SOHVM mutlilevel thresholding of *chromo18*: (a) original slice; (b) histogram of gray-level distribution; (c) Otsu's bi-level threshold; (d) SOHVM result— uncovers inherent bimodal nature of underlying density—most of the image appears to consists of two nearby gray-levels.

8.4.2 Automated Multilevel Thresholding of Biofilm

In this section, the automatic version of the SOHVM is used to extract natural modes of multilevel thresholds from gray-level images. In the first test we run the SOHVM in automatic mode on *chromo18*. The result is shown in Figure 8.12, with a comparison against the popular Otsu's technique [263] for bi-level thresholding (typically used in biofilm characterization software such as ISA [264]). We notice from Figure 8.12, that the SOHVM appears to have found a natural 2-class segmentation of the chromosome data. This result makes sense in fact, due to the inherent bimodal distribution of the gray-level data as seen in Figure 8.12b.

It would seem that the SOHVM, in finding an optimal threshold, does so in a way that is more preserving of structure than Otsu's method. We conjecture that the SOHVM achieves a natural balance between the properties of the SOTM (attempting to maximize the discrimination between classes or clusters mined) while incorporating the necessary topological mining capability that enables it to know when a reasonable solution (for both cluster positions and number of optimal clusters) is found.

In a second test, the SOHVM was allowed to find a natural segmentation of the more complex, heterogeneous biofilm sample *FITC1*. According to the human eye, there appears to be multiple groups of materials present in the image. Again, Otsu's method, which is restricted to a bi-level threshold, is typically used as a preprocessing stage in the analysis of such biofilm images (unless the biologist manually supplies one). The SOHVM in this case finds a natural mode of 25 clusters, which appears to represent a perceptually viable segmentation with respect to the original image. In fact, in further comparison with a multilevel thresholding achieved with an equivalent-sized KM clustering, the SOHVM result appears far more structurally preserving. The SOHVM appears to maintain a set of clusters that efficiently captures the characteristic gray-levels present in the original image, without the need for a user-supplied number for the number of classes to look for. In this sense, the SOHVM represents a more pure unsupervised model, as it does not require separate test runs nor the evaluation of a priori validity indices. It achieves all this in an *online* manner through the information mined and encoded within its topological connections and HME probes.

For typical biofilm analysis in this case, the bi-level threshold shown in Figure 8.13b would often form the basis for *quantification* of average particle volumes, porosity measurements, and other common image properties currently relied upon for biofilm characterization. It would seem that the de-mixing of constituent particles would be a better option before attempting to evaluate such properties. This, however, represents an extremely tedious task on the part of a biologist. The SOHVM represents a very promising avenue for the automation of such in the future. It is believed that analyses based on such segmentations are more likely to yield much higher correlations between image data of such specimens and the biological or chemical conditions governing their growth and ecology. Of course, this remains to be seen and will undoubtedly be the subject of future research effort and collaboration between biologists and signal processing engineers, armed with tools such as the SOHVM.

8.4.3   Multidimensional Feature Segmentation

Perhaps the real potential for the SOHVM lies beyond the simple multilevel thresholding of a single intensity channel. As indicated in preliminary experiments with the SOTM in Chapter 3, such dynamic, self-organizing models represent a useful technique for the fusion of higher order statistics, or channels of information, to be considered in the formulation of viable segmentations. In this section, we consider two multidimensional descriptions of an image voxel for the purpose of segmentation. In both cases presented, we restrict our attention to the addition of features to the previous two single channel test cases *chromo18* and *FITC1*. It is important to note here, that although we are reconsidering single channel information fused with higher order statistics, the exact same approach would be taken in the fusion of information from multiple channels: for example, in an epi-fluorescent dataset with 3 or more channels of intensity information, each overlayed and spatially co-registered within

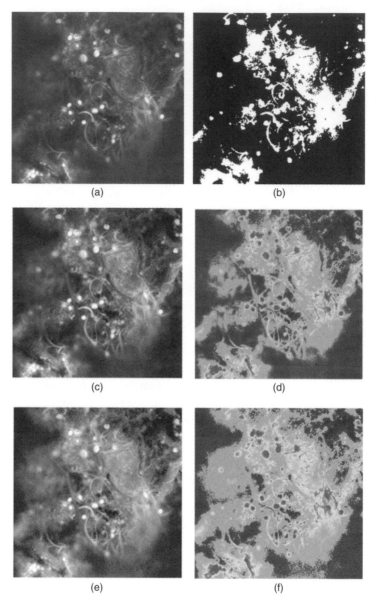

(a)   (b)

(c)   (d)

(e)   (f)

FIGURE 8.13 Automatic SOHVM vs. equivalent KM for the multilevel thresholding of *FITC1*: (a) the original FITC-stained biofilm image showing larger distribution of gray-levels than in *chromo18*; (b) typical Otsu's threshold loses much information about the constituent particles; (c and d) Multilevel threshold obtained with the SOHVM (automatically selected 25 levels); (e and f) K-Means multilevel threshold (where user selected $K = 25$).

the same 3D volume of a specimen. For the purpose of this presentation, however, we preferentially build on the previous examples, thus constrain our investigations to the use of multiple *channels* of statistics rather than separate channels of raw data.

8.4.3.1 Segmentation Based on Textural Properties

In the first example, we consider the SOHVM in an automatic mode, for the segmentation of an adjacent slice in the z-direction of the biofilm volume, to that of *FITC1*, namely *FITC2*. We consider the case when its voxels are each described with first a higher order texture statistic very popular in the signal processing community for the extraction of textural properties of images, namely the Log-Gabor wavelet decomposition [270]. In an effort to maintain the flow of this presentation, we opt for a layman description of this feature; however, the reader is directed to Reference 270 for further detail.

Essentially, the Log-Gabor wavelet represents a bank of oriented filters, over a set of scales and orientations, that are each in turn, convolved with a given image location. For that location, a set of energy values is extracted, depicting the spatial frequency of intensity information present along each *orientation-scale* pairing within that Local region. As texture is often characterized by highly variant intensity information, a GL-based segmentation of homogeneous textures (such as the *hazes* and *dusts* present in many microbiological images) is relatively impossible. The Log-Gabor decomposition captures any periodicity or aperiodicity inherent in such textured regions about a voxel, through its combination of all such filter energies into a single, multidimensional pattern vector (comprising its Log-Gabor energy coefficients).

We consider the texture-based segmentation of *FITC2*, using both the Log-Gabor representation over three scales and six orientations both as the sole pattern vector for each voxel, and in weighted combination with the original GL feature value of the previous section. Figure 8.14 shows the automatic SOHVM based texture segmentations of *FITC2*.

From Figure 8.14b, we see that the SOHVM divides the data into three essential classes based on texture alone. This is feasible, given the hazy regions, tightly packed bacterial regions, and the background. The filter used in this case is perhaps not sufficient, and four scales would yield a better result for capturing textures (as recommended in similar texture metrics used in image and texture retrieval applications [272]), such as those containing very bright, but tiny bacteria scattered in the regions denoted by the arrows. We also note some artifacts in the boundaries of the image, where the regions over which texture can be evaluated are restricted.

In Figure 8.14(c–e), the results of combining Log-Gabor features with GL are shown. In case (c), 20 classes were found. Interestingly, this is approaching the same number of classes automatically found in the GL segmentation of *FITC1*; only the very mild incorporation of texture information (weighted low w.r.t. GL) is enough for the SOHVM to gain some increased level of grouping of related voxels. By increasing the weighting of texture information in (d) and (e), where the class numbers found were 13 and 10, respectively, structural properties begin to emerge. In some ways the segmentations here yield structural properties in a fashion similar to the results of Chapter 4; however, in this case, in a far less arbitrary and more automated fashion.

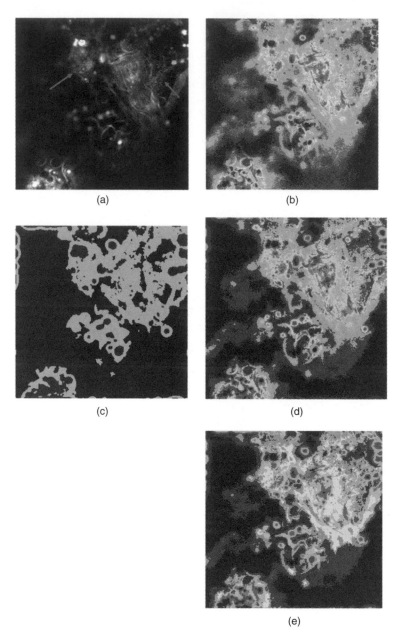

FIGURE 8.14 Automatic SOHVM segmentation of *FITC2* using Log-Gabor feature space: (a) original slice adjacent to *FITC1*; (b) automatic SOHVM segmentation of dominant Log-Gabor patterns; (c–e) $\mathbf{x}_i = [\text{GL, Log-Gabor}]$ feature representation, with weighted features: [1, 0.1], [1, 0.3], and [1, 0.4], respectively.

Of course, much research is needed into an appropriate way of selecting the weights for segmentations using multiple features (perhaps based on some other image statistic extracted from the data). At any rate, it is clear that the SOHVM is fusing this information sensibly.

8.4.3.2 *Segmentation From Local Intensity Statistics*   In the next example, as with the previous, we consider a multidimensional feature description, in this case based on Local intensity features, namely the GL, Local contrast enhancement [273], a Gaussian-filtered version of GL, and a disk-averaged GL of the region surrounding each voxel. The features are shown in Figure 8.15 for the *chromo18* sample. SOTM and SOHVM segmentations are shown in Figure 8.16, under the limitation of 10 nodes. Results indicate that the SOHVM captures structural properties of the chromosomes more efficiently than the SOTM, which tends to over-split the internal chromosome regions.

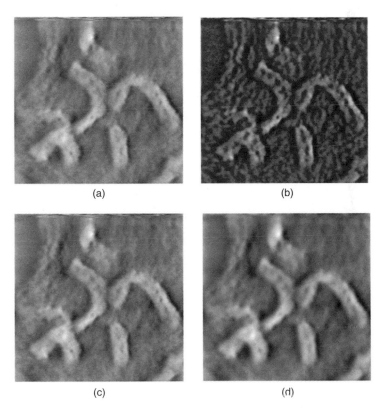

(a)   (b)

(c)   (d)

FIGURE 8.15   Gray-level-based Local voxel statistics, used to form a higher order, multidimensional feature space for SOHVM segmentation of *chromo18*: (a) GL, (b) Local contrast; (c) Gaussian filter using 3 × 3 Local window; (d) Local average over 3 × 3 radius about each voxel.

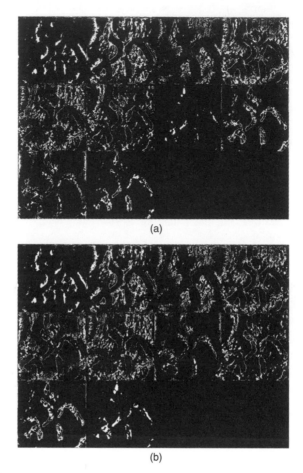

(a)

(b)

FIGURE 8.16 SOTM and SOHVM grouping of higher order voxel statistics for slice 9 of *chromo18*. Restriction was made to finding 10 clusters for visual comparison. SOVHM shows tighter, more compact grouping over the internal chromosome regions. (a) SOTM; (b) SOHVM. Clusters ordered left to right, top to bottom in terms of darkest to brightest GL.

8.5 HARVESTING TOPOLOGIES TO FACILITATE VISUALIZATION

Based on the example presented in the previous section, we consider the information embedded in the SOHVM-discovered topological connections linking clusters. Figure 8.17 shows how the classes are interconnected. Essentially, the links represent the associations between any two given clusters such that some density was found to exist between them (see CHL in Section 7.2.1 in Chapter 7). In the above result, we notice that in fact, although we have grouped the voxels according to a feature set defined in 4D space, we are still able to easily extract related cluster groups through the topological connections. Visually, we can confirm that these connections make sense, particularly, since we have ordered the cluster groups from left to right in

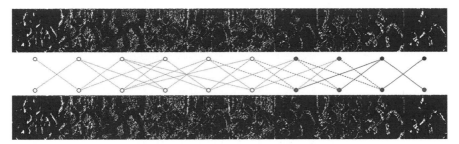

FIGURE 8.17 Harvesting topological associations using the SOHVM—the figure shows topological connections joining related clusters/classes from the multidimensional GL-based segmentation from Section 8.4.3.2. As the statistics are based on GL properties, they have been ordered left to right by ascending GL feature. The SOHVM has automatically mined relationships that reflect this ordering, as demonstrated by the connectivity pattern linking groups.

ascending order by their first feature (namely, the gray-level). As the features used in this example all relate some way to gray-level, the task of visual confirmation becomes relatively simple. We can clearly see that, beginning with the rightmost group (cluster 10), this cluster is most related to cluster 9, and indirectly related (by two hops along the *graph* to clusters 7 and 8.

The spatial location of structures for these clusters confirm that they are all related, in fact, to the chromosome, its more internal components (clusters 9 and 10), and the tightly packed material surrounding the chromosome (7 and 8). In reality, the decision to form links is actually based on all the feature information incorporated into the definition of each pixel; thus, to some extent, these relationships are a reflection of the regional information supplied through the Local contrast and average gray-level in the Local region about each pixel (features 2 and 4).

8.5.1 Topology Aware Opacity and Gray-Level Assignment

The importance of such topological information is this—since we have ordered the cluster groups by one of the features, we note a definite pattern linking clusters from the rightmost segmentations to the leftmost. Such an ordering will most certainly be not so intuitive when many other features are present (e.g., complex features describing texture information). In addition, actual discovery of nodes is not always in the same order. Topological associations thus become important if the computer is then to perform any systematic processing of clusters found. For example, given complex associations between texture patterns mined from an image, how then would one be likely to visualize the result? In 2D, random assignment of gray levels is possible such as that shown in the biofilm segmentations in Section 8.4.2; however, this is not intuitive, and often the gray levels do not highlight true associations in the data; in fact, if per chance two spatially related pixels are part of two different clusters, but are rendered using a similar gray level, then this can impact a user's interpretation of the result.

If we extend this notion to visualization in 3D, a major problem occurs in that in order to view important structures (such as the chromosomes), we need to be able to see *through*, or in fact remove altogether, unrelated material that may be obstructing the path. Typically, volume visualization would be used to view the data; however, requires much effort in terms of manual manipulation of opacity/alpha and gray scales in order to *resolve* possible MOI. This task is a trial and error process and is completely counter-intuitive, with many degrees of freedom (e.g., adjusting a possible 256 gray levels with 256 combinations of alpha settings). Traditional thresholding may be applied to a set of clusters as opposed to raw data; however, at times it is useful to view a particular material within its context. For instance, viewing the central regions of the above chromosomes without their surrounding structure may not offer as much insight into the workings of a biological specimen as viewing in *relation* to its surrounds.

Thus, knowledge of the clusters defining a segmentation, as well as *how* segmented materials are related, may be utilized to intelligently assign appropriate gray levels and opacities to a volume-rendered result. Since the SOHVM is able to capture such associations, the implication for microbiological image visualization is that this process can be automated, or even controlled, through user interaction. The advantage is that the interactions needed to achieve this process are very simple. One possible scenario is through the manipulation of a slider control for cluster selection. Upon selecting a cluster, the topology connections are explored systematically for the assignment of opacity. An example is highlighted in Figure 8.17, where this process might begin at the cluster with the brightest gray-level definition. If there is any limited *a priori* information at this point, that a biologist can make use of for a starting position, then this process can be semi-supervised. For instance, a biologist may know that the structure they are interested in should exhibit a high level of response to a known epi-fluorescent label. Armed with this knowledge, and a backbone segmentation provided by the SOHVM, the biologist may be able to see that a given cluster prototype appears to have extracted a strong value for channel A (in which the marker is known to present). The complete rendering process and visualization task can then be automated from this point, revealing all related material while rendering unrelated information transparent. A user could then in theory, move about the topological *graph* of clusters, exploring relationships inherent in the biological specimen in a natural, simple manner.

Toward this end, we have integrated the SOTM and SOHVM algorithms into a popular software environment called *Avizo* (formerly Amira) [274]. The environment allows for the presentation, visualization, and analysis of scientific data, which makes use of low level OpenGL graphics libraries through a higher level Open Scene-based API.

8.5.2 Visualization of Chromosomes During Mitosis

In the next experiment, we extend the segmentation principles used above, to the extraction of chromosomes from a larger dataset *chromo83*. This 83 slice stack contains more chromosomes from the same orchid root-tip cell, in a more advanced

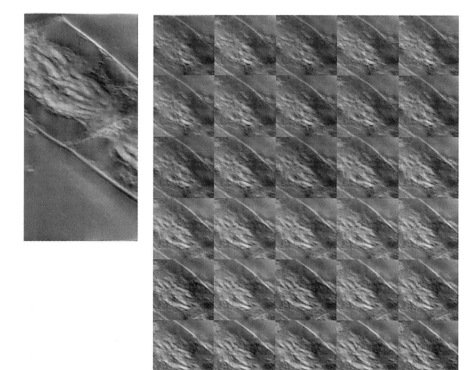

FIGURE 8.18   Sample 3D image stack of orchid root-tip chromosomes from the confocal dataset *chromo83*: (right) slices 36–70 from the 83 slice stack; (left) original size dataset, slice 40. Data is preprocessed using a Hilbert Transform to reconstruct the intensity profile from the raw data. Nomarski Differential Interference Contrast phase-based modality of CLSM was used to capture the image stack (commonly used to image translucent specimens).

state of mitosis, where the chromosomes are unwinding and being drawn to the spindles at either end of the cell. The sheer thickness of this dataset and the density of information within make it difficult to visualize. Figure 8.18 shows a cropped version of the 3D stack of slices that form the dataset.

Figure 8.19 shows the volume rendering of the raw dataset. In this instance, even with some thresholding, it becomes impossible to adequately view the internal structure of the cell under mitosis, without removing much of the information; nor is it viewable in its raw state (embedded in the gray matrix shown). With the SOHVM, a segmentation is thus formed by grouping voxels that have been defined using the same feature space as in Section 8.4.3.2. With the segmentation that results, it becomes far simpler to selectively remove or render to various degrees of transparency, each

FIGURE 8.19 Volume rendering of raw *Chromo83* image stack (top) and SOHVM labeled states (bottom).

of the desired classes. We present a manual example of the concept illustrated in the previous section with the idea that given a topological set of associations, it will become feasible to automate this process. At any rate, even with manual cluster selection, the task of visualization becomes much simpler than if a user manually assigns a mixture of transparencies and gray levels to the raw data and manipulates them until relevant information becomes (if at all), visible.

Segmentation is performed using a similar set of features as with *chromo18*; arbitrary, yet contrasting set of gray levels equal to the number of clusters found

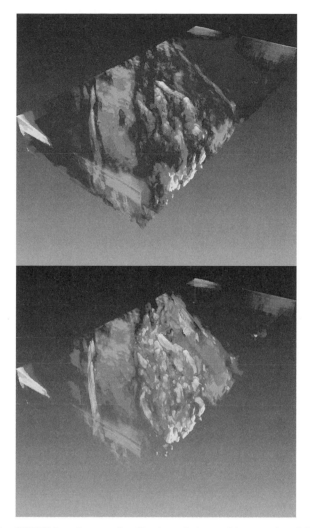

FIGURE 8.20   SOHVM peel away visualization of *chromo83* stages 1 and 2: (top) stage 1; (bottom) stage 2.

are manually assigned following the topological connections discovered by the map, starting with the cluster having the highest GL value. Within *Avizo*, we then manually zero the alpha channel (render it transparent), for each class in succession. This translates into the peel-away process shown in Figures 8.20, 8.21, 8.22, and 8.23.

As can be seen from the resulting figures, the mass of chromosomes unwinding is significantly enhanced with respect to the rendering of raw data. Additionally, the process of segmentation is automatic, and the only steps required at this point by the user are the switching on/off of classes. Thus, the SOHVM has facilitated and greatly

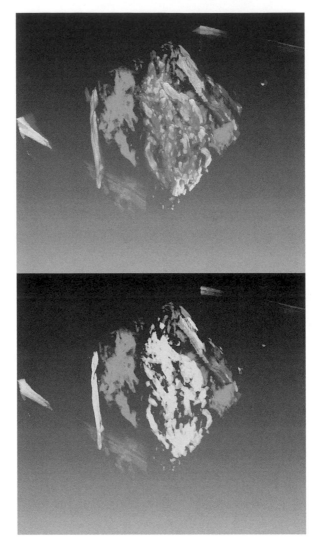

FIGURE 8.21   SOHVM peel away visualization of *chromo83* stages 3 and 4: (top) stage 3; (bottom) stage 4.

simplified the process of extracting and visualizing important structures from within the chromosome specimen.

In terms of its feasibility, here the materials represent what we know to be chromosome material and cell walls. The shape of the structures correlates well with spindle-driven process of cell division (mitosis), where chromatins are known to supercoil together and condense into chromosomes in the central region of the cell, before the two complementary DNA strands forming the chromosome are drawn apart toward the ends of the cell. The converging chromosome material reflects at the

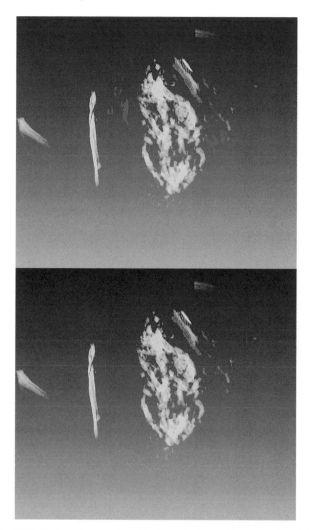

FIGURE 8.22   SOHVM peel away visualization of *chromo83* stages 5 and 6: (top) stage 5; (bottom) stage 6.

ends of the cell reflect this process well, with the added advantage of shedding much light into how this process takes place within 3D space.

8.6 SUMMARY

In comparison to other clustering techniques, both the SOTM and SOHVM algorithms represent useful techniques for the elucidation of microstructure from within 2D and 3D microbiological image data, obtained from various modalities of optical CLSM.

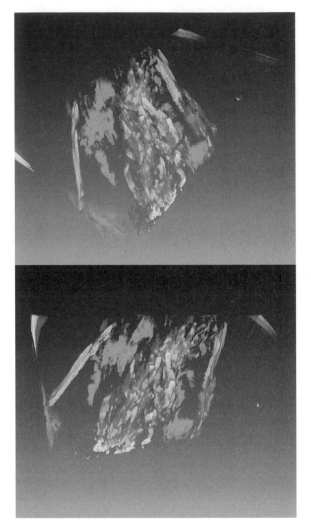

FIGURE 8.23 SOHVM visualization of *chromo83*: stage 3 reoriented, shows chromosome material being drawn to the spindles at either end of the cell during mitosis—(top) from right; (bottom) from left.

We find that the SOHVM is uniquely poised to mine characteristic patterns from unlabeled data without the need for an a posteriori evaluation that requires a search across a range of possible cluster configurations, evaluated using validity analysis against individual runs of fixed algorithms. We show examples of utilizing this automated property of the SOHVM to seek more natural segmentations of gray-level and higher order, multidimensional feature descriptions, with examples for the clustering of texture information and Local gray-level-based statistics. The implications of segmentation for characterization of biological specimens from image data is discussed.

Finally, examples were presented for how the SOHVM can identify inter-class/intercluster relationships, and discuss the implications of this for greatly simplifying the 3D visualization process of microscope data, as indicated with an example of the 3D volume rendering of a large stack of orchid root-tip cells in an advanced state of mitosis.

CHAPTER 9

Closing Remarks and Future Directions

In this book, the overall objective has been to develop a suitable, yet generic framework for the unsupervised mining, grouping, and subsequent topological (relational) description of an appropriate number of characteristic patterns from an input dataset, in the absence of a priori information. The focal points of book lay in the design and development of two novel models for unsupervised learning or data clustering, based on dynamic Self-Organization: namely, the *self-organizing tree map* (SOTM) and *The Self-Organizing Hierarchical Variance Map* (SOHVM).

Specific applications presented outline the utility of these models in applications including modeling and restoration of images corrupted by impulse noise; embedding relevance feedback in automated and semi-automated content-based image retrieval (CBIR); and segmentation and visualization of biomedical image data. In closing, this chapter summarizes the main properties and recommendations in the use of such models and concludes with a discussion of some potential directions for future research and application.

9.1 SUMMARY OF MAIN FINDINGS

9.1.1 Dynamic Self-Organization: Effective Models for Efficient Feature Space Parsing

The SOTM and SOHVM models presented in this book, offer mechanisms that iteratively parse a feature space hierarchically (from coarse down to fine levels of detail). Parsing is achieved stochastically, by allocating new exemplars to regions of feature space in which there is both density and no suitable representative. By allocating exemplars as needed to regions of density, an efficient model of the feature space clusters is built, in contrast to fixed Self-Organizing Map (SOM) based models that often retain exemplars corresponding to regions in feature space containing zero density. The resulting set of exemplars provide a compact model, which can be used as a basis for indexing, classification, and extraction of inherent relationships in the underlying data.

Unsupervised Learning: A Dynamic Approach, First Edition.
Matthew Kyan, Paisarn Muneesawang, Kambiz Jarrah, and Ling Guan.
© 2014 by The Institute of Electrical and Electronics Engineers, Inc. Published by John Wiley & Sons, Inc.

The SOTM and SOHVM models are developed and justified intuitively, through arguments regarding the nature and dynamics of a stochastic, partitional search of the input space. The SOTM evolves from roots in Adaptive Resonance Theory (ART) and traditional SOM-based learning, while the SOHVM draws inspiration from the SOTM along with Hebbian style extensions for learning and correlating input stimuli in the map lattice itself. The SOHVM model, as implied in its naming, extends SOTM hierarchical parsing with the ability to sense Local variance and dynamically adapt associative connections within its map. The importance of these properties are twofold.

1. Reduced chance for cluster prototypes to become trapped in Local minima— identified through more stable solutions when compared with classic models (KM, GMM, FCM, etc.) and even the SOTM;
2. More stable set of associations between clusters found at convergence— demonstrated against other dynamic models (e.g., GNG).

9.1.2   Improved Stability, Integrity, and Efficiency

The SOHVM shows improved efficiency in terms of allocating new prototypes to more viable regions of density in the underlying data space. This translates to a more stable configuration, particularly at higher resolutions of input space considered. This result is best illustrated through Figures 7.13, 7.14, and 7.15, where, under similarly controlled decay schedules, experimental comparisons between the SOTM and the SOHVM show that, at some point in the Global decay of the hierarchical control function, the SOTM network will undergo a rapid proliferation of nodes (prototypes). This can ultimately degrade the integrity of natural clusters previously mined from the data. The SOHVM, by contrast, appears far more resilient to such proliferation. We conjecture that this is on account of its informed search and partitioning strategy. It is important to note that similar proliferation effects occur in Growing Neural Gas (GNG).

In the SOHVM, Hebbian Maximal Eigenfilters (HME) play a significant role in assessing Local orientations for maximal variance in the immediate vicinity of a prototype. As such they can act as a probe or pointer to likely regions of density warranting further division. This is the fundamental difference between the proposed model and its predecessor, the SOTM. Individual HMEs at each node essentially render this process to be Local, rather than Global. While overseen by the Global hierarchical control function as in an SOTM process, the difference here is that the hierarchical control function in the SOHVM serves as an indication of scope, within which insertion may be considered. Ultimately, it is the interplay between Local maximal variances mined thus far that trigger the need for map growth in the region Local to any given cluster prototype. As such, this process is more heavily regulated by the data itself. In the SOTM, this process is effectively blind and thus is more sensitive to spawning nodes in outliers and noisy regions than in the SOHVM.

9.1.3 Adaptive Topologies Promote Consistency and Uncover Relationships

The SOHVM incorporates an additional mechanism of Competitive Hebbian Learning (CHL), to mine intercluster correlations from the data. This mechanism allows the SOHVM to adaptively build and maintain a topological map that reflects the existence of density between clusters found. This first serves to preserve the locations of clusters found previously. An example of this potential is seen in the simple gray-level segmentation of Figure 8.9, where over a number of trials, each allowing for increasingly finer resolutions to be clustered, we see that the SOHVM appears to undergo the least amount of shift in the clusters representative of important structures in the image. This is evidenced through Figure 8.10, where zoomed versions of the labeled clusters are shown comparing the SOHVM, SOTM, self-organizing feature map (SOFM), and K-Means (KM) methods at low and high numbers of cluster prototypes. In the SOHVM case, the pink regions forming the dense centers of the chromosomes in the focal place essentially remain so in both coarse grain and fine grain segmentations. In the other models, more degradation appears.

Both the SOTM and the SOHVM are very effective in finding more important regions of groupings early; however, the SOHVM then works to maintain their relative integrity (should they in fact be representative of actual clusters). We conjecture that this property is by virtue of the combination of topology information (which works to maintain an associative level of cluster position), and the HME probe emanating from any given cluster. In some sense, the HME becomes protective of any density surrounding it, regulating its partitioning.

Cluster validity analysis suggests dynamic Self-Organization yields a more reliable selection of optimal clusters (under a posteriori analysis). Both the SOTM and SOHVM algorithms were subject to cluster validity analysis on both synthetic and real world data. Both were shown to perform well against other popular clustering models particularly in terms of consistency of solution mined from the data. It is conjectured that this is due to the inherent hierarchical nature in which allocation of new cluster prototypes proceeds. In the case of SOHVM, this quality and consistency is more apparent, perhaps due to its more informed hierarchical search.

9.1.4 Online Selection of Class Number

An automatic mode was devised for the SOHVM, such that, in a completely unsupervised manner, it is able to deduce simultaneously, a seemingly optimal number of clusters, their prototypes, and an appropriate topological mapping associating them. Examples were presented for synthetic data, real-world data, and in the mining of natural modes for the multilevel thresholding of biofilm and chromosome data. In a test performed on chromosome data, the SOHVM successfully revealed its inherent bimodal nature. This corroborated with the histogram. For more complex biofilm, visual inspection suggests the mixture of multiple characteristic gray-levels, textures representing bacteria and other biomaterials. The SOHVM was able to mine out a perceptually clear segmentation that appeared to have targeted dominant gray-levels in the image, as compared with a KM result. In the KM, however, the number of classes was specified, while the SOHVM demonstrated self-determination.

9.1.5   Topologies Represent a Useful Backbone for Visualization or Analysis

By formulating a topological backbone of the input space, it becomes possible for clusters in different regions to become, in some sense topologically isolated by virtue of the mapping. As such, the mapping provides a concrete graph or path along which higher level relationships between clusters may be assessed. This, in some sense, could represent a new type of descriptive feature of the input space. One might imagine a graph representation of the topology of input space as a nonparametric descriptor of its distribution. Inexact graph-matching techniques from computer science could represent a viable avenue of future research for comparing topologies mined from input spaces exhibiting similar, yet complex underlying distributions.

In Chapter 8, a more simplistic realization of how topological information can be used for microbiological image visualization is discussed. Essentially, if constrained to movements along a mined topology, a user can conceivably browse through and visualize structures of the data that are related. An example of this was achieved by parsing the topological structure of both a 10-class segmentation of a small stack of chromosomes (18 slices), and a natural segmentation of a large stack of chromosomes (83 slices) at an advanced state of cell mitosis. This process yields a simple peel-away visualization allowing for the visualization of related, yet isolated biomaterials from within the cell. The chromosome material can be clearly seen being drawn along the spindle mechanism toward each end of the dividing cell. Future research effort in this application would need to target appropriate strategies for either the automatic (or user-controlled) traversal of clusters along the topology for the assignment of colors, transparencies, etc., to be used in the rendering process.

The SOHVM was also explored in terms of its relative segmenting abilities on biofilm data using classical texture metrics from the image-processing community. Armed with self-determination of an optimal class number, different weightings were applied to constrain the contribution of texture information fused with gray-level information defining each voxel. The SOHVM was able to mine out extremely clear segmentations that appear to have embedded a certain level of spatial refinement and continuity. This represents a very promising avenue for the purely automatic separation of biomaterials from specimens. Of course, some further research work into the texture description used and an appropriate weighting for mixing gray-level and texture information would need to be conducted. In fact, this result is more desirable than that obtained with the SOTM in early experiments using XY positional information, as the relatively uniform, regular coordinate does not carry any specific informational content, as opposed to the textural feature.

9.2   FUTURE DIRECTIONS

The real advantage of creating a self-organized clustering as opposed to most other clustering methods, lies in the availability of the resulting topological map. Mining the topology, as opposed to assuming one through imposing a predetermined lattice, can be leveraged for very specific tasks. We touch on three major categories of task: namely, dynamic navigation through information repositories; knowledge-assisted visualization; and path-based trajectory analysis. In each category, there is a common theme—where there is topology, there is context, and context can assist in conveying or extracting knowledge.

9.2.1 Dynamic Navigation for Information Repositories

One of the major challenges in search and retrieval relates to the problem of how to effectively present a snapshot of information within a repository and provide the necessary context that can enable a user to browse and locate information of interest. In a CBIR framework, the idea is that an initial query can lead to a collection of results (extracted from the repository based on various similarity metrics). Due to the semantic gap (described in Chapter 6), the content retrieved may not accurately reflect the information need, and thus, the user is given the opportunity to adjust their search, by specifying relevant and irrelevant content from the currently retrieved set. Adaptive learning on this set works to adjust the original query in the hope that a modified search will result in more relevant content.

In Chapter 6, the idea of active learning is presented by working dynamically with a visualization of the retrieved data (shown below in Fig. 9.1a). Assuming an initial query is searched, an alternative to displaying the most similar results across the database is presented. Instead, the most similar cluster and its neighboring clusters are presented in a three-dimensional (3D) visualization, much like the visual thesaurus concept referred to in Figure 6.7a. In this type of approach, the user automatically has the context of nearby or similar content in the repository. Rather than selecting clusters as relevant or not (which can extend the modification of a query to a larger scale than labeling a set of individual retrieved samples), the cluster relating to the best ranked result can be centered in the visualization, and the SOHVM topology connecting nearby clusters can be used in the visualization. The topology can be used to update the query by navigating from the current cluster to nearby clusters, by way of traversing the edges in the SOHVM (Fig. 9.1b). In this way, query modification could be conceived as a combination of navigation and relevance labeling. The traversal through the map structure could also be an indication of the user's interest or information need and could itself be considered in the query modification process.

A related application is information summarization. In simple terms, when one is presented with a repository of information and has no sample query to proceed with in a search, how then does one formulate a query? For instance, take the problem of video summarization: normally, a lengthy sequence of video can only be navigated in a linear fashion—however this does not lend itself to finding interesting clips or sections of video in a rapid way. However, if there was some way to present an overview of important content in the video, then this gives the user an idea of what queries they may wish to pursue.

Summarization is currently only loosely defined, in that what determines a *good* summarization is really a subjective matter. Much like information retrieval, this amounts to what is considered important information to the viewer—which is highly

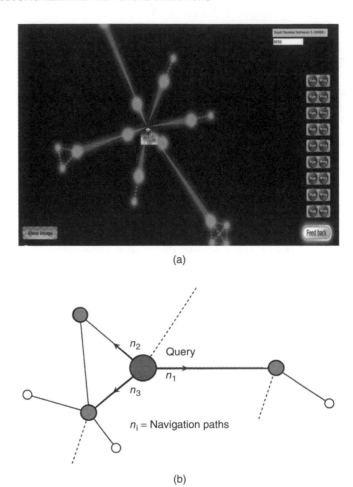

(a)

(b)

FIGURE 9.1   (a) 3D user interference *via* Self-Organizing Tree Map for semiautomatic relevance feedback system. (b) The SOHVM provides an alternative mechanism for navigation—connections in the map providing a path for query modification.

contingent on the application. In surveillance, for instance, this task may be very well defined, for example, a static background is expected, and anything unusual (e.g., motion) could be considered a region of interest. In unstructured video for which the content is not known beforehand, summarization is more open-ended. For instance, a set of key frames may be extracted by an SOM in order to present that which is important to the viewer; the question then becomes how to effectively present this information to the viewer.

    One example might be to rank nodes in the map by their respective densities and present some key frames from these nodes, but favor frames from nodes that are more sparsely located in the map (indicative of quite different visual frames). The structure of the topology could be quickly traversed to find commonly occurring or infrequently occurring frames. In another sense, the structure of the map could act as a guide for video browsing, where the user can begin at a node in the map that has high/low density and the connected nodes display their respective key frames (similar to the process depicted in Fig. 9.1b). The user could navigate any of the nearby nodes (based on their connectivity to the current node being viewed). Summarization and search/ retrieval could be conceived in an SOHVM network as part of the same process.

9.2.2 Interactive Knowledge-Assisted Visualization

An example of automatic clustering and application of color profiles to clustered voxels was presented in Chapter 7, where peel-away visualizations were constructed from the SOHVM map. The idea was initiated for leveraging the topology in applying systematic coloring or opacity mapping to highlight voxels from a given cluster, in the context of their surrounding voxels. This idea naturally extends to the concept of a *dynamic*, *interactive* approach to exploring volumetric datasets, by actively re-rendering the scene based on the user's current cluster of interest.

Volume exploration is an important technique to reveal inner structures and interesting regions in a volumetric dataset. However, exploring the volume is a difficult and nonintuitive task, since there is no prior information available regarding the data distribution. The 3D representation of a volume adds complexity to the whole process. To ease this process, Direct Volume Rendering (DVR) makes use of a Transfer Function (TF), which maps one or more features extracted from the data (the feature space) to different optical properties such as color and opacity.

The TF design is typically a user-controlled process, where the user interacts with different widgets (usually representing feature clusters or 1D/2D histograms) to set color and opacity properties to the feature space. The user can also control some low level properties like number of clusters, cluster variance. Most of the recently proposed DVR methodologies [275–278] are based on this philosophy.

Interacting with the feature space is difficult for the end user, who may not have any knowledge about feature extraction and clustering. Also, these kind of widgets try to represent the feature space directly, putting a restriction on the dimensionality of the feature space. Some methods use alternative ways to represent the higher dimensional feature space through manageable widgets. For instance, in Reference 279 spatial information is encoded in the color values, while opacity is derived through intensity and gradient. But these kinds of alternatives are restrictive in the sense that the clustering or histogram generation is not directly derived from the full feature set. Also, only the specific features used in the proposed methods can be used for all datasets. Volume rendering has a wide range of applications in different fields, and one set of features useful for a specific application might be completely irrelevant in another. Hence, there is a need to make the method independent so that any feature irrespective of its dimensionality can be represented to the user in a visual form while maintaining the topological relationship between various data distributions. This is exactly what an SOM can do. SOM preserves the input data topology and helps to generate a lower dimensional visualization of the clusters. The SOM structure is particularly of interest for DVR because of its visualization capability.

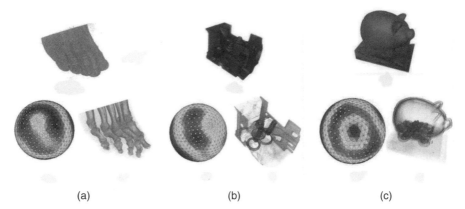

(a)   (b)   (c)

FIGURE 9.2 Rendering results and corresponding spherical SOMs for the three datasets: (a) foot; (b) engine; and (c) piggy bank.

In Figure 9.2, an example is presented of a system that uses a spherical SOM to visualize clusters over voxels in a dataset. Rather than manipulating cluster parameters or optical properties, the user simply interacts with a color-coded SOM lattice representing cluster densities. Due to this visual nature of SOM, there is no need to tweak the cluster parameters and perform operations like split and merge to precisely determine the number of clusters or cluster spread. The user only has to intuitively select or deselect the SOM regions to reveal corresponding structures in a volume. This model is independent of the dimensionality of the feature space. Any feature irrespective of its dimension or complexity can be used with the model, which makes it very robust. In a manner similar to that presented in the previous section, it seems plausible that the exploration task could be considered as a navigation task, where the user traverses the topology of an SOHVM depicted in Figure 9.3. The transfer function could thus be made to adapt to the user's location in the map and embedded in

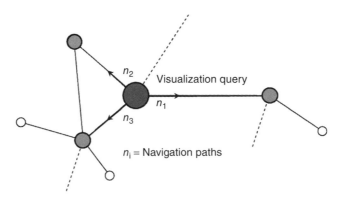

FIGURE 9.3 User interaction via navigation: each new query shows different visualization pixels rendered based on their connectivity to a current query.

the context available from nearby nodes in the map. In this way, the SOHVM could be leveraged for a fully interactive volume exploration, where at each step in the interaction, new nodes become the *visualization query*, with the dataset undergoing a complete re-rendering according to the modified transfer function.

9.2.3 Temporal Data Analysis Using Trajectories

In temporal data, context relates to the states that have led to (or follow) the state in the present time step; the question is, can knowledge of such states assist in the prediction of future states? Or, more specifically, can the collection of states and their layout on the map be indicative of some deeper insight or meaning? We discuss two areas of application in which SOMs have been useful and describe briefly how the dynamic models proposed are applicable.

9.2.3.1 *Video Shot Boundary Detection*   Recent studies have attempted to analyze video data and how it maps onto SOMs. In video, the majority of image sequences exhibit very strong correlation (both spatially and temporally). In this way, the learning conducted on image frames results in a map of key frames that are arranged such that the more proximal frames are visually similar. In fact, this is dependent really on the property used as a descriptor for each frame. For instance, if some motion-related property is used in the learning process, then key frames will be extracted based on motion. Coherent motion and coherent scenes imply relatively smooth changes (in the descriptors) across groups of consecutive frames in the video; thus, a temporal series should map to a relatively smooth trajectory (path) on any SOM.

As an example of this, the authors in Reference 280 propose a method for Video Segmentation and Shot Boundary Detection Using SOMs. Their video shot boundary detection (SBD) algorithm spots discontinuities in the visual stream by monitoring video frame trajectories on SOMs. Their argument is that the SOM space resembles the probability density differences in the feature space and that distances between SOM coordinates give more information than distances between plain features taken from the video stream. SOM can be very helpful in video segmentation. The reason being that consecutive frames in a continuous video segment filmed by a single camera are normally visually similar. In this manner, any transition effects can be categorized into abrupt cuts and gradual transitions based on how fast these changes happen in the video stream. For instance, in cut transitions the change from one shot to another is instantaneous, whereas in the gradual scene change the transition has some duration. In Figure 9.4, a closed-loop spherical SOM is used to separate a video scene into shots based on this principle. Essentially, a sequence of frames can be projected onto the nodes of the map, and a sliding window can be considered over the sequence of nodes. Distances between the nodes in the map space are indicative of whether or not there should be a shot boundary.

In a similar manner, rather than address the shot continuity as a jump on the map, the SOHVM would naturally find such discontinuities as it evolves, as it will update topology and eliminate connections across regions of little to no density in the feature

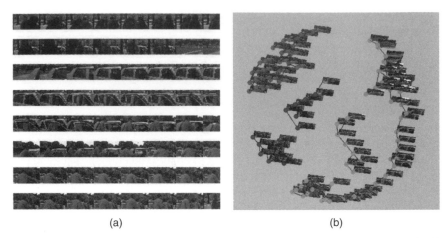

(a)   (b)

FIGURE 9.4 An example of Shot Boundary Detection using the Spherical SOM: (a) video sequence; (b) sequence trajectories on map and their segmentation.

space. There would be no need to consider sliding windows on the projected input sequence.

9.2.3.2 Gesture Recognition Recent trends toward more immersive and interactive computing come with increasing demand for more transparent interfaces between human and computer. Effective interaction, for instance, requires tools that facilitate more natural, human modes of communication. One area under active pursuit (particularly in console gaming), has been the development of technology to understand and interpret human gestural input or *gesture recognition*. Gestures are expressive, meaningful body motions involving physical movements of the fingers, hands, arms, head, face, or body with the intent of (1) conveying meaningful information or (2) interacting with the environment. "Human gestures" incorporate a small subspace of possible human motion. Figure 9.5 shows some examples of human body gestures and hand gestures (sign language).

The idea behind applying SOMs to the problem of gesture recognition is to deal with the challenge of how to effectively parse a sequence of movements into a set of *postures*, then representing or modeling sequences of postures as a gesture. The topological map afforded by the SOM can help in this regard, in much the same way as described for video analysis. In this case, postures are represented by a particular state of sensor values at an instant in time. For instance, Nintendo powerglove, one of the first peripheral interface controllers to recreate human hand movements, uses pitch, yaw, roll, and finger bend; Nintendo Wii sensor uses accelerometer data; Microsoft Kinect uses skeletal tracking of joint positions. Full motion capture technology used in film making and animation can also be used to describe postures, which are then mapped onto the SOM. A gesture can then be represented as a path or trajectory on the map, as traced by projecting a temporal series of postures (Fig. 9.6). Each path can be used to model a type of gesture, or transitions between possible postures

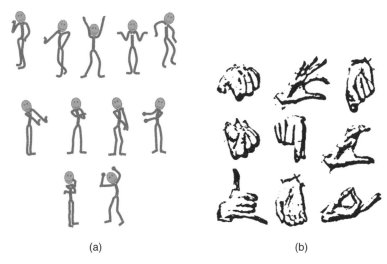

(a)   (b)

FIGURE 9.5 Examples of human gestures: (left) full body gestures; (right) hand gestures (sign language).

for a given gesture can be extracted. Unknown gestures can be recognized through a matching process (template paths) as the path of an unknown gesture is traced on the map.

We present two examples in Figure 9.7 of trajectories mapped onto a spherical SOM of fixed topology and size. In Figure 9.7a, the map was trained on gesture data collected from the Nintendo Powerglove. The dataset presented is from the Australian Sign Language dataset, and the figure shows three different hand signs from the dataset, projected onto the map. In Figure 9.7b, data from a Microsoft Kinect image sensor is presented (skeletal joint positions). In this figure, a set of three gestures from a game of *charades* was captured and projected onto the map. It is quite clear from both graphics in Figure 9.7, that the trajectories mapped are quite

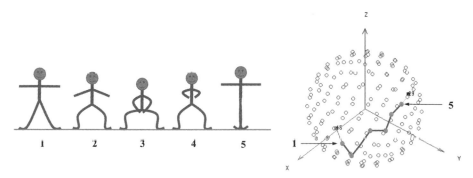

FIGURE 9.6 Temporal sequence of postures representing an arbitrary gesture (of 5 postures)—the mapping of this gesture results in a trajectory on the Spherical SOM.

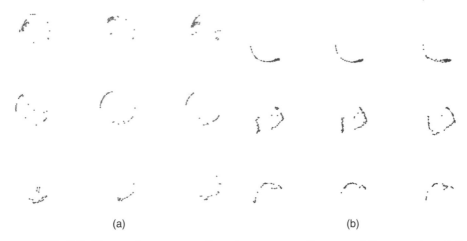

(a)   (b)

FIGURE 9.7 Temporal sequence of postures representing an arbitrary gesture (of 5 postures)—the mapping of this gesture results in a trajectory on the Spherical SOM.

consistent over a similar gesture but quite distinct across different gestures. This is advantageous in recognition, which can be made by comparing paths.

The advantage of SOHVM if applied in this situation is, once again, that nodes reflect regions in feature space of high density, and there are little in regions of low density. The connectivity is representative of the natural paths that a gesture may take through the map. Topology connecting nearby postures can be used to constrain the path in which valid gestures should move; if an incoming sequence does not conform, then it can more readily be neglected in recognition.

A.1 GLOBAL AND LOCAL CONSISTENCY ERROR

Global and Local consistency errors are generally used to assess the relative consistency between two alternative segmentation solutions (often used in image segmentation), under the condition where the number of separate groups in each solution is not necessarily guaranteed to be the same, nor is there any viable method of matching groups across both solutions. In terms of clustering, this technique is useful when we have two clustering solutions obtained from the same input data space, yet have no way of knowing which clusters are meant to represent the same classes across both solutions, or in cases where both solutions have an unequal number of clusters. Consistencies are evaluated according to the way similar data samples are allocated to similar clusters in both solutions. Inconsistencies then occur if, for example, the same two data samples exist in the same cluster in one solution, versus being split across two clusters in the other solution.

Let $\setminus$ and $\| \cdot \|$ denote set difference and cardinality, respectively. Let $R(S, p_i)$ represent the set of pixels corresponding to the region in segmentation S that contains pixel p_i; the Local refinement error (LRE) is defined by

$$\text{LRE}(S_1, S_2, p_i) = \frac{\| R(S_1, p_i) \setminus R(S_2, p_i) \|}{\| R(S_1, p_i) \|} \tag{A.1}$$

The Global Consistency Error (GCE) and Local Consistency Error (LCE) are defined by

$$\text{GCE}(S_1, S_2) = \frac{1}{n} \min \left\{ \sum_i \text{LRE}(S_1, S_2, p_i), \sum_i \text{LRE}(S_2, S_1, p_i) \right\} \tag{A.2}$$

$$\text{LCE}(S_1, S_2) = \frac{1}{n} \sum_i \min \left\{ \text{LRE}(S_1, S_2, p_i), \text{LRE}(S_2, S_1, p_i) \right\} \tag{A.3}$$

Unsupervised Learning: A Dynamic Approach, First Edition.
Matthew Kyan, Paisarn Muneesawang, Kambiz Jarrah, and Ling Guan.
© 2014 by The Institute of Electrical and Electronics Engineers, Inc. Published by John Wiley & Sons, Inc.

Essentially, LRE expresses an error in terms of a weighting of how many pixels are *not* common between the two clusters it belongs to in each solution, versus the size of a cluster. There are two refinement errors per pixel, based on which solution is being considered. LCE then considers the average minimal refinement error between the two solutions, over all pixels. Globally, GCE looks at the minimum cumulative refinement errors over all pixels in each pairing of clusters and averages this over all clusters.

REFERENCES

1. A. M. Turing, "The chemical basis of morphogenesis," *Philosophical Transactions of the Royal Society B*, vol. 237, pp. 5–72, 1952.

2. S. Haykin, *Neural Networks: A Comprehensive Foundation*, 2nd edn. Upper Saddle River (New Jersey): Prentice Hall, Inc., 1999.

3. W. K. Pratt, *Digital Image Processing*. New York: John Wiley & Sons, Inc., 1991.

4. N. Wiener, *Nonlinear Problems in Random Theory*. Cambridge, MA: MIT Press, 1958.

5. Y. Shim, J. Chung, and I. C. Choi, "A comparison study of cluster validity indices using a nonhierarchical clustering algorithm," in *International Conference on Computational Intelligence for Modelling, Control and Automation, and International Conference on Intelligent Agents, Web Technologies and Internet Commerce* (Vienna, Austria), pp. 199–204, 28–30 November, 2005.

6. D. O. Hebb, *The Organization of Behavior: A Neuropsychological Theory*. New York: John Wiley & Sons, Inc., 1949.

7. A. Brazma and J. Vilo, "Gene expression data analysis," *FEBS Letters*, vol. 480, pp. 17–24, 2000.

8. S. Salzberg and S. Cost, "Predicting protein secondary structure with a nearest-neighbor algorithm," *Journal of Molecular Biology*, vol. 227, pp. 371–374, 1992.

9. T. Kohonen, *Self-Organizing Maps*. Berlin: Springer, 1995.

10. J. Randall, L. Guan, W. Li, and X. Zhang, "The hierarchical cluster model for image region segmentation," in *Proceedings of IEEE International Conference on Multimedia and Expo*, vol. 1 (Lausanne, Switzerland), pp. 693–696, August 26–29, 2002.

11. H. Frigui and R. Krishnapuram, "A robust competitive clustering algorithm with applications in computer vision," *IEEE Transactions on Pattern Analysis and Machine Intelligence*, vol. 21, no. 5, pp. 450–465, 1999.

12. W. Reddick, J. Glass, E. Cook, T. Elkin, and R. Deaton, "Automated segmentation and classification of multispectral magnetic resonance images of brain using artificial neural networks," *IEEE Transactions on Medical Imaging*, vol. 6, pp. 911–918, 1997.

13. C. Carpineto and G. Romano, "A lattice conceptual clustering system and its application to browsing retrieval," *Machine Learning*, vol. 24, pp. 95–122, 1996.

14. S. K. Bhatia and J. S. Deogun, "Conceptual clustering in information retrieval," *IEEE Transactions on Systems, Man, and Cybernetics, Part B: Cybernetics*, vol. 28, no. 3, pp. 427–436, 1998.

Unsupervised Learning: A Dynamic Approach, First Edition.
Matthew Kyan, Paisarn Muneesawang, Kambiz Jarrah, and Ling Guan.
© 2014 by The Institute of Electrical and Electronics Engineers, Inc. Published by John Wiley & Sons, Inc.

15. H. M. Abbas and M. M. Fahmy, "Neural networks for maximum likelihood clustering," *Signal Processing*, vol. 36, no. 1, pp. 111–126, 1994.

16. D. Judd, P. Mckinley, and A. K. Jain, "Large-scale parallel data clustering," *IEEE Transactions on Pattern Analysis and Machine Intelligence*, vol. 20, no. 8, pp. 871–876, 1998.

17. D. Lay, *Linear Algebra and Its Applications*. New York: Addison-Wesley, 2000.

18. A. Bell and T. Sejnowski, "The independent components of natural scenes are edge filters," *Vision Research*, vol. 37, no. 23, pp. 3327–3338, 1997.

19. H. Abdi, "Distance," in *Encyclopedia of Measurement and Statistics*. Thousand Oaks (California): SAGE Publications, 2007.

20. P. C. Mahalanobis, "On the generalised distance in statistics," *Proceedings of the National Institute of Science of India*, vol. 12, pp. 49–55, 1936.

21. E. F. Krause, *Taxicab Geometry: An Adventure in Non-Euclidean Geometry*. New York: Dover, 1986.

22. F. Van der Heijden, R. P. W. Duin, D. de Ridder, and D. M. J. Tax, *Classification, Parameter Estimation, and State Estimation: An Engineering Approach Using MATLAB*. Sussex, UK: John Wiley & Sons, Ltd, 2004.

23. B. Batchelor, *Pattern Recognition. Ideas in Practice*, pp. 71–72. New York: Plenum Press, 1978.

24. L. Rigutini and M. Maggini, "A semi-supervised document clustering algorithm based on em," in *Proceedings of the IEEE/WIC/ACM International Conference on Web Intelligence*. Compiegne, France: IEEE Computer Society, 2005.

25. G. R. Xue, C. Lin, Q. Yang, W. S. Xi, H. J. Zeng, Y. Yu, and Z. Chen, "Scalable collaborative filtering using cluster-based smoothing," in *Proceedings of the International ACM SIGIR Conference on Research and Development in Information Retrieval*, pp. 114–121. Salvador, Brazil: ACM, 2005.

26. J. Bennett and S. Lanning, "The netflix prize," in *Proceedings of KDD Cup and Workshop*, vol. 2007 (California), Aug 12, 2007. URL: http://www.cs.uic.edu/~liub/Netflix-KDD-Cup-2007.html

27. G. Linden, B. Smith, and J. York, "Amazon.com recommendations: item-to-item collaborative filtering," *IEEE Internet Computing*, vol. 7, no. 1, pp. 76–80, 2003.

28. A. K. Jain and B. Chandrasekaran, "Dimensionality and sample size considerations in pattern recognition practice," *Handbook of Statistics*, vol. 2, pp. 835–855, 1982.

29. L. Kaufman and P. Rousseeuw, *Finding Groups in Data: An Introduction to Cluster Analysis*. New York: John Wiley & Sons, Inc., 1990.

30. S. Zhong, "Efficient online spherical k-means clustering," in *IEEE International Joint Conference on Neural Networks* (Montreal, Canada), pp. 3180–3185, July 31–August 4, 2005.

31. A. K. Jain and R. C. Dubes, *Algorithms for Clustering Data*. Upper Saddle River, New Jersey: Prentice Hall, Inc., 1988.

32. J. Bezdek and J. Dunn, "Optimal fuzzy partitions: a heuristic for estimating the parameters in a mixture of normal distributions," *IEEE Transactions on Computers*, vol. C24, pp. 835–838, 1975.

33. D. E. Gustafson and W. C. Kessel, "Fuzzy clustering with a fuzzy covariance matrix," *IEEE Conference on Decision and Control*, vol. 17, pp. 761–766, 1978.

34. R. Babuška, P. Van der Veen, and U. Kaymak, "Improved covariance estimation for Gustafson– Kessel clustering," in *Proceedings of the 2002 IEEE International Conference on Fuzzy Systems*, vol. 2, pp. 1081–1085, May 12–17, 2002.

35. I. Gath and A. Geva, "Unsupervised optimal fuzzy clustering," *IEEE Transactions on Pattern Analysis and Machine Intelligence*, vol. 11, no. 7, pp. 773–780, 1989.

36. G. Xuan, W. Zhang, and P. Chai, "Em algorithms of Gaussian mixture model and hidden Markov model," in *IEEE International Conference on Image Processing* (Thessaloniki, Greece), pp. 145–148, October 7–10, 2001.

37. R. Redner and H. Walker, "Mixture densities, maximum likelihood and the EM algorithm," *SIAM Review*, vol. 26, no. 2, pp. 195–239, 1984.

38. E. Gokcay and J. C. Principe, "Information theoretic clustering," *IEEE Transactions on Pattern Analysis and Machine Intelligence*, Vol. 24, no. 2, pp. 158–171, 2002.

39. F. Masulli and S. Rovetta, "A new approach to hierarchical clustering for the analysis of genomic data," in *Proceedings of the International Conference on Neural Networks* (Montreal, Canada), July 31–August 4, 2005.

40. B. S. Everitt, S. Landau, and M. Leese, *Cluster Analysis*. London, UK: Arnold, 2001.

41. J. H. Ward and M. E. Hook, "Application of a hierarchical clustering procedure to a problem of grouping profiles," *Educational and Psychological Measurement*, vol. 23, pp. 69–81, 1963.

42. R. A. Jarvis and E. A. Patrick, "Clustering using a similarity measure based on shared near neighbors," *IEEE Transactions on Computers*, vol. C22, pp. 1025–1034, 1973.

43. W. Dzwinel, D. Yuen, Y. Kaneko, K. Boryczko, and Y. Ben-Zion, "Multi-resolution clustering analysis and 3-d visualization of multitudinous synthetic earthquakes," *Visual Geosciences*, vol. 8, no. 1, pp. 1–32, 2003.

44. Y. Boykov and V. Kolmogorov, "An experimental comparison of min-cut/max-flow algorithms for energy minimization in vision," *IEEE Transactions on Pattern Analysis and Machine Intelligence*, vol. 26, no. 9, pp. 1124–1137, 2004.

45. J. Shi and J. Malik, "Normalized cuts and image segmentation," *IEEE Transactions on Pattern Analysis and Machine Intelligence*, vol. 22, no. 8, pp. 888–905, 2000.

46. P. K. Simpson, "Fuzzy min– max neural networks. I. Classification," *IEEE Transactions on Neural Networks*, vol. 3, pp. 776–786, 1992.

47. D. B. Fogel and P. K. Simpson, "Evolving fuzzy clusters," *International Conference on Neural Networks*, pp. 1829–1834, San Francisco, California, March 28–April 1, 1993.

48. D. B. Fogel and P. K. Simpson, "Experiments with evolving fuzzy clusters," *Proceedings of the Second Annual Conference on Evolutionary Programming*, La Jolla, CA. February 25–26, 1993. pp. 90–97, 1993.

49. J. Rissanen, "Universal coding, information, prediction, and estimation," *IEEE Transactions on Information Theory*, vol. 30, pp. 629–636, 1984.

50. A. Ghozeil and D. B. Fogel, "Discovering patterns in spatial data using evolutionary programming," *Proceedings of the First Annual Conference on Genetic Programming.*, pp. 521–527, (Stanford, California) July 28–31, 1996.

51. U. Maulik and S. Bandyopadhyay, "Genetic algorithm-based clustering technique," *Pattern Recognition*, vol. 33, no. 9, pp. 1455–1465, 2000.

52. G. Folino, A. Forestiero, and G. Spezzano, "Swarming agents for discovering clusters in spatial data," in *Proceedings of the Second International Symposium on Parallel and Distributed Computing*. IEEE Computer Society, 2003.

53. E. Oja, "Unsupervised learning in neural computation," *Theoretical Computer Science*, vol. 287, no. 1, pp. 187–207, 2002.

54. B. S. Y. Lam and H. Yan, "Cluster validity for DNA microarray data using a geometrical index," in *International Conference on Machine Learning and Cybernetics* (Guangzhou, China), pp. 3333–3339, August 18–21, 2005.

55. K. Y. Yeung, D. R. Haynor, and W. L. Ruzzo, "Validating clustering for gene expression data," *Bioinformatics*, vol. 17, no. 4, p. 309, 2001.

56. H. Akaike, "A new look at the statistical model identification," *IEEE Transactions on Automatic Control*, vol. 19, no. 6, pp. 716–723, 1974.

57. G. Schwarz, "Estimating the dimension of a model," *The Annals of Statistics*, vol. 6, no. 2, pp. 461–464, 1978.

58. A. Tritschler and R. Gopinath, "Improved speaker segmentation and segments clustering using the Bayesian information criterion," in *European Conference on Speech Communication and Technology*, Budapest, Hungary, September 5–9, 1999. URL: http://www.informatik.uni-trier.de/~ley/db/conf/interspeech/eurospeech1999.html

59. U. Maulik and S. Bandyopadhyay, "Performance evaluation of some clustering algorithms and validity indices," *IEEE Transactions on Pattern Analysis and Machine Intelligence*, vol. 24, no. 12, pp. 1650–1654, 2002.

60. J. C. Bezdek, *Pattern Recognition with Fuzzy Objective Function Algorithms*. Norwell, MA: Kluwer Academic Publishers, 1981.

61. X. L. Xie and G. Beni, "A validity measure for fuzzy clustering," *IEEE Transactions on Pattern Analysis and Machine Intelligence*, vol. 13, no. 8, pp. 841–847, 1991.

62. J. Dunn, "A fuzzy relative of the ISODATA process and its use in detecting compact well-separated clusters," *Cybernetics and Systems*, vol. 3, no. 3, pp. 32–57, 1973.

63. J. C. Bezdek and N. R. Pal, "Some new indexes of cluster validity," *IEEE Transactions on Systems, Man, and Cybernetics, Part B: Cybernetics*, vol. 28, no. 3, pp. 301–315, 1998.

64. T. Caliński and J. Harabasz, "A dendrite method for cluster analysis," *Communications in Statistics—Simulation and Computation*, vol. 3, no. 1, pp. 1–27, 1974.

65. Y. Shim, J. Chung, and I. Choi, "A comparison study of cluster validity indices using a nonhierarchical clustering algorithm," in *International Conference on Computational Intelligence for Modelling, Control and Automation, and International Conference on Intelligent Agents, Web Technologies and Internet Commerce*, vol. 1, Vienna, Austria, November 28–30, 2005.

66. B. S. Y. Lam and H. Yan, "Assessment of microarray data clustering results based on a new geometrical index for cluster validity," *Soft Computing—A Fusion of Foundations, Methodologies and Applications*, vol. 11, no. 4, pp. 341–348, 2007.

67. D. Hebb, *The Organisation of Behaviour*. New York: John Wiley & Sons, Inc., 1949.

68. T. Kohonen, "Self-organized formation of topologically correct feature maps," *Biological Cybernetics*, vol. 43, no. 1, pp. 59–69, 1982.

69. S. Grossberg, "Adaptive pattern classification and universal recoding: I. Parallel development and coding of neural feature detectors," *Biological Cybernetics*, vol. 23, no. 3, pp. 121–134, 1976.

70. S. Grossberg, "Adaptive pattern classification and universal recoding: II. Feedback, expectation, olfaction, illusions," *Biological Cybernetics*, vol. 23, no. 4, pp. 187–202, 1976.

71. A. Takeuchi and S. Amari, "Formation of topographic maps and columnar microstructures in nerve fields," *Biological Cybernetics*, vol. 35, pp. 63–72, 1979.

72. P. Erdi and G. Barna, "Self-organizing mechanism for the formation of ordered neural mappings," *Biological Cybernetics*, vol. 51, pp. 93–101, 1984.

73. M. Corttrel and J. C. Fort, "A stochastic model of retinotopy: a self organizing process," *Biological Cybernetics*, vol. 53, pp. 405–411, 1986.

74. T. Kohonen, *Self-Organization and Associative Memory*. Springer, 1989.

75. G. A. Carpenter and S. Grossberg, "Associative learning, adaptive pattern recognition, and cooperative–competitive decision making by neural networks," in *Hybrid and Optical Computing* (H. Szu, ed.). SPIE, 1987.

76. G. Carpenter and S. Grossberg, "The art of adaptive pattern recognition by a self-organizing neural network," *Computer*, vol. 21, no. 3, pp. 77–88, 1988.

77. G. A. Carpenter and S. Grossberg, "Neural dynamics of category learning and recognition: attention, memory consolidation, and amnesia," in *Brain Structure, Learning, and Memory* (J. Davis, R. Newburgh, and E. Wegman, eds). AAAS Symposium Series, 1986.

78. M. Georgiopoulos, G. L. Heileman, and J. Huang, "Convergence properties of learning in art 1," *Neural Computation*, vol. 2, pp. 502–509, 1990.

79. T. Kohonen, "The self-organizing map," *Proceedings of the IEEE*, vol. 78, no. 9, pp. 1464–1480, 1990.

80. D. J. Wilshaw and C. Malsburg, "A marker induction mechanism for the establishment of ordered neural mappings: its application to the retinotectal problem," *Philosophical Transactions of the Royal Society of London*, vol. B287, no. 9, pp. 203–243, 1979.

81. T. Martinez and K. Schulten, "A 'neural-gas' network learns topologies," *Artificial Neural Networks*, vol. 1, pp. 397–402, 1991.

82. R. Mukkulainen, "Script recognition with hierarchical feature maps," *Connection Science*, vol. 2, no. 1, pp. 83–101, 1990.

83. M. Dittenbach, D. Merkl, and A. Rauber, "The growing hierarchical self-organization map," in *Proceedings of the International Joint Conference on Neural Networks (IJCNN)*, vol. 6, pp. 15–19. Como, Italy: IEEE Computer Society, July 2000.

84. M. Dittenbach, A. Rauber, D. Merkl, "Recent advances with the growing hierarchical self-organizing map," in *Advances in Self-Organising Maps*, pp. 140–145. Springer, 2001.

85. M. Dittenbach, A. Rauber, and D. Merkl, "Uncovering hierarchical structure in data using the growing hierarchical self organizing map," *Neurocomputing*, vol. 48, no. 1–4, pp. 199–216, 2002.

86. M. Dittenbach, D. Merkl, and A. Rauber, "Hierarchical clustering of document archives with the growing hierarchical self-organizing map," *International Conference on Artificial Neural Networks*, pp. 500–505. Vienna, Austria August 21–25, 2001.

87. P. Koikkalainen and E. Oja, "Self-organizing hierarchical feature maps," in *International Joint Conference on Neural Networks* (San Diego, CA), pp. 279–284, June 17–21, 1990.

88. J. Pakkanen, J. Iivarinen, and E. Oja, "The evolving tree—a novel self-organizing network for data analysis," *Neural Processing Letters*, vol. 20, no. 3, pp. 199–211, 2004.

89. B. Fritzke, "Growing cell structures—a self-organizing network for unsupervised and supervised learning," *Neural Networks*, vol. 7, no. 9, pp. 1441–1460, 1994.

90. B. Fritzke, "Growing grid—a self-organizing network with constant neighborhood range and adaptation strength," *Neural Processing Letters*, vol. 2, no. 5, pp. 9–13, 1995.

91. B. Fritzke, "A growing neural gas network learns topologies." *Advances in neural information processing systems*, vol. 7 pp. 625–632, 1995.

92. T. M. Martinez, "Competitive hebbian learning rule forms perfectly topology preserving maps," in *International Conference on Artificial Neural Networks (ICANN)* (Amsterdam, The Netherlands), pp. 427–434, March 28–April 1, 1993.

93. D. DeSieno, "Adding a conscience to competitive learning," in *IEEE International Conference on Neural Networks*, vol. I (San Diego, CA), pp. 117–124, July 24–27, 1988.

94. C. Hung and S. Wermter, "A dynamic adaptive self-organising hybrid model for text clustering," in *Proceedings of the Third IEEE International Conference on Data Mining* (Florida), pp. 75–82, November 19–22, 2003.

95. H. Kong and L. Guan, "Detection and removal of impulse noise by a neural network guided adaptive median filter," in *IEEE International Conference on Neural Networks*, vol. 2, Australia, November 27–December 1, 1995.

96. J. A. Kangas, T. Kohonen, and J. T. Lassksonen, "Variants of self-organizing maps," *IEEE Transactions on Neural Networks*, vol. 1, no. 1, pp. 93–99, 1990.

97. A. V. Skorokhod, *Studies in the Theory of Random Processes*. Reading, MA: Addison-Wesley, 1965.

98. S. Grossberg, "On learning and energy–entropy dependence in recurrent and nonrecurrent signed networks," *Journal of Statistical Physics*, vol. 1, pp. 319–350, 1969.

99. B. Kosko, "Unsupervised learning in noise," *IEEE Transactions on Neural Networks*, vol. 1, pp. 44–57, 1990.

100. D. E. Rumelhart and D. Zipser, "Feature discovery by competitive learning," *Cognitive Science*, vol. 9, pp. 75–112, 1985.

101. B. Kosko, "Stochastic competitive learning," *IEEE Transactions on Neural Networks*, vol. 2, no. 5, pp. 522–529, 1991.

102. H. C. Andrews and B. R. Hunt, *Digital Image Restoration*. Englewood Cliffs, NJ: Prentice Hall, Inc., 1977.

103. R. R. Lawrence, R. S. Marvin, and E. S. Carolyn, "Applications of a non-linear smoothing algorithm to speech processing," *IEEE Transactions on Acoustics, Speech, and Signal Processing*, vol. ASSP-23, pp. 552–557, 1975.

104. Y. H. Lee and S. A. Kassam, "Generalized median filtering and related nonlinear filtering techniques," *IEEE Transactions on Acoustics, Speech, and Signal Processing*, vol. ASSP-33, pp. 672–683, 1985.

105. R. Bernstein, "Adaptive nonlinear filters for simultaneous removal of different kinds of noise in images," *IEEE Transactions on Circuits and Systems*, vol. CAS-34, pp. 1275–1291, 1987.

106. N. Wiener, *Nonlinear Problems in Random Theory*. MIT Press, 1958.

107. J. W. Tukey, *Exploratory Data Analysis*. Addison-Wiley, 1977.

108. D. R. K. Brownrigg, "The weighted median filter," *Communications of the ACM*, vol. 27, pp. 807–818, 1984.

109. S. J. Ko and Y. H. Lee, "Center weighted median filters and their applications to image enhancement," *IEEE Transactions on Circuits and Systems*, vol. CAS-38, pp. 984–993, 1991.

110. O. Yli-Harja, J. Astola, and Y. Neuvo, "Analysis of the properties of median and weighted median filters using threshold logic and stack filter representation," *IEEE Transactions on Signal Processing*, vol. 39, pp. 395–410, 1991.

111. G. R. Arce and M. P. McLoughlin, "Theoretical analysis of max/median filters," *IEEE Transactions on Acoustics, Speech, and Signal Processing*, vol. ASSP-35, pp. 60–69, 1987.

112. A. Nieminen, P. Heinonen, and Y. Neuvo, "A new class of detail-preserving filters for image processing," *IEEE Transactions on Pattern Analysis and Machine Intelligence*, vol. PAMI-9, pp. 74–90, 1987.

113. G. R. Arce and R. E. Foster, "Detail-preserving ranked-order based filters for image processing," *IEEE Transactions on Acoustics, Speech, and Signal Processing*, vol. ASSP-37, pp. 83–98, 1989.

114. A. Kundu, S. K. Mitra, and P. P. Vaidyanathan, "Application of two-dimensional generalized mean filtering for removal of impulse noises from images," *IEEE Transactions on Acoustics, Speech, and Signal Processing*, vol. ASSP-32, pp. 600–609, 1984.

115. I. Pitas and A. Venetsanopoulos, "Nonlinear mean filters in image processing," *IEEE Transactions on Acoustics, Speech, and Signal Processing*, vol. ASSP-34, pp. 573–584, 1986.

116. H. Lin and A. N. Willson, "Median filters with adaptive length," *IEEE Transactions on Circuits and Systems*, vol. CAS-35, pp. 675–690, 1988.

117. J. E. Kenneth, "Minimum mean squared error impulse noise estimation and cancellation," *IEEE Transactions on Signal Processing*, vol. 43, pp. 1651–1662, 1995.

118. E. Abreu, M. Lightstone, S. K. Mitra, and K. Arakawa, "A new efficient approach for the removal of impulse noise from highly corrupted images," *IEEE Transactions on Image Processing*, vol. 5, pp. 1012–1025, 1996.

119. B. I. Justusson, "Median filtering: statistical properties," in *Two-Dimensional Digital Signal Processing* (T. S. Huang, ed.). Berlin/Heidelberg: Springer-Verlag, 1981.

120. H. Kong and L. Guan, "Noise-exclusive adaptive filtering for removing impulsive noise in digital images," *IEEE Transactions on Circuits and Systems*, vol. 45, pp. 422–428, 1998.

121. H. Kong and L. Guan, "A new approach for Gaussian and uniform distributed impulse noise images," *Journal of Electronic Imaging*, vol. 7, pp. 36–44, 1998.

122. J. B. Bednar and T. L. Watt, "Alpha-trimmed means and their relationship to the media filters," *IEEE Transactions on Acoustics, Speech, and Signal Processing*, vol. ASSP-32, pp. 145–153, 1984.

123. A. Lev, S. W. Zucker, and A. Rosenfeld, "Iterative enhancement of noise images," *IEEE Transactions on Systems, Man and Cybernetics*, vol. SMC-7, pp. 435–442, 1977.

124. M. P. McLoughlin and G. R. Arce, "Deterministic properties of the recursive separable median filter," *IEEE Transactions on Acoustics, Speech, and Signal Processing*, vol. ASSP-35, pp. 98–106, 1987.

125. W. W. Boles, M. Kanefsky, and M. Simaan, "Recursive two-dimensional median filtering algorithms for fast image root extraction," *IEEE Transactions on Circuits and Systems*, vol. 35, pp. 1323–1326, 1988.

126. L. Guan and H. Kong, "An efficient algorithm for impulse noise removal in cable TV transmission," *Journal of Real-Time Imaging*, vol. 4, pp. 113–124, 1998.

127. Q. Zhang and R. K. Ward, "Impulse noise correction in TV transmission," *IEEE Transactions on Consumer Electronics*, vol. 41, no. 3, pp. 731–737, 1996.

128. H. Kong and L. Guan, "A neural network guided adaptive filter for the removal of impulse noise in digital images," *Neural Networks*, vol. 9, no. 3, pp. 373–378, 1996.

129. Y. Rui, T. S. Huang, and S. Mehrotra, "Content-based image retrieval with relevance feedback in MARS," in *IEEE International Conference on Image Processing* (Santa Barbara, CA), pp. 815–818, October 26–29, 1997.

130. K. Jarrah, M. Kyan, S. Krishnan, and L. Guan, "Computational intelligence techniques and their applications in content-based image retrieval," in *IEEE International Conference on Multimedia and Expo* (Toronto, Canada), pp. 33–36, July 9–12, 2006.

131. D. Marr, "Vision: a computational investigation into the human presentation and processing of visual information," in *Two Dimensional Digital Signal Processing* (T. S. Huang, ed.). New York: W.H. Freeman and Company, 1982.

132. S. M. J. and D. H. Ballard, "Indexing via color histograms," in *IEEE International Conference on Computer Vision* (Osaka, Japan), pp. 390–393, December 4–7, 1990.

133. Y. Rui, Efficient indexing, browsing and retrieval of image/video content. PhD thesis, University of Illinois, Urbana Champaign (Illinois), 1999.

134. P. Muneesawang, Retrieval of image/video content by adaptive machine and user interaction. PhD thesis, University of Sydney, Sydney, Australia, 2002.

135. M. Stricker and M. Orengo, "Similarity of color images," in *SPIE Storage and Retrieval for Image and Video Databases* (San Jose, CA), pp. 381–392, February 9–10, 1995.

136. B. S. Manjunath, P. Salembier, and T. Sikora, *Introduction to MPEG-7 Multimedia Content Description Interface*. John Wiley & Sons, Ltd, 2002.

137. J. R. Smith and S. F. Chang, "Automated binary texture feature sets for image retrieval," in *IEEE International Conference on Acoustics, Speech and Signal Processing* (Atlanta, GA), pp. 2239–2242, May 7–10, 1996.

138. M. H. Gross, R. Koch, L. Lippert, and A. Dreger, "Multiscale image texture analysis in wavelet spaces," *IEEE International Conference on Image Processing*, vol. 3, pp. 412–416, November 13–16, 1994.

139. A. Kundu and J. L. Chen, "Texture classification using QMF bank-based subband decomposition," *CVGIP: Graphical Models and Image Processing*, vol. 54, no. 5, pp. 369–384, 1992.

140. P. Muneesawang and L. Guan, "Multiresolution-histogram indexing and relevance feedback learning for image retrieval," in *IEEE International Conference on Image Processing* (Vancouver, Canada), pp. 526–529, September 10–13, 2000.

141. K. Jarrah, P. Muneesawang, I. Lee, and L. Guan, "Minimizing human– machine interactions in automatic image retrieval," in *IEEE Canadian Conference on Electrical and Computer Engineering* (Niagara Falls, Canada), pp. 1589–1592, May 2–5, 2004.

142. W. Y. Ma and B. S. Manjunath, "A comparison of wavelet transform features for texture image annotation," *IEEE International Conference on Image Processing*, vol. 2, pp. 256–259, October 23–26, 1995.

143. D. Zhang, A. Wong, M. Indrawan, and G. Lu, "Content-based image retrieval using gabor texture features," in *IEEE Pacific-Rim Conference on Multimedia* (Sydney, Australia), pp. 392–395, December 13–15, 2000.

144. E. Persoon and K. S. Fu, "Shape discrimination using Fourier descriptors," *IEEE Transactions on System, Man and Cybernetics*, vol. 7, no. 3, pp. 170–179, 1977.

145. Y. Rui, A. C. She, and T. S. Huang, "Modified Fourier descriptors for shape representation—a practical approach," in *International Workshop on Image Database and Multimedia Search*, (Amsterdam, The Netherlands), August 22–23, 1996.

146. Q. Chen, E. Petriu, and X. Yang, "A comparative study of Fourier descriptors and Hu's seven moment invariants for image recognition," in *IEEE Canadian Conference on Electrical and Computer Engineering* (Niagara Falls, Canada), pp. 103–106, May 2–5, 2004.

147. M. K. Hu, "Visual pattern recognition by moment invariants," *IRE Transactions on Information Theory*, vol. IT-8, pp. 179–187, 1962.

148. S. Paschalakis and P. Lee, "Pattern recognition in gray level images using moment based invariant features," in *IEEE Conference on Image Processing and its Applications*, vol. 1, pp. 245–249, July 13–15, 1999.

149. S. Theodoridis and K. Koutroumbas, *Pattern Recognition*, 2nd edn. Elsevier Science, 2003.

150. Y. Rui, T. S. Huang, M. Ortega, and S. Mehrotra, "Relevance feedback: a power tool for interactive content-based image retrieval," *IEEE Transactions on Circuits and Systems for Video Technology*, vol. 8, no. 5, pp. 644–655, 1998.

151. P. Muneesawang and L. Guan, "A non-linear RBF model for adaptive content-based image retrieval," in *International Symposium on Multimedia Information Processing* (University of Sydney, Australia), pp. 188–191, December 13–15, 2000.

152. Y. Li, An effective shape descriptor for content-based image retrieval. PhD thesis, Ryerson University, Toronto, Canada, 2006.

153. G. Salton and M. J. McGill, *Introduction to Modern Information Retrieval*. New York: McGraw Hill, 1983.

154. T. Gevers and A. W. M. Smeulders, "Pictoseek: Combining color and shape invariant features for image retrieval," *IEEE Transactions on Image Processing*, vol. 9, pp. 102–119, 2000.

155. E. Di Sciascio and M. Mongiello, "Drawsearch: a tool for interactive content-based image retrieval over the net," in *SPIE Storage and Retrieval for Image and Video Databases*, pp. 561–572, January 26–29, 1999, San Jose, CA.

156. I. J. Cox, M. L. Miller, T. P. Minka, T. V. Papathoman, and P. N. Yianilos, "The Bayesian image retrieval system, pichunter: theory, implementation, and psychophysical experiments," *IEEE Transactions on Image Processing*, vol. 9, no. 1, pp. 20–37, 2000.

157. T. Sigitani, Y. Liguni, and H. Maeda, "Image interpolation for progressive transmission by using radial basis function networks," *IEEE Transactions on Neural Networks*, vol. 10, no. 2, pp. 381–390, 1999.

158. N. Ejaz and W. Baik, "Video summarization using a network of radial basis function," *Multimedia Systems*, vol. 18, pp. 483–497, 2012.

159. D. DeMenthon, V. Kobla, and D. Doermann, "Video summarization by curve simplification," in *ACM International Conference on Multimedia* (Bristol, England), pp. 211–218, September 12–16, 1998.

160. P. Mundur, Y. Rao, and Y. Yesha, "Keyframe-based video summarization using Delaunay clustering," *International Journal on Digital Libraries*, vol. 6, no. 2, pp. 219–232, 2006.

161. M. Furini, F. Geraci, M. Montangero, and M. Pellegrini, "Stimo: still and moving video storyboard for the web scenario," *Multimedia Tools and Applications*, vol. 46, no. 1, pp. 47–69, 2010.

162. S. E. F. de Avila, A. P. B. Lopes, L. J. Antonio, and A. A. Araujo, "Vsumm: a mechanism designed to produce static video summaries and a novel evaluation method," *Pattern Recognition Letters*, vol. 32, no. 1, pp. 56–68, 2011.

163. V. Dordevic, N. Reljin, and I. Reljin, "Identifying and retrieving of audio sequences by using wavelet descriptors and neural network with user's assistance," in *IEEE EUROCON The International Conference on Computer as a Tool* (Belgrade, Serbia and Montenegro), pp. 167–170, November 21–24, 2005.

164. G. Chen, T. J. Wang, and P. Herrera, "A novel music retrieval system with relevance feedback," in *IEEE International Conference on Innovative Computing Information and Control* (Kaohsiung, Taiwan), pp. 158–162, June 18–20, 2008.

165. T. Amin, M. Zeytinoglu, and L. Guan, "Application of Laplacian mixture model to image and video retrieval," *IEEE Transactions on Multimedia*, vol. 9, no. 7, pp. 1416–1429, 2007.

166. G.-H. Cha, "A context-aware similarity search for a handwritten digit image database," *The Computer Journal*, vol. 53, no. 8, pp. 1291–1301, 2010.

167. G.-H. Cha, "Capturing contextual relationship for effective media search," *Multimedia Tools and Applications*, vol. 56, pp. 351–364, 2012.

168. H. Tabout, A. Souissi, and A. Sbihi, "Region-based automated relevance feedback in algae image retrieval," *International Journal of Computer Science and Network Security*, vol. 7, no. 12, pp. 124–131, 2007.

169. T. Amin, Application of Laplacian mixture model to image and video retrieval. PhD thesis, Ryerson University, Toronto, Canada, 2004.

170. K. H. Yap, K. Wu, and C. Zhu, "Knowledge propagation in collaborative tagging for image retrieval," *Journal of Signal Processing Systems*, vol. 59, no. 2, pp. 163–175, 2010.

171. R. Zhang and L. Guan, "A collaborative Bayesian image retreival framework," in *IEEE International Conference on Acoustics, Speech and Signal Processing* (Taipei, Taiwan), pp. 1953–1956, April 19–24, 2009.

172. R. Zhang and L. Guan, "Multimodal image retrieval via Bayesian information fusion," in *IEEE International Conference on Multimedia and Expo* (New York), pp. 830–833, June 28–July 3, 2009.

173. J. Peng, B. Bhanu, and S. Qing, "Probabilistic feature relevance learning for content-based image retrieval," *Computer Vision and Image Understanding*, vol. 75, no. 1, pp. 150–164, 1999.

174. N. S. Kojić, S. K. Čabarkapa, G. J. Zajić, and B. D. Reljin, "Implementation of neural network in CBIR systems with relevance feedback," *Journal of Automatic Control*, vol. 16, no. 1, pp. 41–45, 2006.

175. S. Cabarkapa, N. Kojic, V. Radosavljevic, G. Zajic, and B. Reljin, "Adaptive content-based image retrieval with relevance feedback," in *IEEE EUROCON The International Conference on Computer as a Tool* (Belgrade, Serbia and Montenegro), pp. 147–150, November 21–24, 2005.

176. P. Muneesawang, H. S. Wong, J. Lay, and L. Guan, "Learning and adaptive characterization of visual contents in image retrieval systems," in *Handbook on*

Neural Networks for Signal Processing (Y. H. Hu and J.-N. Hwang, eds). CRC Press, 2001.

177. Y. Zhao, Y. Zhao, and Z. Zhu, "Relevance feedback based on query refining and feature database updating in CBIR system," in *IASTED International Conference on Signal Processing, Pattern Recognition and Applications* (Innsbruck, Austria), Track: 520-081, February 15–17, 2006.

178. X. He, O. King, W. Y. Ma, M. Li, and H. J. Zhang, "Learning a semantic space from user's relevance feedback for image retrieval," *IEEE Transactions on Circuits and Systems for Video Technology*, vol. 13, no. 1, pp. 39–48, 2003.

179. K. Shkurko and X. Qi, "A radial basis function and semantic learning space based composite learning approach to image retrieval," in *IEEE International Conference on Acoustics, Speech and Signal Processing* (Hawaii), pp. I-945–I-948, April 15–20, 2007.

180. M. R. Azimi-Sadjadi, J. Salazar, and S. Srinivasan, "An adpatable image retreival system with relevance feedback using kernel machines and selective sampling," *IEEE Transactions on Image Processing*, vol. 18, no. 7, pp. 1645–1659, 2009.

181. V. Radosavljevic, S. Kojic, S. Cabarkapa, G. Zajic, I. Reljin, and B. Reljin, "An image retrieval system with users relevance feedback," in *Workshop on Image Analysis for Multimedia Interactive Services* (Incheon, Korea), pp. 9–12, April 19–21, 2006.

182. G. Cha, "Non-metric similarity ranking for image retrieval," in *International Conference on Database and Expert Systems Application* (Krakw, Poland), pp. 853–862, September 4–8, 2006.

183. D. Zhou, O. Bousquet, T. N. Lal, J. Weston, and B. Schlkopf, "Learning with local and global consistency," *Advances in Neural Information Processing Systems*, vol. 16, pp. 321–327, 2004.

184. S. Tong and E. Chang, "Support vector machine active learning for image retrieval," in *ACM International Conference on Multimedia* (Ottawa, Canada), pp. 107–118, September 30–October 5, 2001.

185. L. Wu, C. Faloutsos, K. Sycara, and T. R. Payne, "Falcon: feedback adaptive loop for content-based retrieval," in *International Conference on Very Large Databases* (Cairo, Egypt), pp. 297–306, September 10–14, 2000.

186. Y. Boykov and V. Kolmogorov, "An experimental comparison of min-cut/max-flow algorithms for energy minimization in vision," *IEEE Transactions on Pattern Analysis and Machine Intelligence*, vol. 26, no. 9, pp. 1124–1137, 2004.

187. N. Zhang and L. Guan, "Graph cuts in content-based image classification and retrieval with relevance feedback," in *Pacific-Rim Conference on Multimedia* (Hong Kong), pp. 30–39, December 10–14, 2007.

188. K. Wu and K. H. Yap, "Content-based image retrieval using fuzzy perceptual feedback," *Multimedia Tools and Applications*, vol. 32, no. 3, pp. 235–251, 2007.

189. S. Rudinac, M. Uscumlic, M. Rudinac, G. Zajic, and B. Reljin, "Global image search vs. regional search in CBIR systems," in *IEEE International Workshop on Image Analysis for Multimedia Interactive Services*, pp. 14–17, June 6–8, 2007, Santorini, Greece.

190. R. Ding, X. Ji, and L. Zhu, "Research on the relevance feedback-based image retrieval in digital library," *Proceedings of World Academy of Science, Engineering and Technology*, vol. 25, pp. 48–52, 2007.

191. P. Muneesawang and L. Guan, "Automatic machine interactions for content-based image retrieval using a self-organizing tree map architecture," *IEEE Transactions on Neural Network*, vol. 13, no. 4, pp. 821–834, 2002.

192. R. Yan, A. Hauptmann, and R. Jin, "Multimedia search with pseudo-relevance feedback," in *International Conference on Image and Video Retrieval* (Illinois), pp. 238–247, July 24–25, 2003.

193. R. Yan, A. Hauptmann, and R. Jin, "Negative pseudo-relevance feedback in content-based video retrieval," in *Proceedings of the Eleventh ACM International Conference on Multimedia* (California), pp. 343–346, November 02–08, 2003.

194. L. S. Kennedy and S. F. Chang, "A reranking approach for context-based concept fusion in video indexing and retrieval," in *ACM International Conference on Image and Video Retrieval* (Amsterdam, The Netherlands), pp. 333–340, July 9–11, 2007.

195. Y. Wu, Q. Tian, and T. S. Huang, "Discriminant-EM algorithm with application to image retrieval," in *IEEE Conference on Computer Vision and Pattern Recognition* (South Carolina), pp. 222–227, June 13–15, 2000.

196. M. F. A. Hady and F. Schwenker, "Semi-supervised learning," in *Handbook of Neural Information Processing*, pp. 215–239. Berlin/Heidelberg: Springer-Verlag, 2013.

197. T. Joachims, "Transductive inference for text classification using support vector machines," in *International Conference on Machine Learning* (Bled, Slovenia), pp. 200–209, June 27–30, 1999.

198. L. Wang, K. Chan, and Z. Zhang, "Bootstrapping SVM active learning by incorporating unlabelled images for image retrieval," in *IEEE Computer Society Conference on Computer Vision and Pattern Recognition* (Wisconsin), pp. I629–I634, June 18–20, 2003.

199. S. Rudinac, M. Larson, and A. Hanjalic, "Exploiting visual reranking to improve pseudo-relevance feedback for spoken-content-based video retrieval," in *International Workshop on Image Analysis for Multimedia Interactive Services* (London, UK), pp. 17–20, May 6–8, 2009.

200. K. Wu and K. H. Yap, "Fuzzy SVM for content-based image retrieval: a pseudo-label support vector machine framework," *IEEE Computational Intelligence Magazine*, vol. 2, no. 1, pp. 10–16, 2006.

201. J. He, M. Li, Z. Li, H. J. Zhang, H. Tong, and C. Zhang, "Pseudo relevance feedback based on iterative probabilistic one-class SVMs in web image retrieval," in *Pacific-Rim Conference on Multimedia* (Tokyo, Japan), pp. 213–220, November 30–December 3, 2004.

202. J. H. Hsiao, C. S. Chen, and M. S. Chen, "Visual-word-based duplicate image search with pseudo-relevance feedback," in *IIEEE International Conference on Multimedia and Expo* (Hannover, Germany), pp. 669–672, June 23–26, 2008.

203. R. He, Y. Zhu, and W. Zhan, "Using local latent semantic indexing with pseudo relevance feedback in web image retrieval," in *International Joint Conference on INC, IMS, and IDC* (Seoul, South Korea), pp. 1354–1357, August 25–27, 2009.

204. K. Kise, Y. Wuotang, and K. Matsumoto, "Document image retrieval based on 2d density distributions of terms with pseudo relevance feedback," in *IEEE International Conference on Document Analysis and Recognition* (Edinburgh, Scotland), pp. 488–492, August 3–6, 2003.

205. J. G. Carbonell, Y. Yang, R. E. Frederking, R. D. Brown, Y. Geng, and D. Lee, "Translingual information retrieval: a comparative evaluation," in *International Joint Conference on Artificial Intelligence* (Aichi, Japan), August 23–29, 1997.

206. Y. Liu, T. Mei, X. S. Hua, J. Tang, X. Wu, and S. Li, "Learning to video search rerank via pseudo preference feedback," in *IEEE International Conference on Multimedia and Expo*, pp. 297–300, (Hannover, German) June 23–26, 2008.

207. M. Torjmen, K. Pinel-Sauvagnat, and M. Boughanem, "Using pseudo-relevance feedback to improve image retrieval results," in *Workshop of the Cross-Language Evaluation Forum* (Budapest, Hungary), pp. 665–673, September 19–21, 2007.

208. O. El Demerdash, L. Kosseim, and S. Bergler, "Image retrieval by inter-media fusion and pseudo-relevance feedback," in *Workshop of the Cross-Language Evaluation Forum* (Aarhus, Denmark), pp. 605–611, September 17–19, 2008.

209. N. Maillot, J. P. Chevallet, V. Valea, and J. H. Lim, "IPAL inter-media pseudo-relevance feedback approach to ImageCLEF 2006 photo retrieval," in *Workshop of the Cross-Language Evaluation Forum* (Alicante, Spain), September 20–22, 2006.

210. T. Deselaers, D. Keysers, and H. Ney, "Fire—flexible image retrieval engine: ImageCLEF 2004 evaluation," in *Multilingual Information Access for Text, Speech and Images Workshop*, pp. 688–698. Springer, 2004.

211. K. Sauvagnat, Modele flexible pour la recherche d'information dans des corpus de documents semi-structuráes. PhD thesis, Université Toulouse III—Paul Sabatier, Toulouse, France, 2005.

212. O. El Demerdash, S. Bergler, and L. Kosseim, "Image query expansion using semantic selectional restrictions," in *Workshop of the Cross-Language Evaluation Forum* (Corfu, Greece), pp. 150–156, September 30–October 2, 2009.

213. P. Munesawang and L. Guan, "Adaptive video indexing and automatic/semi-automatic relevance feedback," *IEEE Transactions on Circuits and Systems for Video Technology*, vol. 15, no. 8, pp. 1032–1046, 2005.

214. Y. Freund, H. S. Seung, E. Shamir, and N. Tishby, "Selective sampling using the query by committee algorithm," *Machine Learning*, vol. 28, no. 2– 3, pp. 133–168, 1997.

215. D. D. Lewis and J. Catlett, "Heterogeneous uncertainty sampling for supervised learning," in *International Conference on Machine Learning*, (New Jersey), pp. 148–156, July 10–13, 1994.

216. P. Munesawang, "Image retrieval system using semi-automatic relevance feedback through 3d model," *MUT Engineering Transactions*, vol. 1, pp. 7–18, 2012.

217. M. Tinkler, "Visual thesaurus," *U.S. Patent Application 10/962,245*, 2004.

218. W. H. Hsu, L. S. Kennedy, and S. F. Chang, "Reranking methods for visual search," *IEEE on Multimedia*, vol. 3, no. 14, pp. 14–22, 2007.

219. J. Randall, L. Guan, X. Zhang, and W. Li, "Investigations of the self-organizing tree map," in *Proceedings of International Conference on Neural Information Processing*, vol. 2, pp. 724–728, 1999.

220. K. Jarrah, S. Krishnan, and G. L., "Automatic content-based image retrieval using hierarchical clustering algorithms," in *International World Congress on Computational Intelligence* (Vancouver, Canada), pp. 6564–6569, June 16–21, 2006.

221. K. Jarrah, M. Kyan, I. Lee, and L. Guan, "Application of image visual characterization and soft feature selection in content-based image retrieval," in *SPIE Multimedia Content*

Analysis, Management, and Retrieval (San Jose, CA), pp. 101–109, January 17–19, 2006.

222. M. Kyan, L. Guan, and S. Liss, "Refining competition in the self-organising tree map for unsupervised biofilm image segmentation," *Neural Networks*, vol. 18, no. 5–6, pp. 850–860, 2005.

223. J. Yang and V. Honavar, "Feature subset selection using a genetic algorithm," *IEEE Intelligent Systems*, vol. 13, no. 2, pp. 44–49, 1998.

224. P. Muneesawang and L. Guan, "Minimizing user interaction by automatic and semi-automatic relevance feedback for image retrieval," in *IEEE International Conference on Image Processing* (Rochester), pp. 601–604, September 22–25, 2002.

225. M. Kyan, K. Jarrah, P. Muneesawang, and L. Guan, "Strategies for unsupervised multimedia processing: self-organizing trees and forests," *IEEE Computational Intelligence Magazine*, vol. 1, no. 2, pp. 27–40, 2006.

226. D. E. Goldberg, *Genetic Algorithms in Search, Optimization, and Machine Learning*. New York: Addison-Wesley, 1998.

227. M. Mitchell, *An Introduction to Genetic Algorithms*. Cambridge MA: MIT Press, 1998.

228. C. Darwin, *The Origin of Species by Means of Natural Selection or the Preservation of Favored Races in the Struggle for Life*. New York: Book League of America, 1929.

229. I. Rechenberg, *Evolutionsstrategie; Optimierung technischer Systeme nach Prinzipien der biologischen Evolution. Mit einem Nachwort von Manfred Eigen*. Stuttgart: Frommann-Holzboog, 1973.

230. H.-P. Schwefel, *Numerische Optimierung von Computer-Modellen mittels der Evolutionsstrategie*, vol. 26. Basel/Stuttgart: Birkhaeuser, 1977.

231. L. Fogel, A. Owens, and M. Walsh, *Artificial Intelligence Through Simulated Evolution*. John Wiley & Sons, 1966.

232. A. S. Fraser, "Simulation of genetic systems by automatic digital computers. I. Introduction," *Australian Journal of Biological Science*, vol. 10, pp. 484–491, 1957.

233. A. S. Fraser, "Simulation of genetic systems by automatic digital computers. II. Effects of linkage on rates of advance under selection," *Australian Journal of Biological Science*, vol. 10, pp. 492–499, 1957.

234. G. J. Friedman, "Digital simulation of an evolutionary process," *General Systems Yearbook*, vol. 4, pp. 171–184, 1959.

235. W. W. Bledsoe, "The use of biological concepts in the analytical study of systems," *ORSA–TIMS National Meeting*, 1961.

236. H. J. Bremermann, "Optimization through evolution and recombination," in *Proceedings of the Conference on Self-Organizing Systems* (M. C. Yovits, G. T. Jacobi, and G. D. Golstine, eds), pp. 93–106. Spartan Books, 1962.

237. J. Reed, R. Toombs, and N. A. Barricelli, "Simulation of biological evolution and machine learning," *Journal of Theoretical Biology*, vol. 17, pp. 319–342, 1967.

238. S. W. R. and M. Zhang, "Classification strategies for image classification in genetic programming," in *IEEE International Conference on Image and Vision Computing* (Palmerston North, New Zealand), pp. 402–407, November 26–28, 2003.

239. S. Zehang, Y. Xiaojing, G. Bebis, and S. J. Louis, "Neural-network-based gender classification using genetic search for eigen-feature selection," in *IEEE International*

Joint Conference on Neural Networks, pp. 2433–2438, (Honolulu, Hawaii) May 12–17, 2002.

240. M. Hilaga, Y. Shinagawa, T. Kohmura, and T. Kunii, "Topology matching for fully automatic similarity estimation of 3d shapes," in *Proceedings of the ACM Annual Conference on Computer Graphics* (New York), pp. 203–212, August 12–17, 2001.

241. Corel (1999) *Corel gallery magic 65000*, www.corel.com

242. F. G. Lobo, D. E. Goldberg, and M. Pelikan, "Time complexity of genetic algorithms on exponentially scaled problems," in *Proceedings of The Genetic and Evolutionary Computation Conference*, pp. 151–158. Morgan Kaufmann Publishers, 2000.

243. T. Martinetz and K. K. Schulten, "A neural-gas network learns topologies," *Artificial Neural Network*, vol. I, pp. 397–402, 1991.

244. T. M. Martinez, "Competitive hebbian learning rule forms perfectly topology preserving maps," in *International Conference on Artificial Neural Networks* (Amsterdam, The Netherlands), pp. 427–434, May 25–27, 1993.

245. E. Oja, "A simplified neuron model as a principal component analyzer," *Journal of Mathematical Biology*, vol. 15, pp. 267–273, 1982.

246. G. S. Stent, "A physiological mechanism for Hebb's postulate of learning," in *Proceedings of the National Academy of Sciences of the United States of America*, vol. 70, pp. 997–1001, 1973.

247. D. DeSieno, "Adding a conscience to competitive learning," in *IEEE International Conference on Neural Networks* (San Diego, CA), pp. 117–124, July 24–24, 1988.

248. B. Balasko, J. Abonyi, B. Feil, "Department of Process Engineering University of Veszprem, Veszprem, Hungary". *Fuzzy Clustering and Data Analysis Toolbox: for use with Matlab*, Feb 27, 2009, 2005. www.mathworks.com/matlabcentral/fileexchange/

249. D. J. Newman, S. Hettich, C. L. Blake, and C. J. Merz, UCI repository of machine learning databases. PhD thesis, Department of Information and Computer Science, University of California, Irvine, Irvine, CA, 1998.

250. J. Kovaevi and R. F. Murphy, "Molecular and cellular bioimaging." *IEEE Signal Processing Magazine*, p. 19, May 2006.

251. F. Aguet, J. L. Vonesch, C. Vonesch, and M. Unser, "The colored revolution of bioimaging." *IEEE Signal Processing Magazine*, pp. 20–31, May 2006.

252. R. J. Palmer and C. Sternberg, "Modern microscopy in biofilm research: confocal microscopy and other approaches," *Current Opinion in Biotechnology*, vol. 10, no. 3, pp. 263–268, 1999.

253. C. K. Reddy and F. B. Dazzo, "Computer-assisted segmentation of bacteria in color micrographs." *Microscopy and Analysis Magazine*, pp. 5–7, The Americas Edition, Sep 2004.

254. F. He, J. Jablonska, S. Winkelbach, W. Lindenmaier, A. P. Zeng, B. Ma, and K. E. J. Dittmar, "Six-color segmentation of multicolor images in the infection studies of listeria monocytogenes," *Microscopy Research and Technique*, vol. 7, pp. 171–178, 2007.

255. E. Labruyere, V. Meas-Yedid, N. Guillen, C. Zimmer, and J.-C.Olivio-Marin, "Segmentation and tracking of migrating cells in videomicroscopy with parametric active contours: a tool for cell-based drug testing," *IEEE Transactions in Medical Imaging*, vol. 21, no. 10, pp. 1212–1221, 2002.

256. N. Pal and S. Pal, "A review on image segmentation techniques," *Pattern Recognition*, vol. 26, no. 9, pp. 1277–1294, 1993.

257. Y. Boykov and V. Kolmogorov, "An experimental comparison of min-cut/max-flow algorithms for energy minimization in vision," *IEEE Transactions on Pattern and Machine Intelligence (PAMI)*, vol. 26, pp. 1124–1137, 2004.

258. Y. Tu, G. Euskirchen, W. Ward, M. Chalfie, and D. C. Prasher, "Green fluorescent protein as a marker for gene expression," *Science*, vol. 263, no. 5148, pp. 802–805, 1994.

259. S. N. Liss, "Microbial flocs suspended biofilms," in *Encyclopedia of Environ. Microbiology* (G. Sutton, ed.), pp. 2000–2012. New York: John Wiley & Sons, Inc., 2002.

260. M. H. F. Wilkinson, "Automated and manual segmentation techniques in image analysis of microbes," in *Imaging, Morphometry, Fluorometry and Motility Techniques and Applications* (M. H. F. Wilkinson and F. Schut, eds). New York: John Wiley & Sons, Inc., 1998.

261. H. Beyenal, G. Harkin, Z. Lewandowski, and X. Yang, "Evaluation of biofilm image thresholding methods," *Water Research*, vol. 35, no. 5, pp. 1149–1158, 2001.

262. T. W. Ridler and S. Calvard, "Picture thresholding using an iterative selection method," *IEEE Transactions on Systems, Man and Cybernetics*, vol. SMC-8, pp. 630–632, 1978.

263. N. A. Otsu, "Threshold selection method from gray-level histograms," *IEEE Transactions on Systems Man and Cybernetics*, vol. 9, no. 1, pp. 62–66, 1979.

264. H. Beyenal, "Image Structure Analyzer (ISA) to analyze biofilm images," ASM Conference on Biofilms. March 25–29, 2007, Quebec City, Canada.

265. P. Baveye, "Comment on evaluation of biofilm image thresholding methods," *Water Research*, vol. 36, pp. 805–806, 2002.

266. J. Kittler and J. Illingworth, "Minimum error thresholding," *Pattern Recognition*, vol. 19, pp. 41–47, 1986.

267. J. Besag, "On the statistical analysis of dirty pictures (with discussion)," *Journal of the Royal Statistical Society. Series B*, vol. 48, pp. 259–302, 1986.

268. Z. Lewandowksi, H. Beyenal, and G. Harkin, "Quantifying biofilm structure: facts and fiction," *Biofouling*, vol. 20, no. 1, pp. 1–23, 2004.

269. C. Tolle, "Suboptimal minimum cluster volume cover-based method for measuring fractal dimension," *IEEE Transactions on Pattern Analysis and Machine Intelligence*, vol. 25, no. 1, pp. 32–41, 2003.

270. P. Kovesi, "Image features from phase congruency." *VIDERE: Journal of computer vision research*, vol. 1, no. 3, pp. 1–26, 1999.

271. C. W. Therrien, *Decision estimation and classification: An Introduction to Pattern Recognition and Related Topics*, pp. 215–227. New York: John Wiley & Sons, Inc., 1989.

272. B. Manjunath and W. Y. Ma, "Edgeflow: a technique for boundary detection and image segmentation," *IEEE Transactions on Image Processing*, vol. 9, pp. 1375–1388, 2000.

273. R. Gonzalez and R. Woods, *Digital Image Processing*, 2nd edn. Prentice Hall, Inc., 2002.

274. Mercury Computer Systems. *Amira 4.1.1. Developer Pack*, June 1, 2006. www.amiravis.com

275. G. Kindlmann and J. W. Durkin, "Semi-automatic generation of transfer functions for direct volume rendering," in *Proceedings of the IEEE Symposium on Volume Visualization*, (New York), pp. 79–86, October 19–20, 1998.

276. B. Nguyen, W. Tay, C. Chui, and S. Ong, "A clustering-based system to automate transfer function design for medical image visualization," *The Visual Computer*, vol. 28, pp. 181–191, 2012.

277. Y. Wang, W. Chen, J. Zhang, T. Dong, G. Shan, and X. Chi, "Efficient volume exploration using the Gaussian mixture model," *IEEE Transactions on Visualization and Computer Graphics*, vol. 17, pp. 1560–1573, 2011.

278. M. Selver, M. Alper, and C. Guzeli, "Semiautomatic transfer function initialization for abdominal visualization using self-generating hierarchical radial basis function networks," *IEEE Transactions on Visualization and Computer Graphics*, vol. 15, pp. 395–409, 2009.

279. S. Roettger, M. Bauer, and M. Stamminger, "Spatialized transfer functions," in *Proceedings of the IEEE/Eurographics Symposium on Visualization*, pp. 271–278, (Leeds, United Kingdom) June 1–3, 2005.

280. H. Muurinen and J. Laaksonen, "Video segmentation and shot boundary detection using self-organizing maps," in *Scandinavian Conference on Image Analysis*, (Aalborg, Denmark), pp. 770–779, June 10–14, 2007

Unsupervised Learning: A Dynamic Approach, First Edition.
Matthew Kyan, Paisarn Muneesawang, Kambiz Jarrah, and Ling Guan.
© 2014 by The Institute of Electrical and Electronics Engineers, Inc. Published by John Wiley & Sons, Inc.

IEEE Press Series on
COMPUTATIONAL INTELLIGENCE

Series Editor, **David B. Fogel**

The IEEE Press Series on Computational Intelligence includes books on neural, fuzzy, and evolutionary computation, and related technologies, of interest to the engineering and scientific communities. Computational intelligence focuses on emulating aspects of biological systems to construct software and/or hardware that learns and adapts. Such systems include neural networks, our use of language to convey complex ideas, and the evolutionary process of variation and selection. The series highlights the most-recent and groundbreaking research and development in these areas, as well as the important hybridization of concepts and applications across these areas. The audiences for books in the series include undergraduate and graduate students, practitioners, and researchers in computational intelligence.

Reinforcement Learning and Approximate Dynamic Programming for Feedback Control. Edited by Frank L. Lewis and Derong Liu. 2012. 978-1118-10420-0

Complex-Valued Neural Networks: Advances and Applications. Edited by Akira Hirose. 2013. 978-1118-34460-6

Unsupervised Learning: A Dynamic Approach. Matthew Kyan, Paisarn Muneesawang, Kambiz Jarrah, Ling Guan. 2014. 978-0470-27833-8